2014 Provincial and Inaugural Regional Competitiveness Analysis

Safeguarding Indonesia's Growth Momentum

Lee Kuan Yew School of Public Policy
ASIA COMPETITIVENESS INSTITUTE

About ACI

The Asia Competitiveness Institute (ACI) was established in August 2006 as a research centre at the Lee Kuan Yew School of Public Policy (LKYSPP), National University of Singapore (NUS). It aims to build the intellectual leadership and network for understanding and developing competitiveness in the Asia region. ACI seeks to contribute to the enhancement of inclusive growth, living standards and institutional governance through competitiveness research on sub-national economies in Asia. It identifies mitigating issues and challenges for potential public policy interventions through close collaboration with regional governments, business corporations, policy think-tanks and academics.

ACI's value proposition may be encapsulated in an acronym:

Analytical inputs to initiate policies for policy-makers and business leaders in Asia

Capacity building to enable others through improvement in productivity and efficiency

Intellectual leadership to create pragmatic models of competitiveness and inclusive growth.

The Institute's core research competencies can also be encapsulated in this acronym describing our evidence-based assessments conducted on public policies for **A**SEAN in the context of the rise of **C**HINA and **I**NDIA.

Vision and Mission

- The overarching vision of ACI is to build up its research credibility with policy impact, contributing as a professional think-tank.
- The mission is to establish our niche as a leading policy think-tank in Asia by identifying competitiveness, promoting competition and synergising complementarities amongst Asian economies and business corporations.
- We will articulate, entice discourse and shape agendas in the arena of public policies amongst Asian governments.
- We will undertake evidence-based assessments of public policy outcomes, their effectiveness and impact on inclusivity.

Asia Competitiveness Institute | Lee Kuan Yew School of Public Policy | National University of Singapore
469A Bukit Timah Road, Level 2 Tower Block, Singapore 259770
Tel: (65) 6516 5025 Fax: (65) 6467 8714 http://spp.nus.edu.sg/ACI

NUS National University of Singapore

2014 Provincial and Inaugural Regional Competitiveness Analysis

Safeguarding Indonesia's Growth Momentum

Tan Khee Giap
Co-Director, Asia Competitiveness Institute
Lee Kuan Yew School of Public Policy
National University of Singapore

Nurina Merdikawati
Research Associate, Asia Competitiveness Institute
Lee Kuan Yew School of Public Policy
National University of Singapore

Mulya Amri
Research Associate, Asia Competitiveness Institute
Lee Kuan Yew School of Public Policy
National University of Singapore

Tan Kong Yam
Co-Director, Asia Competitiveness Institute
Lee Kuan Yew School of Public Policy
National University of Singapore

Reviewers

Luky Eko Wuryanto
Deputy Minister for Infrastructure and Regional Development
Coordinating Ministry for Economic Affairs, Indonesia

Umar Juoro
Member of National Economic Council (KEN), Indonesia

Lee Kuan Yew School of Public Policy
Asia Competitiveness Institute
NUS National University of Singapore
World Scientific

Published by

World Scientific Publishing Co. Pte. Ltd.
5 Toh Tuck Link, Singapore 596224
USA office: 27 Warren Street, Suite 401-402, Hackensack, NJ 07601
UK office: 57 Shelton Street, Covent Garden, London WC2H 9HE

British Library Cataloguing-in-Publication Data
A catalogue record for this book is available from the British Library.

2014 PROVINCIAL AND INAUGURAL REGIONAL COMPETITIVENESS ANALYSIS
Safeguarding Indonesia's Growth Momentum

ISBN 978-981-4667-49-4
ISBN 978-981-4704-64-9 (pbk)

In-house Editor: Dong Lixi

Typeset by Stallion Press
Email: enquiries@stallionpress.com

Printed in Singapore

Contents

Foreword

The Asia Competitiveness Institute's (ACI) flagship research project on the competitiveness analysis for 33 Indonesian provinces has attracted widespread local and international interests. At various stages of the research, the ACI engaged policymakers, academia, and business sector, which are proven to be critical as boosting competitiveness requires multi-stakeholder effort. As the then Chairman of Indonesian Employers' Association (APINDO) and currently sits in its advisory board, I value this research effort in promoting healthy competition amongst provinces to eventually lift Indonesia's competitiveness as a whole.

To maintain its growth momentum, Indonesia has to address a number of challenges. Productivity is one of them. Labour productivity can be improved through better education system and training. This is not only the responsibility of the government but also employers, big and small companies alike. Faster knowledge and technology transfer to local industry ensures Indonesia to be on track in its industrialisation development strategy. Commitment to better infrastructure is also of primary importance to increase efficiency. All in all, aligned with the ACI's approach, collaboration among stakeholders is needed for Indonesia to resolve these perennial issues.

With the ACI's inaugural research analysing regional competitiveness, on top of provincial-level, the current attention is now shifting to a more balanced regional development. Indonesia, from western Sabang to eastern Merauke, has abundant potential waiting to be unleashed. I am confident that the ACI does provide robust analysis on the regional landscape, elaborating its strengths and weaknesses, as well as development strategies.

I strongly hope the ACI will continue its excellent research work on Indonesia's competitiveness. Unique strategy, not one-size-fits-all, is valuable in this context given each province's background and performance. From the APINDO, we are proud to be the ACI's partner in this unprecedented research effort and we would ensure continuous support to the study.

Sofjan Wanandi
Chief Expert Staff
For Vice President of Indonesia

Preface

The Asia Competitiveness Institute (ACI) has proven to live up to its name, being at the competitive edge of delving into Indonesia's provincial and regional competitiveness. This is one of its kind that targets both local and international audiences. Continuity of the research, now at its second edition, is a hallmark of well-received flagship publication as the world expects Indonesia to undertake transformation under the new leadership of President Joko Widodo. It is inevitable that the new President inherits perennial problems that span from lack of infrastructure to corruption. Regional disparity, as also highlighted in the ACI findings, remains real. As a well-reputed public figure for running a clean government and getting things done, hopes are high for his presidency to navigate Indonesia to take its rightful position as an economic powerhouse and engine of growth for the region and beyond.

It will also be interesting to witness how Indonesia pivots towards strengthening its maritime power after decades of negligence. The maritime vision suits the archipelagic nation that desperately needs seamless connectivity across islands, including those of outermost, forefront and least developed islands. Advancing sea-based infrastructure will also enhance Indonesia's integration into various international strategic partnerships, including the ACI's Asia Economic Connectivity Vision 2030 (AECV 2030).

The key to success is commitment for better governance to accelerate Indonesia's development, given the complexity in streamlining multiple layers of government. It is important for the long-standing and high priority structural reforms to be implemented in a complex institutional and decentralised framework. This is not an easy task for Indonesia, but is certainly not an impossible one.

The ACI's extensive research on the competitiveness of each Indonesia's province and region helps to resolve the information gap on their relative performance as compared to their peers. Such comprehensive annual 'check-up' is necessary to devise development strategies going forward. The results are not only ranking per se, but also detailed composition of their strengths and weaknesses that require further policy attention. Topical research study on competitiveness drivers through Geweke causal analysis further enriches the collective insights of rigorous studies on Indonesia's current state of development.

Aligned with the Lee Kuan Yew School of Public Policy's mission to raise the standards of governance in Asia, improve the lives of its people and contribute to the transformation of the region, this book clearly represents our action in the making. More exciting work related to the ACI's deep interests in Indonesia's research will persist, further building up evidence-based policy recommendations useful for the government and other stakeholders. For Indonesia as a whole, the rewards for action — as well as the costs of complacency — are too high. This is the momentum for Indonesia to take giant strides towards transformation.

Professor Kishore Mahbubani
Dean
Lee Kuan Yew School of Public Policy
National University of Singapore

Acknowledgements

The Asia Competitiveness Institute (ACI) has been committed to track the competitiveness of various Asian economies across the years. With the Indonesian economy's growing prominence in the world, in-depth study on Indonesia's provincial-level competitiveness across the years provides distinct insights into the unique potentials, opportunities, and challenges ahead. In this second edition, the inaugural regional competitiveness analysis that puts together provinces into clusters is introduced to further verify the Master Plan for Acceleration and Expansion of Indonesia's Economic Development (MP3EI). More specialised topic on Geweke causal analysis offers richer understanding into the contextual aspect that drives the competitiveness.

This report benefitted from the discussions with a number of policy makers in Indonesia through various forums. We thank the President's Delivery Unit for Development Monitoring and Oversight (UKP4) for co-organising Inter-Ministerial Roundtable Forum and extend our appreciation to high-level government and state-owned enterprises officials for useful research suggestions. We also received valuable feedback on preliminary findings from Dr Luky Eko Wuryanto, Deputy Minister for Infrastructure and Regional Development, the Coordinating Ministry for Economic Affairs of Indonesia and Mr Umar Juoro, then Member of the National Economic Council (KEN) appointed by the President of Republic of Indonesia, as both participated as discussants in a Review Seminar held at the Lee Kuan Yew School of Public Policy, National University of Singapore, on August 4, 2014. Their discussant notes are included in the respective chapters.

For each regional chapter, we have received research contributions from Indonesian graduates from Master in Public Policy and Master in Public Administration at the Lee Kuan Yew School of Public Policy, National University of Singapore. They are as follows:

Chapter 3 Sumatra Region: Rizky Novrianto and Bonifasius Agung Nugroho
Chapter 4 Java Region: Ririn Radiawati Kusuma and Raisa Annisa
Chapter 5 Kalimantan Region: Dessy Septiane Sukendar
Chapter 6 Sulawesi Region: Fenny Karlavita Siregar
Chapter 7 Bali–Nusa Tenggara Region: Fakhridho Susrahadiansyah Bagus Pratama
Chapter 8 Maluku–Papua Region: Edwina Frisdiantiny

We, in particular, would like to extend our appreciation for encouragement and solid support from Professor Kuntoro Mangkusubroto, then Head of UKP4, and Mr Mahendra Siregar, then Chairman of Indonesia Investment Coordinating Board (BKPM) at various stages of this research.

This report is the result of a strong partnership among the business sector, government, and academia. We are grateful for the collaboration with the Indonesian Employers' Association (APINDO) and continued support from its then chairman, Mr Sofjan Wanandi. We would also like to thank various local government offices and universities for their cooperation in hosting forums in their premises and participating in our perception surveys.

The coordination and execution of field trips would not have been possible without the excellent work by Yap Xin Yi, Muhammad Fadhel Jamali, Shanty Citra Eka Vebriani Yusup, Dedy Permadi, and Dr Riawati Jahja. We also thank Faizal Rianto and Faisal Rachman for valuable research assistance and extented ACI's researchers including Dr Linda Low, Adjunct Professor Ramkishen Rajan, Sangiita Yoong Wei Cher, Yuan Randong, Nie Tongxin, and Kartik Rao for their research inputs. Our appreciation is also extended to the staff of World Scientific who tirelessly ensure that our published work is of the highest quality.

Finally, we are immensely grateful to Dean Kishore Mahbubani and for the research funding from the Ministry of Trade and Industry Singapore in supporting this unprecedented effort, without which, such extensive book would not have been possible.

Tan Khee Giap, Nurina Merdikawati, Mulya Amri, and Tan Kong Yam
Asia Competitiveness Institute, Lee Kuan Yew School of Public Policy
National University of Singapore

About the Authors

Tan Khee Giap is a Co-Director of the Asia Competitiveness Institute (ACI) and Associate Professor at the Lee Kuan Yew School of Public Policy, National University of Singapore. He is also the Chairman of the Singapore National Committee for Pacific Economic Cooperation. Upon graduating with a PhD from University of East Anglia, England, in 1987 under the Overseas Research Scheme awarded by the Committee of Vice-Chancellors and Principals of the Universities of the United Kingdom, he joined the banking sector as a treasury manager and served as secretary to the Assets and Liabilities Committee for three years. Thereafter he taught at the Department of Economics and Statistics, National University of Singapore, 1990–1993. Dr Tan joined Nanyang Technological University in 1993 and was Associate Dean, Graduate Studies Office, 2007–2009. Dr Tan has consulted extensively with the various government ministries, statutory boards and government-linked companies of the Singapore Government. He has also served as a consultant to international agencies such as the Asian Development Bank, Asian Development Bank Institute, United Nations Industrial Development Group, World Gold Council, ASEAN Secretariat, Central Policy Unit of Hong Kong, Kerzner International, Las Vegas Sands and Marina Bay Sands. Dr Tan is the lead author for eight books and published widely in international refereed journals. His current research interests include econometric forecasting, Cost of Living Index, Global Liveable Cities Index and competitiveness analysis on 31 provinces in China, 35 states in India and ASEAN-10 economies. Dr Tan was Deputy President of the Singapore Economic Society, 2004. He served in the 2002 Economic Review Committee (ERC), served as Chairman of the Task Force on Portable Medical Benefits (PMB), served as the Deputy Chairman of the IPS Forum for Economic Restructuring (IFER) in 2003 and served as a member of the Resource Panel of the Government Parliamentary Committee for Transport and Government Parliamentary Committee for Finance and Trade since 2007. Dr Tan has extensively advised and guided multinational corporations leading to public listings especially those companies from Mainland China and Taiwan. He is also currently an Independent Director of the publicly listed Artivision, BreadTalk Group, Boustead Projects and TEE Land.

Nurina Merdikawati is a Research Associate at the Asia Competitiveness Institute (ACI) at the Lee Kuan Yew School of Public Policy (LKYSPP), National University of Singapore. Nurina graduated with a Master's degree in Public Policy from the LKYSPP with a specialisation in economic policy analysis. She was a Mochtar Riady Scholar and on the Dean's list. Nurina received her Bachelor's degree in Economics (Second Upper) from Nanyang Technological University, Singapore. She has worked with the Central Bank of Indonesia as a visiting researcher and held an internship at the Centre for Strategic and International Studies (CSIS) in Jakarta. At ACI, Nurina is co-ordinating the research on Indonesia's competitiveness analysis at the provincial and regional levels and the country's agriculture productivity. Prior to ACI, she spearheaded data management, collection, and analysis for INSEAD eLab projects and the Global Talent Competitiveness Index. Additionally, Nurina conducted firm-level studies on building business performance and competitiveness with new information and communications technology (ICTs), country-level studies on payment systems, and talent competitiveness.

Mulya Amri is a Research Associate at the Asia Competitiveness Institute (ACI) and PhD candidate at the Lee Kuan Yew School of Public Policy, National University of Singapore. He has 13 years of working experience in the private, public, and non-profit sectors. Before starting his PhD studies in 2011, Mulya worked in Singapore with HOK, a global planning and architecture consultancy firm, and with Jurong Consultants, the consultancy arm of Singapore's JTC Corporation, which is responsible for the planning, development and management of numerous industrial parks in Singapore. Prior to moving to Singapore, Mulya worked with international development agencies such as UNDP, UN-HABITAT, and the World Bank on projects related to urban and housing development, and community-driven development in various Indonesian regions. He was also a co-founder of COMBINE Resource Institution, an NGO based in Yogyakarta, Indonesia, working to strengthen community-based information systems. Together with Tan Khee Giap, Linda Low and Tan Kong Yam, Mulya co-wrote *Competitiveness Analysis and Development Strategies for 33 Indonesian Provinces*, published by World Scientific in 2013. He has also written book chapters on inter-municipal co-operation (published by GIZ), human settlements (published by the Ministry of Public Works, Indonesia), community media, and Corporate Social Responsibility (published by Indonesia Business Links). Mulya graduated with a Bachelor's degree from Institut Teknologi Bandung (ITB), Indonesia, and was awarded a Fulbright Scholarship to study for a Master's degree in Urban Planning at the University of California, Los Angeles (UCLA), and a Chevening award to study at the London School of Economics and Political Science (LSE).

Tan Kong Yam is a Co-Director of the Asia Competitiveness Institute (ACI) at the Lee Kuan Yew School of Public Policy, National University of Singapore. He is also Professor of Economics at the Nanyang Technological University. From June 2002 to June 2005, he was a senior economist at the World Bank office in Beijing where he worked on issues of macro stabilisation, integration of the fragmented domestic market, banking reform, international trade and investment, energy security as well as regional inequality. In 2004, he was a member of the World Bank expert group on the eleventh five-year plan (2006–10) for the State Council in China. The expert group provided the Chinese Government with analyses and policy recommendations on urbanization, regional inequality, innovation policy, energy and water policy as well as strategy on banking reform. Prior to that, he was the chief economist of the Singapore Government (1999–2002) and Head, Department of Business Policy, Faculty of Business Administration at the National University of Singapore. He is a graduate of Princeton (1975–79, class of 1931 scholar, Paul Volcker Thesis prize) and Stanford University (1980–83), where he completed his Master's and PhD in three years. Prior to joining NUS, he has worked at the Hoover Institution at Stanford University, World Bank, the Monetary Authority of Singapore, and was the Director of Research at the Ministry of Trade and Industry in Singapore. His research interests are in international trade and finance, economic and business trends in the Asia Pacific region and economic reforms in China. He has published ten books and numerous articles in major international journals including *American Economic Review*, *World Bank Economic Review*, *Long Range Planning*, *Australian Journal of Management* etc on economic and business issues in the Asia Pacific region. He served as a board member at the Singapore Central Provident Fund Board (1984–96) and the National Productivity Board (1989–90). He has also consulted for many organizations including Temasek, GIC, Citigroup, IBM, ATT, BP, ABN-AMRO, Ikea, Bank of China, China Construction Bank, People's Bank of China, EDB, Areva, Capitaland, Guangdong provincial government, Samsung, Mauritius Government, Ministry of Trade and Industry, Mobil, and Singapore Technology, amongst others.

List of Provinces

	Name of Province in Bahasa	Name of Province in English
1	Aceh	Aceh
2	Bali	Bali
3	Banten	Banten
4	Bengkulu	Bengkulu
5	DI Yogyakarta	DI Yogyakarta
6	DKI Jakarta	DKI Jakarta
7	Gorontalo	Gorontalo
8	Jambi	Jambi
9	Jawa Barat	West Java
10	Jawa Tengah	Central Java
11	Jawa Timur	East Java
12	Kalimantan Barat	West Kalimantan
13	Kalimantan Selatan	South Kalimantan
14	Kalimantan Tengah	Central Kalimantan
15	Kalimantan Timur	East Kalimantan
16	Kepulauan Bangka Belitung	Bangka Belitung Islands
17	Kepulauan Riau	Riau Islands
18	Lampung	Lampung
19	Maluku	Maluku
20	Maluku Utara	North Maluku
21	Nusa Tenggara Barat	West Nusa Tenggara
22	Nusa Tenggara Timur	East Nusa Tenggara
23	Papua	Papua
24	Papua Barat	West Papua
25	Riau	Riau
26	Sulawesi Barat	West Sulawesi
27	Sulawesi Selatan	South Sulawesi
28	Sulawesi Tengah	Central Sulawesi
29	Sulawesi Tenggara	Southeast Sulawesi
30	Sulawesi Utara	North Sulawesi
31	Sumatera Barat	West Sumatra
32	Sumatera Selatan	South Sumatra
33	Sumatera Utara	North Sumatra

List of Abbreviations

ACI	Asia Competitiveness Institute
ADB	Asian Development Bank
AEC	ASEAN Economic Community
AECV 2030	Asia Economic Connectivity Vision 2030
AIIB	Asian Infrastructure Investment Bank
ALKI	*Alur Laut Kepulauan Indonesia (Indonesia's Archipelagic Sea Lanes)*
AMDAL	*Analisis Dampak Lingkungan* (Environmental Impact Assessment)
APINDO	*Asosiasi Pengusaha Indonesia* (Indonesian Employers' Association)
APJII	*Asosiasi Penyelenggara Jasa Internet Indonesia* (Association of Internet Service Providers in Indonesia)
ASEAN	Association of Southeast Asian Nations
B2B	Business-to-Business
BKPM	*Badan Koordinasi Penanaman Modal* (Indonesia's Investment Coordinating Board)
BLK	*Balai Latihan Kerja* (Vocational Training Centre)
BPD	*Bank Pembangunan Daerah* (Regional Development Bank)
BPS	*Biro Pusat Statistik* (Central Statistical Bureau)
BRT	Bus Rapid Transit
CPO	Crude Palm Oil
CSR	Corporate Social Responsibility
DEA	Data Envelopment Analysis
EYE	Education for Youth Employment
FDI	Foreign Direct Investment
FMCG	Fast-Moving Consumer Goods
GCR	Global Competitiveness Report
GDP	Gross Domestic Product
GRDP	Gross Regional Domestic Product
HDI	Human Development Index
HRD	Human Resources Development
ICT	Information and Communications Technology
INDO-DAPOER	Indonesia Database for Policy and Economic Research
JICA	Japan International Corporation Agency
KBA	Key Biodiversity Area
KP3EI	*Komite Percepatan dan Perluasan Pembangunan Ekonomi Indonesia* (Committee for Acceleration and Expansion of Indonesia's Economic Development)
KPP	*Kursus Para Profesi* (Para Professional Course)
KSPP	*Klaster Sentra Produksi Pertanian* (Agricultural Production Centres)
LNG	Liquified Natural Gas
MAC	Middle-class and Affluent Consumers

MICE	Meetings, Incentives, Conferences and Exhibitions
MIFEE	Merauke Integrated Food and Energy Estate
MNCs	Multinational Corporations
MP3EI	*Masterplan Percepatan dan Perluasan Pembangunan Ekonomi Indonesia* (Master Plan for Acceleration and Expansion of Indonesia's Economic Development)
MRT	Mass Rapid Transit
NJOP	*Nilai Jual Objek Pajak* (Sales Value of the Tax Object)
NPLCT	North Pulau Laut Coal Terminal
NTT	*Nusa Tenggara Timur* (East Nusa Tenggara)
PELINDO	*PT. Pelabuhan Indonesia* (Port of Indonesia Ltd.)
PON	*Pekan Olahraga Nasional* (National Sports Week)
PPP	Public Private Partnership
PT KAI	*PT Kereta Api Indonesia* (Indonesian Railway Corporation)
R&D	Research and Development
RPJMD	*Rencana Pembangunan Jangka Menengah Daerah* (Provincial Medium–Term Development Plan)
RPJMN	*Rencana Pembangunan Jangka Menengah National* (National Medium–Term Development Plan)
RPJPN	*Rencana Pembangunan Jangka Panjang Nasional* (National Long–Term Development Plan)
RUU PPDK	*Rencana Undang-undang Percepatan Pembangunan Daerah Kepulauan* (Law on Acceleration of Development in Archipelagic Areas)
SEZ	Special Economic Zone
SMEs	Small and Medium-sized Enterprises
SMK	*Sekolah Menengah Kejuruan* (Vocational High School)
SOE	State-Owned Enterprise
TC	Technological Change
TEC	Technical Efficiency Change
TEU	Twenty-foot Equivalent Units
TFP	Total Factor Productivity
UKP4	*Unit Kerja Presiden bidang Pengawasan dan Pengendalian Pembangunan* (President's Delivery Unit for Development Monitoring and Oversight)
UN-REDD	United Nations Initiative for Reducing Emissions from Deforestation and Forest Degradation
UP4B	*Unit Percepatan Pembangunan Provinsi Papua dan Provinsi Papua Barat* (Unit for the Acceleration of Development in Papua and West Papua)
VLCC	Very Large Crude Carrier
WCY	World Competitiveness Yearbook

List of Tables and Figures

Chapter 3

Chapter 4

Chapter 5

Chapter 6

Chapter 1

2014 Competitiveness Ranking and Simulation Study for 33 Indonesian Provinces: An Annual Update

1. INTRODUCTION

1.1 Background and Notes

This book, updated to 2014, is the second in the annual series by the Asia Competitiveness Institute (ACI)[1] to analyse the competitiveness of Indonesia's sub-national entities.[2] The analysis highlights relevant development strategies as Indonesia joins other emerging economies and assumes its rightful competitive place in Southeast Asia.

Incorporating suggestions from our partners and stakeholders[3], this book contains both provincial competitiveness ranking, as well as competitiveness analysis and development strategies of six regions. These are defined by the country's Master Plan for Acceleration and Expansion of Indonesia's Economic Development 2011–2025 (MP3EI) as six "economic corridors".[4] This new shift in emphasis from 33 chapters for 33 provinces to six chapters for each of the six Indonesian regions is to highlight a cluster approach to galvanise and synergise efforts across-the-board.

Chapter 1 presents updates on the analysis of competitiveness rankings and simulation studies for the 33 provinces for 2014 based on 2011 data.[5] Chapter 2 provides the overview of the ACI's inaugural regional competitiveness ranking. The following chapters 3–8 provide greater details for each region by analysing their comparative strengths and weaknesses, as well as development strategies.

Going beyond provincial and regional competitiveness rankings, this 2014 publication also features one chapter on more specific aspects of competitiveness. In Chapter 9, the ACI uses Geweke causality[6] in probing into provinces with particularly high and low competitiveness levels to explain the main factors that account for their performance. We analyse two highly competitive provinces, East Java and East Kalimantan, in contrast to two provinces with low competitiveness, East Nusa Tenggara and North Maluku. By applying Geweke's analysis, we identify how different factors interplay with each other in determining their respective competitiveness.

---

[1] Tan Khee Giap *et al.*, *Competitiveness Analysis and Development Strategies for 33 Indonesian Provinces* (Singapore: World Scientific, 2013) marks the first in the series. Subsequent journal article can be found in Tan Khee Giap and Mulya Amri, "Subnational Competitiveness and National Performance: Analysis and Simulation for Indonesia," *Journal of Centrum Cathedra (JCC): The Business and Economics Research Journal* Vol. 6, No. 2 (2013):173–192. See also other ACI studies with the same competitiveness framework: Tan Khee Giap *et al.*, *Annual Analysis of Competitiveness, Development Strategies and Public Policies on ASEAN-10: 2000–2010* (Singapore: Pearson, 2013); Tan Khee Giap *et al.*, *Annual Analysis of Competitiveness, Simulation Studies and Development Perspective for 34 Greater China Economies: 2000–2010* (Singapore: World Scientific, 2013); and Tan Khee Giap *et al.*, *Annual Analysis of Competitiveness, Simulation Studies and Development Perspective for 35 States and Federal Territories of India: 2000–2010* (Singapore: World Scientific, 2013).

[2] Results of the 2013 study were based on data from 2010. Results for the 2014 competitiveness are updated to 2011. Conventionally, due to collation, compilation and publication of official data, such a lag of data before reaching end-users is acceptable.

[3] The ACI held Review Seminar on *Safeguarding Indonesia's Growth Momentum: Enhancing Regional Competitiveness, Increasing Productivity and Improving Layers of Government* on August 4, 2014, to solicit comments and suggestions from policy advisers and scholars. Concurrently, the annual field trip to 33 provinces, where meetings and discussions were held with business owners (facilitated by Indonesian Employers' Association (APINDO)), government officials, and academics, had also generated input and feedback.

[4] Coordinating Ministry for Economic Affairs, *Master Plan for Acceleration and Expansion of Indonesia's Economic Development 2011–2025 (MP3EI)* (Jakarta: Coordinating Ministry for Economic Affairs, 2011).

[5] North Kalimantan, the newly created province in 2012, is not yet included pending availability of data.

[6] John Geweke, "Measurement of linear dependence and feedback between multiple time series," *Journal of the American Statistical Association* Vol. 77, No. 378 (1982): 304–313.

Finally, Chapter 10 provides concluding remarks that sum up the gist from each chapter that paves the way forward. It also briefly elaborates the ACI's future research agenda on the role of decentralisation and governing institutions in economic development, agricultural productivity, and potential middle-income trap.

1.2 Motivation, Objectives and Expected Contributions

Indonesia is confidently claiming its place as one of the world's rising "middle powers".[7] The 1997 Asian Financial Crisis coupled with abrupt political transition in 1998 brought the country's economy down temporarily.[8] However, Indonesia quickly regained political stability and showed remarkable economic resilience to rebound. Since 2002, the annual Gross Domestic Product (GDP) growth has been consistently above 4.5%. Since 2005, GDP growth has been hovering around 6% per year — except in 2009 during Global Financial Crisis when growth rate dipped slightly to 4.63%.

As the largest country in Southeast Asia, Indonesia's economic growth is expected to bring greater regional stability by creating positive spillover effects to its neighbours, especially members of the Association of Southeast Asian Nations (ASEAN). A study by the ACI on the competitiveness of ASEAN-10 countries for 2000–2010 found that a 1% increase in Indonesia's GDP correlates with a 0.25% increase in Singapore's GDP.[9] As Indonesia and Singapore further strengthen their economic ties, both bilaterally and within the framework of ASEAN Economic Community (AEC), there is greater awareness on how Indonesia's economic growth brings mutual benefit to both countries.

There are a number of lessons in which Indonesia could learn from the international marketplace of ideas. One of such lessons comes from the People's Republic of China, which has managed to maintain around 10% growth rate over multiple decades. One of the keys to China's success is setting in place a system that encourages healthy competition among sub-national entities (provinces, cities, municipalities, etc.), where incentives are given to local leaders who perform well. In some instances, due to the autonomy of local and provincial governments, the Chinese fiscal system has been dubbed as "market-preserving federalism".[10]

Indonesia's decentralisation laws, ratified in 1999 and updated in 2004, promote a system where the authority to address local matters (except for foreign affairs, defence, justice, finance, religion, natural resources, and state administration) rests in the hands of sub-national governments. The laws also stipulate that fiscal resources will be made available in a balanced manner to enable sub-national governments to conduct this role. The laws open the possibility to enable healthy competition and collaboration among sub-national governments towards inclusive economic growth. With this paradigm, each province, city, and district should clearly understand their strengths and weaknesses. On top of that, they are also expected to understand and act upon the strengths and weaknesses of their neighbouring provinces.

This study is conducted by the ACI as a professional and neutral party with empirical factual results. The intention of the study is for relevant region or province to better understand the competitiveness among Indonesia's sub-national peers, identify strategies to improve their situation, and promote a mindset of healthy competition and collaboration among regions. Such peer review among regions can trigger the development of more sustainable economic fundamentals in Indonesia and promote further ASEAN cooperation. The ACI intends to conduct this research annually so that the competitiveness profile of Indonesian provinces and regions is not just captured once as a portrait, but continuously to enable a study into the dynamics of competitiveness over time.

More specifically, for Indonesia's central government agencies, this research is expected to give further insights on the different development levels (including disparities) related to competitiveness across Indonesia's provinces and regions in a concise and policy-friendly language. For provincial stakeholders, be it the

[7] Andrew Cooper and Jongryn Mo, "Middle Power Leadership and the Evolution of the G20," *Global Summitry Journal* Vol. 1 (2013): 1–14.

[8] Steven Radelet and Jeffrey D. Sachs, "The East Asian Financial Crisis: Diagnosis, Remedies, Prospects," *Brookings Papers on Economic Activity* Vol. 1 (1998): 1–90.

[9] Tan Khee Giap *et al.*, *Annual Analysis of Competitiveness, Development Strategies and Public Policies on ASEAN-10: 2000–2010.*

[10] Barry R. Weingast, "The Economic Role of Political Institutions: Market-Preserving Federalism and Economic Development," *Journal of Law, Economics, & Organisation* Vol. 11, No. 1 (1995): 1–31.

government or businesses, this research can be used as a benchmark to measure their province's competitiveness in relation to the other provinces in the country, and to identify critical areas which need further attention. For investors, either from within Indonesia or abroad, this research could serve as a rough map of investment potentials and challenges in different parts of Indonesia. For academics, professors, and researchers around the world, this study is hoped to contribute to the literature on economic development in Indonesia's regions and spawn more intellectual creativity.

2. RESEARCH METHODOLOGY

2.1 Existing Literature on Competitiveness Reviews

The notion of regional or *in-situ* competitiveness has been explored in various ways. Initially, in the 1980s, "competitiveness" was considered as a part of the private sector domain, especially in relation to firm performance.[11] Over time, the discourse expanded onto the domain of macroeconomics, as shown by the establishment of "Council on Competitiveness" or similar institution in various advanced industrialised countries. Some scholars acknowledge that it is primarily firms that compete, not nations, regions, or places.[12] However, the performances of those firms depend on various factors that are embedded in the firms' location. These include quality of labour and infrastructure, governance, costs of doing business, as well as the performance of competing and complementary firms around the area.[13]

Two of the most highly cited cross-country competitiveness studies at the moment are the World Competitiveness Yearbook (WCY)[14] and the Global Competitiveness Report (GCR)[15]. The WCY defines competitiveness as composed of four factors: (a) economic performance, (b) government efficiency, (c) business efficiency, and (d) infrastructure. Each factor is further made up of five criteria, so that there are 20 criteria in total. The WCY uses equal weights such that each criterion contributes 5% weight, and each factor contributes 25% weight to the overall competitiveness index.[16] Most of the data used are statistical indicators sourced from international, regional, and national organisations. However, substantial perception data sourced from executive surveys supplement the statistical data.

The GCR breaks down its Global Competitiveness Index into three sub-indices: (a) basic requirements, (b) efficiency enhancers, and (c) innovation and sophistication factors.[17] Each of the three sub-indices has a different number of pillars. The basic requirements sub-index has four pillars: institutions, infrastructure, macroeconomic environment, and health and primary education. The efficiency enhancers sub-index is composed of six pillars: higher education and training, goods market efficiency, labour market efficiency, financial market development, technological readiness, and market size. Lastly, the innovation and sophistication factors sub-index consists of two pillars: business sophistication and innovation. Most of the data that make up these pillars and sub-indices come from executive opinion surveys.

2.2 The ACI's Competitiveness Framework

The ACI's approach to competitiveness is holistic, integrated, and systemic, encompassing all different factors that collectively shape the ability of a nation, region, or province to achieve substantial and inclusive economic development over a sustained period of time.

---

[11] Michael Porter, *Competitive Strategy* (New York: Free Press, 1980).

[12] Paul Krugman, "Competitiveness: a dangerous obsession," *Foreign Affairs* Vol. 73 (1994): 28–44.

[13] See Gillian Bristow, *Critical Reflections on Regional Competitiveness: Theory, Policy, and Practice* (New York: Routledge, 2010); Roberto Camagni, "On the Concept of Territorial Competitiveness: Sound or Misleading?" *Urban Studies* Vol. 39, No. 13 (2002): 2395–2411; and Michael Kitson, Ronald L Martin, and Peter Tyler, "Regional Competitiveness: An Elusive Yet Key Concept?" *Regional Studies* Vol. 38, No. 9 (2004): 999–1000 for further details.

[14] International Institute for Management Development (IMD), *IMD World Competitiveness Yearbook* (Lausanne: IMD, 2014).

[15] World Economic Forum (WEF), *The Global Competitiveness Report 2013–2014* (Geneva: WEF, 2014).

[16] IMD, *IMD World Competitiveness Yearbook.*

[17] WEF, *The Global Competitiveness Report 2013–2014.*

Figure 1.1. The ACI's Competitiveness Framework

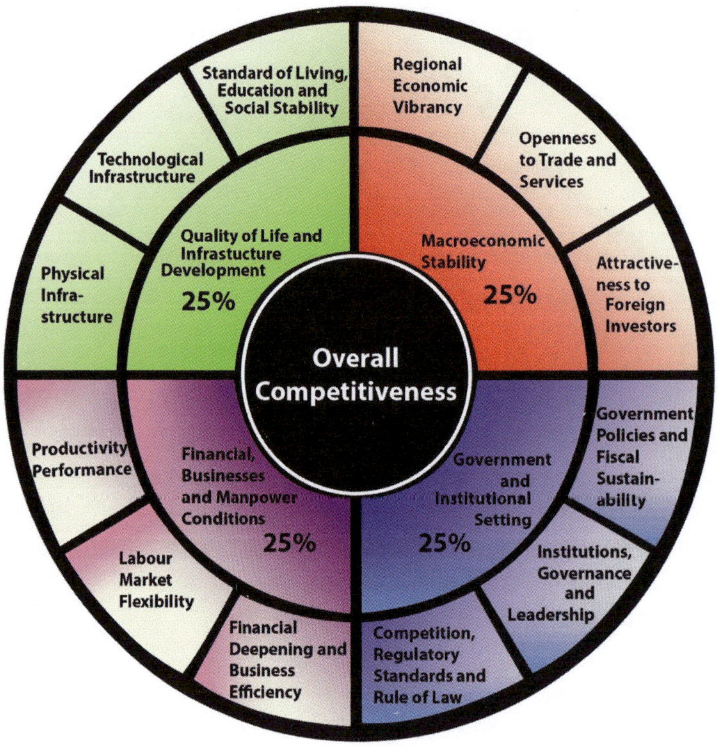

Source: Asia Competitiveness Institute

In line with this comprehensive approach, the ACI defines competitiveness through four different environments: (a) Macroeconomic Stability, (b) Government and Institutional Setting, (c) Financial, Businesses and Manpower Conditions, and (d) Quality of Life and Infrastructure Development. As visualised in Figure 1.1, each contributes the same weight (25%) to the Overall Competitiveness index.

The ACI's competitiveness framework further drills down to nested approach, wherein each of the four environments is further divided into three sub-environments (each sub-environment is nested within a specific environment). Therefore, there are 12 sub-environments altogether. Each sub-environment contributes the same weight (33.3%) towards its respective environment's index.

In aggregating sub-environments into environments, and environments into an overall ranking, the ACI uses a simple averaging mechanism with equal weights. While assigning different weights for different indicators with varying levels of importance may seem appropriate, the implementations are as controversial. Thus, to achieve a balanced view towards the different factors that make up an overall notion of competitiveness, we use equal weights across all indicators.

Two environments are predominantly economic, while the other two incorporate political, institutional, social, and physical attributes. Altogether, there are 12 sub-environments.

1. Macroeconomic Stability, encompassing aggregated economic conditions in the province, includes the following sub-environments:

    a) Regional Economic Vibrancy,
    b) Openness to Trade and Services,
    c) Attractiveness to Foreign Investors.

2. Government and Institutional Setting, covering efficacy of government institutions as well as expectations of progress in the public sector, includes the following sub-environments:

    a) Government Policies and Fiscal Sustainability,
    b) Institutions, Governance and Leadership,
    c) Competition, Regulatory Standards and Rule of Law.

3. Financial, Businesses and Manpower Conditions, representing the performance and potential of firms as well as conditions that managers face in running their companies, includes the following sub-environments:
   a) Financial Deepening and Business Efficiency,
   b) Labour Market Flexibility,
   c) Productivity Performance.
4. Quality of Life and Infrastructure Development, combining infrastructure with basic social services, includes the following sub-environments:
   a) Physical Infrastructure,
   b) Technological Infrastructure,
   c) Standard of Living, Education and Social Stability.

2.3 Indicators and Data Sources

For the 2014 study on Indonesia's 33 provinces and six regions, the ACI uses 104 unique indicators, as compared to 91 indicators used in 2013 study. See Appendix 1 for the complete list of indicators.

To a certain extent, having additional indicators ensures more robust interpretation of the aggregated sub-environment score. Uneven distribution of indicators across sub-environments (due to data availability) is acknowledged, but it is not an issue. Regardless of the number of indicators in a sub-environment, they will simply average out. This also allows a certain amount of flexibility in adding or removing indicators when updating the index in the future, as long as the overall structure of the 12 sub-environments nested within the four environments does not change.

Data for the 104 indicators used in this study came from various sources. Most of the data (79 out of 104 indicators, approximately 76%) were from the year 2011, taken from official sources, such as the Central Statistical Bureau (BPS), Central Bank (*Bank Indonesia*), Ministry of Health, etc. These were secondary quantitative data, such as Gross Regional Domestic Product (GRDP), export, import, length of paved roads, etc. Due to lag in data availability, the latest available data at the time of collection in mid-2013 came from 2011.

A smaller portion of the data (25 out of 104 indicators, approximately 24%) was sourced through perception surveys conducted in each province in the second half of 2013. Three types of stakeholders were surveyed separately in each province: (1) business owners and operators, (2) provincial government, and (3) academics. Responses from the three different stakeholders were aggregated at the province level, with the intention that one stakeholder group can provide a balancing view for the other stakeholders.

Due to resource limitations, the sampling method was purposive sampling, instead of random sampling. The ACI collaborated with local partners with knowledgeable respondents. For business owners and operators, the surveys were done in collaboration with the Indonesian Employers' Association (APINDO), which has chapters in each province and invited their members to participate in the survey. For government respondents, the surveys were supported by the Coordinating Ministry for Economic Affairs, which provided reference letters to the governors of the 33 provinces. The provincial government, in turn, invited representatives from various provincial government departments to participate in the survey. For academics, the ACI collaborated with universities in each province, most often with the school of economics and business, but not exclusively so. The university or school then invited their lecturers, researchers, and graduate students to participate in the survey.

The surveys were conducted using an electronic response system, where questions were presented on a computer projector, and participants were to key in their answers using keypads or "clickers". Facilitators from the ACI were present in each survey to read the questions and give clarifications when needed. In a rare case where an electronic survey could not be conducted, respondents were given paper-based survey forms to fill in. The fact that the surveys were done in face-to-face manner also provided good opportunity for the ACI to discuss specific topics in more detail with relevant parties who are knowledgeable about their province.

The surveys managed to capture a total of 1,973 respondents. Of these, 725 were business owners and operators, 698 were academics, and 550 were provincial government officials. The number of respondents is equivalent to about 60 respondents per province on average (1,973 respondents divided by 33 provinces). Out of these 60 respondents, typically 22 were business owners and operators, 21 were academics, and 17 were provincial government officials.[18]

2.4 The Standardised Score

Upon completion of data collection, the next step is to determine how to aggregate the different types of data into one coherent way of analysis. There are 104 different indicators used in this research, each in different value or quantity terms, such as Length of Paved Roads in kilometres and survey results in Likert Scale. How do we resolve these differences in the measurement units?

We use a statistical methodology of 'standardised score'. The standardised score is a relative comparison to see how well the performance of a certain province or region is, in comparison to the average province or region. Therefore, the unit of measurement is no longer relevant. The standardised score has no unit of measurement because it simply measures relative performance among provinces or regions, whatever the indicator is. In statistical terms, it measures how many standard deviations away is each province or region from the average province or region. See Appendix 2 for technical explanation on computing the rankings.

If a province or region has a standardised score of zero, it is basically an average performer in terms of that particular indicator. Having a negative score means the province or region performs below average. Having a positive score, on the other hand, means above-average performance. The further away the score is from zero, the further away is the performance of said province or region from the national average.

The standardised scores for each indicator are then systematically aggregated, firstly at the sub-environment level, followed by re-aggregation at the environment level, and finally, at the overall level. This allows for comparison of performance between the 33 provinces (or six regions) at different levels, from the Overall Competitiveness to specific indicators.

To ensure more robust calculation of the standardised score, there has been an update to the algorithm used in this year's study compared to that of the previous year. In the previous year[19], standardisation was conducted only once at the indicator level. No further standardisation was conducted afterwards (i.e. when aggregating the indicators into 12 sub-environments, four environments, and one Overall Competitiveness). By contrast, in this current volume, standardisation was conducted after each aggregation. As such, there were four standardisations conducted: (1) at the indicator level, (2) after aggregating indicators into sub-environments, (3) after aggregating sub-environments into environments, and (4) after aggregating environments into Overall Competitiveness. The update in methodology resulted in wider spread between the minimum and maximum scores for the 33 provinces, which means that the score difference has become slightly more pronounced.

2.5 *What-if* Simulation

A competitiveness ranking in itself seems like a beauty contest. It identifies who are doing well and who are facing challenges, but stops short of giving more constructive advice on improving the rankings.

We go one step beyond by tackling the "so what" question. What is the policy implication of a competitiveness ranking result for a particular province? The data available allow us to do an in-depth analysis of the performance of each province according to the different indicators, sub-environments, and environments. By analysing the data, we are able to identify not only the Overall Competitiveness ranking, but also specific

[18] Out of the 99 surveys that were planned (three in each of the 33 provinces), only 96 could be conducted. Three provincial governments were not surveyed due to technical difficulties. They were the provincial governments of Riau, Riau Islands, and Central Kalimantan. For these three cases, proxy scores were used to represent the survey results of the provincial government. However, surveys with the other two stakeholders (academics and businesses) for these three provinces were successfully conducted.

[19] Tan Khee Giap *et al.*, *Competitiveness Analysis and Development Strategies for 33 Indonesian Provinces.*

indicators for which the province is doing well or struggling. This allows us to come up with policy recommendations for each province.

The ACI's *what-if* competitiveness simulation is based on the improvement of each province's top 20% weakest indicators by policies, and a re-calculation of the standardised score based on such improvement.

To conduct the simulation, we firstly looked at each province and sorted the different indicators for each province from the highest to the lowest score. This allowed us to identify the top 20% weakest indicators of each province. Next, we raised the scores of these 20% weakest indicators moderately to match the average score. This means that the scores of these indicators are raised to zero, if previously negative. If they are already zero or positive, then no changes are made to the scores.

Once these scores were raised, we re-calculated the ranking with the assumption that other provinces remained constant. Therefore, this policy simulation was done one-by-one for each province. Each province would then have a new and improved standardised score. This allowed us to answer the question: if a particular province improves on its weakest indicators while assuming that other provinces remain constant, how would that province's competitiveness ranking improve?

The *what-if* competitiveness simulation was conducted only for the 33 provinces and not for the six regions due to limited number of cases.

3. ANALYSIS ON ACI'S PROVINCIAL COMPETITIVENESS RANKING

Having explained the methodology for constructing the ACI's Competitiveness Index, we now examine the results of the competitiveness ranking of Indonesian provinces for 2014.[20] The ranking is derived from sorting the standardised score for each province. Thus, an analysis of the ranking results should be done in conjunction with a review of the standardised scores.

3.1 Competitiveness Ranking of 33 Provinces — Rank and Score by Environment

Quantitative Spread — Overall Competitiveness

The Overall Competitiveness ranking (Table 1.1) is an aggregate of four specific competitiveness environments. Detailed discussion on the four environments will follow afterwards.

For Overall Competitiveness, there are several components to take note in terms of standardised scores: the spread (maximum and minimum scores), the average, and the median.

From the spread, we see that the scores range from a maximum of 3.3580 to a minimum of –1.7075. The province with the maximum score is DKI Jakarta, which is the top rank. The province with minimum score is North Maluku, ranked as the 33rd. With a closer look at the range, however, we find that except for DKI Jakarta, the other 32 provinces fall under the range of 1.8152 (East Java) to –1.7075 (North Maluku). DKI Jakarta, thus, can be considered an 'outlier' as its score (3.3580) is significantly much higher than the other provinces.

Including DKI Jakarta, the average performing province (score of zero) is somewhere between that occupying the 12th (Banten, 0.1672) and the 13th position (Aceh, –0.0109). The median is always in the middle, which is the province holding 17th position (West Sumatra, –0.2179). We can see that the average score (zero, at position between 12th and 13th) is higher than the median score (–0.2179, at 17th position), which means that the average is skewed upwards towards DKI Jakarta's high score.

With closer scrutiny, we also find several "jumps" in the standardised scores. The gap between the top scorer (DKI Jakarta) and the runner up (East Java) has been pointed out. However, wide gaps also exist between the provinces occupying the top five positions, as well as between those occupying the bottom five positions. Towards the middle part of Table 1.1, gaps occur between the provinces in the 11th, 12th, and 13th position (Riau Islands, Banten, and Aceh).

[20] As previously mentioned, the hard data are based on 2011 and the soft data are from 2013. For more details, please see section 2.3.

Table 1.1. 2014 Overall Competitiveness: Ranking and Score

2014 Rank	2013 Rank	Province	2014 Score
1	1	DKI Jakarta	3.3580
2	2	East Java	1.8152
3	3	East Kalimantan	1.5566
4	5	Central Java	1.3262
5	4	West Java	1.0834
6	6	DI Yogyakarta	0.7047
7	11	South Sulawesi	0.6684
8	13	South Kalimantan	0.4884
9	10	Riau	0.3731
10	14	North Sulawesi	0.3109
11	8	Riau Islands	0.2901
12	7	Banten	0.1672
13	16	Aceh	−0.0109
14	9	Bali	−0.0179
15	26	Central Kalimantan	−0.0754
16	12	South Sumatra	−0.1676
17	17	West Sumatra	−0.2179
18	22	West Kalimantan	−0.2234
19	19	North Sumatra	−0.2594
20	29	Bangka Belitung Islands	−0.2756
21	23	Central Sulawesi	−0.3553
22	28	West Nusa Tenggara	−0.3733
23	31	Maluku	−0.5685
24	20	Lampung	−0.5773
25	21	West Sulawesi	−0.5870
26	30	West Papua	−0.7013
27	25	Jambi	−0.7379
28	15	Gorontalo	−0.7549
29	18	Southeast Sulawesi	−0.7833
30	27	Bengkulu	−0.9576
31	24	Papua	−1.2268
32	33	East Nusa Tenggara	−1.5634
33	32	North Maluku	−1.7075

Source: Asia Competitiveness Institute

Geographic Spread — Overall Competitiveness

The Overall Competitiveness ranking can also be viewed on a map of Indonesian provinces, as seen in Figure 1.2. On the map, provinces are colour-coded based on three groups: Top 10 positions (green), Bottom 10 positions (red), and Middle 13 positions (yellow). Several points could be highlighted from Figure 1.2. First, we see a noticeable geographic concentration of high-competitiveness and low-competitiveness provinces, although less pronounced than the 2013 ranking. The top performing provinces are still dominated by Java, where five out of six Java provinces (except Banten) are in the Top 10. However, the five remaining Top 10 provinces are now more evenly spread, with two from Kalimantan (East Kalimantan at third and South Kalimantan at eighth),

Figure 1.2. 2014 Map of Overall Competitiveness Ranking

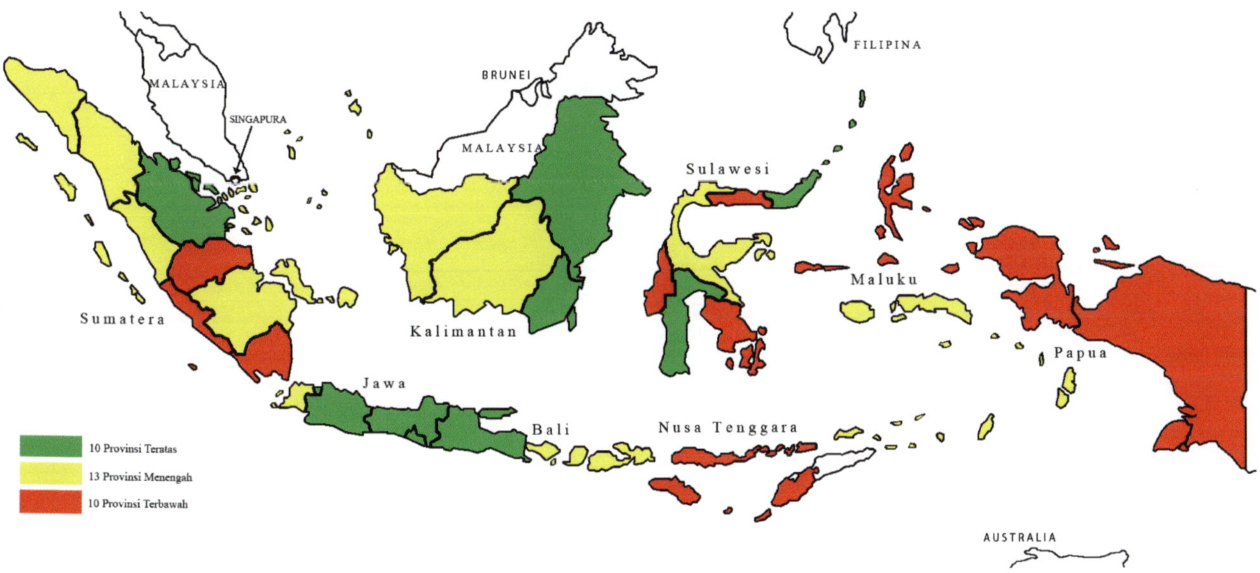

Source: Asia Competitiveness Institute

two from Sulawesi (South Sulawesi at seventh and North Sulawesi at 10th), and one from Sumatra (Riau at ninth).

Provinces in eastern Indonesia still dominate the Bottom 10, but the disparity is less pronounced compared to the 2013 ranking. Three provinces from the easternmost region occupy the Bottom 10 (North Maluku (33rd), Papua (31st), and West Papua (26th)), along with three provinces from Sulawesi (Southeast Sulawesi (29th), Gorontalo (28th), and West Sulawesi (25th)), three provinces from Sumatra (Bengkulu (30th), Jambi (27th), and Lampung (24th)), and East Nusa Tenggara at 32nd.

Some general conclusions can be drawn about the geographic spread of Overall Competitiveness: (1) Provinces in Java are very competitive, (2) Provinces in Kalimantan are relatively competitive, (3) Provinces in Sumatra and Sulawesi show mixed competitiveness, and (4) Provinces in Bali, Nusa Tenggara, Maluku, and Papua are generally less competitive. It is important to note, especially for policymakers, that given Indonesia's archipelagic spread, distance and connectivity matter in competitiveness. Soft infrastructure, such as information and communications technology (ICT), is as vital.

Quantitative Spread — Macroeconomic Stability

As seen from Table 1.2 for Macroeconomic Stability, we see that the scores range from a maximum of 4.6199 to a minimum of –0.9008. The province topping the rank with the maximum score is DKI Jakarta. The province with the minimum score is East Nusa Tenggara, ranked at 33rd. There is a huge gap in score between DKI Jakarta in the first position (4.6199) and East Java in the second position (1.7543). Excluding the top three performing provinces, a more symmetrical score range between East Kalimantan (fourth, 0.7591) and East Nusa Tenggara (33rd, –0.9008) can be seen.

The average performing province (score of zero) is between that occupying the 11th (South Sulawesi) and the 12th position (South Sumatra). The median position is held by West Sulawesi at the 17th position, with a score of –0.3447. Similar to Table 1.1 for Overall Competitiveness, we see that the average score (zero, 11th–12th) is higher than the median score. This means that the average is also skewed upwards towards DKI Jakarta's, East Java's, and West Java's high scores. However, the score differences are even more extreme, highlighting major disparities in this environment.

Several "jumps" in the standardised scores are also observable, such as between the provinces in the first, second, third, and fourth positions (DKI Jakarta, East Java, West Java, and East Kalimantan, respectively). Another large gap occurs between the province occupying seventh position (Banten, 0.3737) and eighth position (Riau, 0.1504).

Table 1.2. 2014 Macroeconomic Stability: Ranking and Score

2014 Rank	2013 Rank	Province	2014 Score
1	1	DKI Jakarta	4.6199
2	2	East Java	1.7543
3	3	West Java	1.2443
4	4	East Kalimantan	0.7591
5	5	Riau Islands	0.5828
6	6	Central Java	0.4649
7	7	Banten	0.3737
8	9	Riau	0.1504
9	10	North Sumatra	0.1047
10	12	South Kalimantan	0.1037
11	15	South Sulawesi	0.0628
12	16	South Sumatra	–0.0586
13	20	North Sulawesi	–0.1281
14	19	West Papua	–0.2456
15	21	Central Kalimantan	–0.2519
16	32	Central Sulawesi	–0.3223
17	28	West Sulawesi	–0.3447
18	8	Bali	–0.3730
19	13	Bangka Belitung Islands	–0.3985
20	14	Jambi	–0.4055
21	24	West Kalimantan	–0.4102
22	18	DI Yogyakarta	–0.4499
23	31	Southeast Sulawesi	–0.4697
24	11	Papua	–0.4765
25	27	Gorontalo	–0.4955
26	25	West Sumatra	–0.5170
27	22	West Nusa Tenggara	–0.5226
28	33	Aceh	–0.5510
29	17	Lampung	–0.5659
30	23	Maluku	–0.6522
31	30	Bengkulu	–0.7948
32	26	North Maluku	–0.8863
33	29	East Nusa Tenggara	–0.9008

Source: Asia Competitiveness Institute

Geographic Spread — Macroeconomic Stability

The map for Macroeconomic Stability (Figure 1.3) similarly shows a noticeable geographic clustering of high-competitiveness and low-competitiveness provinces. Top performing provinces are still dominated by Java, where five out of six Java provinces (except DI Yogyakarta) are in the Top 10. The five remaining Top 10 provinces are clustered around the Malacca Strait (Riau Islands at fifth place, Riau at eighth place, and North Sumatra at ninth place) and along the eastern coast of Kalimantan (East Kalimantan at fourth place and South Kalimantan at 10th place).

Figure 1.3. 2014 Map of Macroeconomic Stability Ranking

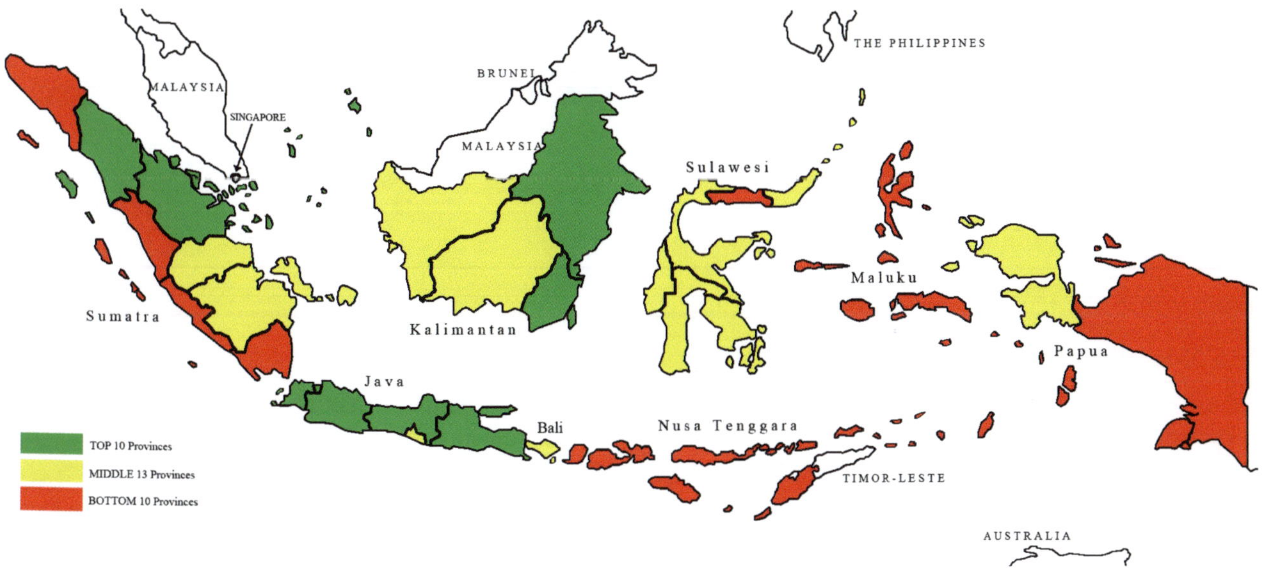

Source: Asia Competitiveness Institute

Provinces in the Bottom 10 also tend to cluster together. The clusters are the Maluku and Papua islands cluster (North Maluku (32nd), Maluku (30th), and Papua (24th)), the Nusa Tenggara cluster (East Nusa Tenggara (33rd) and West Nusa Tenggara (27th)), and the Sumatra's western coast cluster (Bengkulu (31st), Lampung (29th), Aceh (28th), and West Sumatra (26th)), as well as Gorontalo (25th) in Sulawesi.

Some general conclusions can be drawn about the geographic spread of Macroeconomic Stability: (1) Provinces in Java are very competitive, (2) Provinces in Kalimantan are relatively competitive, (3) Provinces in Sumatra and Sulawesi show mixed competitiveness, and (4) Provinces in Bali, Nusa Tenggara, Maluku, and Papua are generally less competitive.

Quantitative Spread — Government and Institutional Setting

For Government and Institutional Setting, as per Table 1.3, we see that the scores range from a maximum of 2.0408 (DKI Jakarta, first) to a minimum of –2.4930 (North Maluku, 33rd). This range is more symmetrical, meaning that no province is strongly pulling the average score towards either direction (upwards or downwards).

The average performing province (score of zero) is between that occupying the 18th (Gorontalo) and the 19th position (Central Kalimantan). The median position is held by South Sumatra at the 17th position, with score of 0.0560. The average score (zero, 18th–19th) is lower than the median score (0.0560, 17th), which means that the average is skewed slightly downwards towards the low performing provinces, especially by North Maluku's low score.

There are gaps or "jumps" in score throughout the board, but none is as extreme as those seen in Table 1.2 (Macroeconomic Stability). The biggest gap exists between North Maluku at the 33rd position (–2.4930) and East Nusa Tenggara at the 32nd position (–1.5920). This calls for attention as North Maluku is rather far behind other provinces in terms of Government and Institutional Setting.

The other noticeable gap is seen between DKI Jakarta at first place (2.0408) and Central Java at second place (1.5230). However, this gap is not as big as those shown in Table 1.1 and Table 1.2, implying that DKI Jakarta cannot be complacent.

Table 1.3. 2014 Government and Institutional Setting: Ranking and Score

2014 Rank	2013 Rank	Province	2014 Score
1	1	DKI Jakarta	2.0408
2	3	Central Java	1.5230
3	7	South Sulawesi	1.3156
4	17	East Kalimantan	1.2568
5	2	East Java	1.1538
6	9	West Java	1.0261
7	4	DI Yogyakarta	1.0260
8	10	North Sulawesi	0.7359
9	13	Aceh	0.6563
10	12	West Sulawesi	0.4997
11	11	South Kalimantan	0.4630
12	14	Central Sulawesi	0.4109
13	18	West Kalimantan	0.3906
14	27	Riau	0.3109
15	19	West Nusa Tenggara	0.2010
16	29	Bangka Belitung Islands	0.0711
17	6	South Sumatra	0.0560
18	8	Gorontalo	0.0392
19	24	Central Kalimantan	–0.1041
20	33	Maluku	–0.1633
21	21	Lampung	–0.2466
22	15	Southeast Sulawesi	–0.3328
23	5	Banten	–0.3767
24	16	Bali	–0.4068
25	23	West Sumatra	–0.4596
26	25	Jambi	–0.8221
27	6	North Sumatra	–1.0464
28	22	Papua	–1.1625
29	28	West Papua	–1.2482
30	20	Bengkulu	–1.3418
31	29	Riau Islands	–1.3806
32	32	East Nusa Tenggara	–1.5920
33	31	North Maluku	–2.4930

Source: Asia Competitiveness Institute

Geographic Spread — Government and Institutional Setting

Figure 1.4 shows some noticeable clustering of high-competitiveness and low-competitiveness provinces. The top performing provinces are still dominated by Java, where five out of six Java provinces (except Banten) are in the Top 10. The remaining Top 10 provinces are clustered at Makassar Strait (South Sulawesi at third, West Sulawesi at 10th, and East Kalimantan at fourth), as well as North Sulawesi at eighth and Aceh at ninth position.

Figure 1.4. 2014 Map of Government and Institutional Setting Ranking

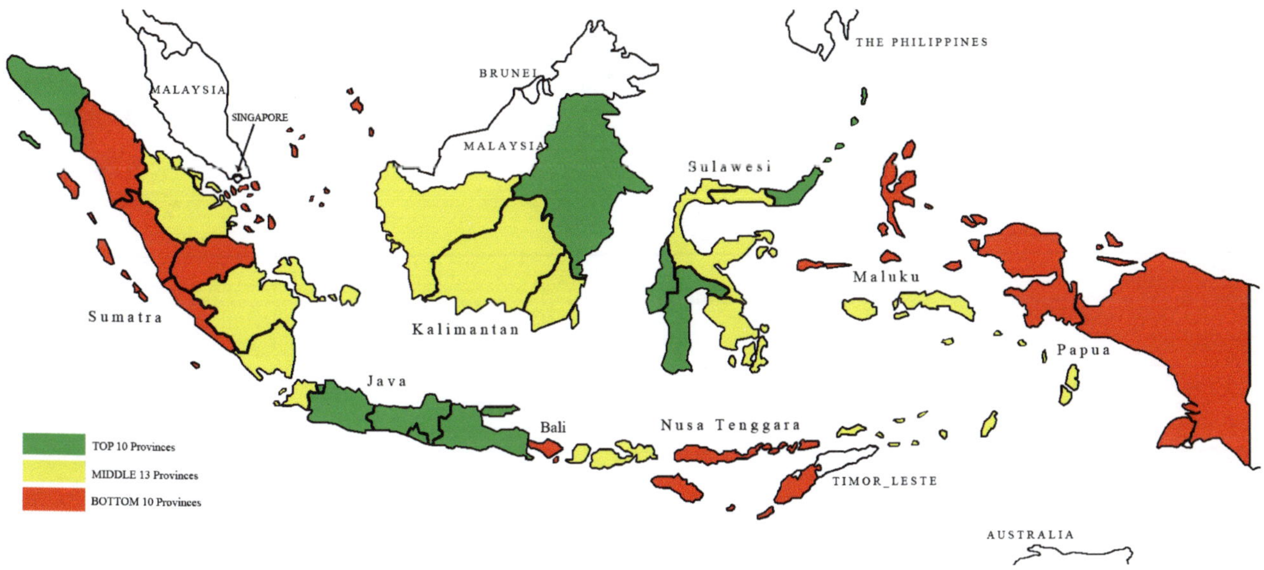

Source: Asia Competitiveness Institute

Provinces in the Bottom 10 also have tendency to cluster: the Maluku and Papua cluster (North Maluku (33rd), Papua (28th), and West Papua (29th)), the Bali–Nusa Tenggara cluster (East Nusa Tenggara (32nd) and Bali (24th)), and the Sumatra's western coast cluster (Bengkulu (30th), West Sumatra (25th), and North Sumatra (27th)), as well as other Sumatra provinces such as Jambi (26th) and Riau Islands (31st).

The following general conclusions can be made in regard to the geographic spread of Government and Institutional Setting: (1) Provinces in Java are competitive, (2) Provinces in Sulawesi and Kalimantan are quite competitive, and (3) Provinces in Sumatra, Maluku, Papua, Bali, and Nusa Tenggara regions are generally less competitive.

Quantitative Spread — Financial, Businesses and Manpower Conditions

From Table 1.4, the scores for Financial, Businesses and Manpower Conditions range from a maximum of 3.0912 (DKI Jakarta, first) to a minimum of –1.4229 (Gorontalo, 33rd). This range is not symmetrical with more upward pull towards DKI Jakarta's high score, but at least, the disparity in the scores is not as extreme as that of Macroeconomic Stability (Table 1.2).

The average performing province (score of zero) lies between the 13th (DI Yogyakarta) and the 14th position (Bangka Belitung Islands). The median position is held by Bali (17th) with a score of –0.1215. The average score (zero, 13th–14th) is higher than the median score (–0.1215, 17th), which means that the average is skewed upwards towards the highest score.

Gaps in scores are also observed across–the–board, most notably between DKI Jakarta at first (3.0912) and Central Java at second position (1.9709). It is also pronounced among East Kalimantan (fourth, 1.6325), West Java (fifth, 1.0829), and Riau Islands (sixth, 0.5307).

Other score gaps exist between DI Yogyakarta (13th, 0.1481) and Bangka Belitung Islands (14th, –0.0252), as well as between Banten (22nd, –0.3739) and Maluku (23rd, –0.6059).

Geographic Spread — Financial, Businesses and Manpower Conditions

Based on Figure 1.5, clustering of provinces as high-competitiveness and low-competitiveness remains noticeable. Four of the Top 10 provinces are located in Java (except Banten and DI Yogyakarta). The remaining top-performing provinces are clustered at Kalimantan Region (East Kalimantan (fourth), West Kalimantan (eighth), and Central Kalimantan (ninth)), along Malacca Strait that is close to Singapore and Malaysia (Riau Islands (sixth) and Riau (seventh)), and South Sulawesi at 10th position.

Table 1.4. 2014 Financial, Businesses and Manpower Conditions: Ranking and Score

2014 Rank	2013 Rank	Province	2014 Score
1	1	DKI Jakarta	3.0912
2	4	Central Java	1.9709
3	3	East Java	1.9106
4	2	East Kalimantan	1.6325
5	5	West Java	1.0829
6	9	Riau Islands	0.5307
7	6	Riau	0.5280
8	14	West Kalimantan	0.3419
9	25	Central Kalimantan	0.2953
10	12	South Sulawesi	0.2899
11	7	Papua	0.1943
12	17	West Papua	0.1808
13	18	DI Yogyakarta	0.1481
14	32	Bangka Belitung Islands	–0.0252
15	27	South Kalimantan	–0.0642
16	30	North Sulawesi	–0.0709
17	13	Bali	–0.1215
18	8	South Sumatra	–0.2306
19	15	West Sumatra	–0.2855
20	28	West Nusa Tenggara	–0.3124
21	21	North Sumatra	–0.3303
22	22	Banten	–0.3739
23	11	Maluku	–0.6059
24	26	Bengkulu	–0.6401
25	23	Aceh	–0.6762
26	10	Lampung	–0.6816
27	24	Central Sulawesi	–0.8586
28	29	Jambi	–0.8646
29	33	East Nusa Tenggara	–1.0432
30	19	West Sulawesi	–1.0802
31	31	North Maluku	–1.1722
32	16	Southeast Sulawesi	–1.3371
33	20	Gorontalo	–1.4229

Source: Asia Competitiveness Institute

Provinces in the Bottom 10 also exhibit clustering: the Sulawesi cluster with four provinces (Gorontalo (33rd), Southeast Sulawesi (32nd), West Sulawesi (30th), and Central Sulawesi (27th)), and the southern Sumatra cluster with three provinces (Jambi (28th), Lampung (26th), and Bengkulu (24th)).

With this, general conclusions can be drawn regarding the geographic spread of Financial, Businesses and Manpower Conditions: (1) Provinces in Java and Kalimantan are competitive, (2) Provinces in Sumatra show mixed performance, (3) Provinces in Sulawesi tend to be less competitive, with the exception of South Sulawesi which has made it into the Top 10, and (4) Provinces in Maluku, Papua, Bali, and Nusa Tenggara regions are generally less competitive.

Figure 1.5. 2014 Map of Financial, Businesses and Manpower Conditions Ranking

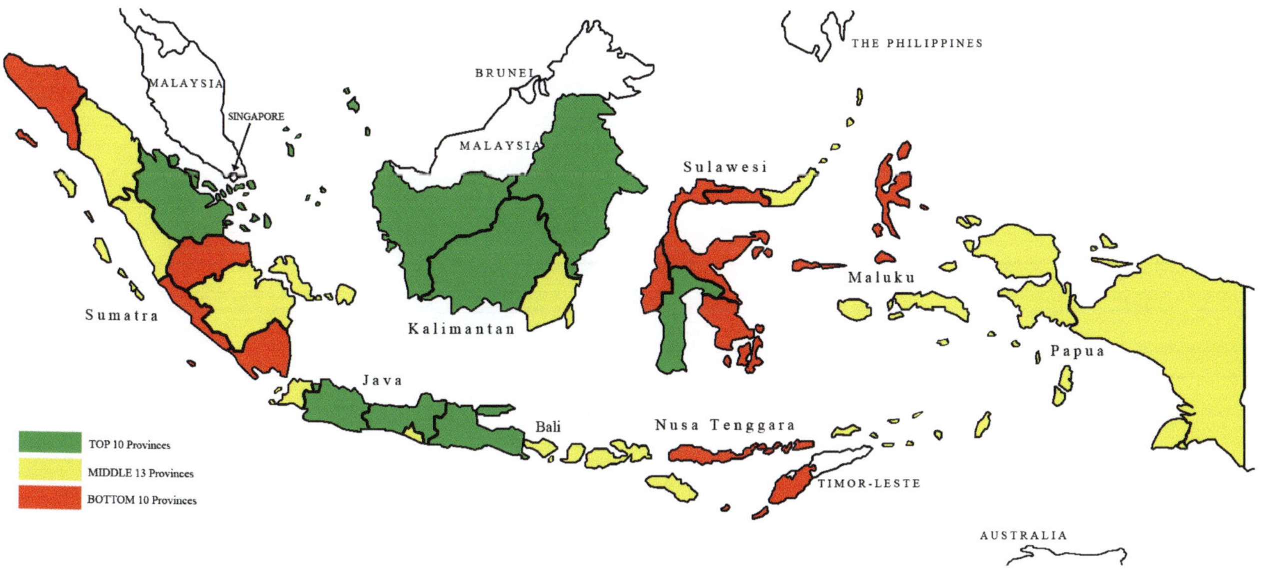

Source: Asia Competitiveness Institute

Quantitative Spread — Quality of Life and Infrastructure Development

Based on Table 1.5 for Quality of Life and Infrastructure Development, the scores range from a maximum of 1.6479 (DI Yogyakarta, first) to a minimum of –2.6847 (Papua, 33rd). The maximum and minimum scores are not symmetrical, with the minimum score being greater in absolute terms. However, if we take away Papua (33rd) from Table 1.5, we would find a more symmetrical spread.

The average performing province (score of zero) is between that occupying the 16th (Riau) and the 17th position (Central Kalimantan). The median position (17th) is held by Central Kalimantan with a score of –0.1932. The average province is practically the same as the median province. This means that the average is relatively not skewed towards either direction.

There are only a few score gaps throughout the board, but the main gap deserves attention, especially because it occurs between the province at 33rd (Papua, –2.6847) and 32nd position (East Nusa Tenggara, –1.7266).

Another gap occurs between the province at 27th (Gorontalo, –0.6620) and 28th position (West Papua, –1.0478), although the difference is not that large. It can be concluded that for Quality of Life and Infrastructure Development, there is generally a normal distribution of scores, with the exception of Papua at 33rd that is quite far behind other provinces.

Geographic Spread — Quality of Life and Infrastructure Development

Reviewing Figure 1.6, there is no noticeable clustering of high-competitiveness provinces, except perhaps slightly along the Makassar Strait (East Kalimantan (second), South Kalimantan (sixth), and South Sulawesi (ninth)). The other Top 10 provinces include four provinces from Java (DI Yogyakarta (first), DKI Jakarta (third), East Java (fourth), and Banten (seventh)), one from Bali (eighth), and two from Sumatra (Riau Islands (fifth) and Aceh (10th)).

Provinces in the Bottom 10, however, do show a tendency to cluster. These clusters are seen especially in the eastern regions of the country, such as the Maluku and Papua islands (North Maluku (31st), Papua (33rd), and West Papua (28th)), as well as the Nusa Tenggara cluster (East Nusa Tenggara (32nd) and West Nusa Tenggara (26th). The remaining Bottom 10 provinces are quite spread out in Sulawesi (West Sulawesi (29th), Gorontalo (27th), and Southeast Sulawesi (24th)), Kalimantan (West Kalimantan (30th)), and Sumatra (Bangka Belitung Islands (25th)).

Table 1.5. 2014 Quality of Life and Infrastructure Development: Ranking and Score

2014 Rank	2013 Rank	Province	2014 Score
1	2	DI Yogyakarta	1.6479
2	4	East Kalimantan	1.5912
3	1	DKI Jakarta	1.5515
4	8	East Java	1.2914
5	3	Riau Islands	1.2437
6	9	South Kalimantan	1.1414
7	6	Banten	0.9396
8	5	Bali	0.8412
9	10	South Sulawesi	0.5816
10	16	Aceh	0.5340
11	14	West Sumatra	0.5287
12	7	North Sulawesi	0.5097
13	13	Central Java	0.5052
14	15	North Sumatra	0.3987
15	12	West Java	0.2935
16	11	Riau	0.2667
17	20	Central Kalimantan	–0.1932
18	17	South Sumatra	–0.3311
19	19	Jambi	–0.3915
20	23	Central Sulawesi	–0.4258
21	22	Bengkulu	–0.4465
22	26	Lampung	–0.4492
23	24	Maluku	–0.4920
24	18	Southeast Sulawesi	–0.4970
25	21	Bangka Belitung Islands	–0.5751
26	29	West Nusa Tenggara	–0.6226
27	25	Gorontalo	–0.6620
28	28	West Papua	–1.0478
29	30	West Sulawesi	–1.0508
30	27	West Kalimantan	–1.0744
31	31	North Maluku	–1.1959
32	32	East Nusa Tenggara	–1.7266
33	33	Papua	–2.6847

Source: Asia Competitiveness Institute

Some general conclusions can be drawn about the geographic spread of Quality of Life and Infrastructure Development: (1) There are no geographic concentrations among the Top 10 provinces, (2) The Bottom 10 provinces are still largely found in eastern Indonesia, (3) Provinces in Sulawesi and Kalimantan show mixed results, and (4) Provinces in Sumatra generally show medium levels of competitiveness.

Figure 1.6. 2014 Map of Quality of Life and Infrastructure Development Ranking

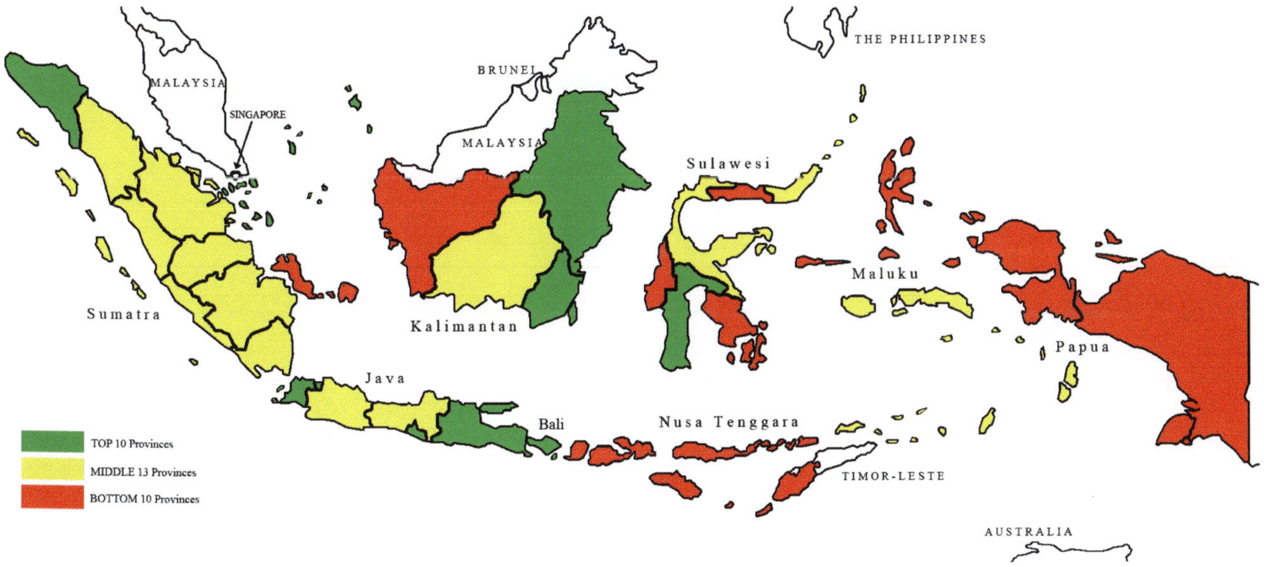

Source: Asia Competitiveness Institute

3.2 *What-if* Competitiveness Simulation

Overall Competitiveness

Next, we focus on the results of the *what-if* competitiveness simulation of Indonesian provinces for 2014. Table 1.6 shows the ranking for each province along with their standardised scores, before and after policy simulation. The results that were presented previously are "as it is" or before simulation was conducted.

Policy simulation results for Overall Competitiveness (Table 1.6) show that different provinces have different potentials to improve their rankings and scores. After simulation, which increases the scores of each province's top 20% weakest indicators (while assuming that other provinces' remain constant), some provinces are shown to be able to jump ranks substantially while others shift one or two positions.

Some of the provinces that show potential to jump multiple ranks include Bengkulu (+9), North Sumatra (+10), West Sulawesi (+10), Gorontalo (+12), and Southeast Sulawesi (+12). These provinces have potentials, but their weakest indicators drag them down heavily. By focusing on improving the top 20% weakest indicators, these provinces demonstrate that they can claim substantially higher ranking.

The *what-if* simulation is a static simulation, in which the simulation is conducted one province at a time. Each province's weakest scores were raised and the competitiveness ranking for each of the 33 provinces was subsequently re-calculated with the assumption that other provinces did not change their scores. This indicates that the rankings and scores presented in Table 1.6 cannot be compared vertically (one province against another), but should be read horizontally as the level of improvement (in ranking and in score) that each province could potentially achieve after the policy simulation.

In addition, since each province's simulation is done one-by-one, it is possible that more than one province improve to reach the same rank. For example, as per Table 1.6, if each province improves their top 20% weakest indicators, then Banten, DI Yogyakarta, South Kalimantan, Riau Islands, and South Sulawesi all have an opportunity to claim the sixth position.

With Tables 1.7 to 1.10, we present the policy simulation results according to each of the four competitiveness environments.

Table 1.6. 2014 *What-if* Competitiveness Simulation on Overall Competitiveness

	Rank		Score	
Province	**Before**	**After**	**Before**	**After**
Aceh	13	9	−0.0109	0.4435
Bali	14	8	−0.0179	0.4905
Banten	12	6	0.1672	0.7066
Bengkulu	30	21	−0.9576	−0.3074
DI Yogyakarta	6	6	0.7047	1.0265
DKI Jakarta	1	1	3.3580	3.8194
Gorontalo	28	16	−0.7549	−0.1438
Jambi	27	19	−0.7379	−0.2430
West Java	5	3	1.0834	1.5466
Central Java	4	3	1.3262	1.6647
East Java	2	2	1.8152	2.0867
West Kalimantan	18	13	−0.2234	0.1228
South Kalimantan	8	6	0.4884	0.7051
Central Kalimantan	15	10	−0.0754	0.3036
East Kalimantan	3	3	1.5566	1.7378
Bangka Belitung Islands	20	13	−0.2756	0.0669
Riau Islands	11	6	0.2901	0.8687
Lampung	24	16	−0.5773	−0.1280
Maluku	23	16	−0.5685	−0.1353
North Maluku	33	24	−1.7075	−0.6193
West Nusa Tenggara	22	13	−0.3733	0.0812
East Nusa Tenggara	32	26	−1.5634	−0.7392
Papua	31	22	−1.2268	−0.4056
West Papua	26	13	−0.7013	0.0108
Riau	9	7	0.3731	0.6588
West Sulawesi	25	15	−0.5870	−0.0813
South Sulawesi	7	6	0.6684	0.9327
Central Sulawesi	21	13	−0.3553	0.0507
Southeast Sulawesi	29	17	−0.7833	−0.2152
North Sulawesi	10	8	0.3109	0.6265
West Sumatra	17	12	−0.2179	0.1676
South Sumatra	16	13	−0.1676	0.1205
North Sumatra	19	9	−0.2594	0.3738

Source: Asia Competitiveness Institute

Macroeconomic Stability

In regard to Macroeconomic Stability (Table 1.7), a number of provinces have the potential to improve by a large margin. These include Aceh (+14), Lampung, West Sumatra, and Central Sulawesi (each +12), and Maluku (+10).

Table 1.7. 2014 *What-if* Competitiveness Simulation on Macroeconomic Stability

Province	Rank		Score	
	Before	**After**	**Before**	**After**
Aceh	28	14	–0.5510	–0.2148
Bali	18	13	–0.3730	–0.1205
Banten	7	7	0.3737	0.3737
Bengkulu	31	28	–0.7948	–0.5509
DI Yogyakarta	22	14	–0.4499	–0.1564
DKI Jakarta	1	1	4.6199	4.6337
Gorontalo	25	18	–0.4955	–0.3522
Jambi	20	18	–0.4055	–0.3543
West Java	3	3	1.2443	1.3331
Central Java	6	6	0.4649	0.5050
East Java	2	2	1.7543	1.7543
West Kalimantan	21	17	–0.4102	–0.3350
South Kalimantan	10	8	0.1037	0.1987
Central Kalimantan	15	13	–0.2519	–0.1300
East Kalimantan	4	4	0.7591	0.9050
Bangka Belitung Islands	19	16	–0.3985	–0.3226
Riau Islands	5	5	0.5828	0.7487
Lampung	29	17	–0.5659	–0.3424
Maluku	30	20	–0.6522	–0.4086
North Maluku	32	26	–0.8863	–0.5133
West Nusa Tenggara	27	16	–0.5226	–0.2712
East Nusa Tenggara	33	31	–0.9008	–0.6951
Papua	24	17	–0.4765	–0.3450
West Papua	14	13	–0.2456	–0.0744
Riau	8	8	0.1504	0.2949
West Sulawesi	17	16	–0.3447	–0.2783
South Sulawesi	11	8	0.0628	0.1912
Central Sulawesi	16	14	–0.3223	–0.2237
Southeast Sulawesi	23	19	–0.4697	–0.3911
North Sulawesi	13	9	–0.1281	0.1314
West Sumatra	26	14	–0.5170	–0.1921
South Sumatra	12	12	–0.0586	–0.0304
North Sumatra	9	8	0.1047	0.2165

Source: Asia Competitiveness Institute

Government and Institutional Setting

In regard to Government and Institutional Setting (Table 1.8), three provinces have the potential to improve by a large margin. These include North Maluku (+13), North Sumatra (+12), and Riau Islands (+11).

Table 1.8. 2014 *What-if* Competitiveness Simulation on Government and Institutional Setting

	Rank		Score	
Province	**Before**	**After**	**Before**	**After**
Aceh	9	8	0.6563	0.8811
Bali	24	15	–0.4068	0.2455
Banten	23	15	–0.3767	0.2415
Bengkulu	30	24	–1.3418	–0.4342
DI Yogyakarta	7	6	1.0260	1.1139
DKI Jakarta	1	1	2.0408	2.2274
Gorontalo	18	14	0.0392	0.3625
Jambi	26	20	–0.8221	–0.1290
West Java	6	6	1.0261	1.1238
Central Java	2	2	1.5230	1.6160
East Java	5	4	1.1538	1.2735
West Kalimantan	13	11	0.3906	0.4760
South Kalimantan	11	10	0.4630	0.5516
Central Kalimantan	19	16	–0.1041	0.1555
East Kalimantan	4	3	1.2568	1.3198
Bangka Belitung Islands	16	16	0.0711	0.1959
Riau Islands	31	20	–1.3806	–0.1914
Lampung	21	17	–0.2466	0.0521
Maluku	20	19	–0.1633	0.0218
North Maluku	33	20	–2.4930	–0.2294
West Nusa Tenggara	15	14	0.2010	0.3185
East Nusa Tenggara	32	26	–1.5920	–0.7498
Papua	28	26	–1.1625	–0.7991
West Papua	29	23	–1.2482	–0.3640
Riau	14	10	0.3109	0.5364
West Sulawesi	10	10	0.4997	0.6199
South Sulawesi	3	2	1.3156	1.5080
Central Sulawesi	12	9	0.4109	0.6554
Southeast Sulawesi	22	16	–0.3328	0.1201
North Sulawesi	8	6	0.7359	1.0247
West Sumatra	25	16	–0.4596	0.1325
South Sumatra	17	16	0.0560	0.1803
North Sumatra	27	15	–1.0464	0.1802

Source: Asia Competitiveness Institute

Financial, Businesses and Manpower Conditions

In regard to Financial, Businesses and Manpower Conditions (Table 1.9), these provinces have the potential to make major improvement: Gorontalo (+15), Bengkulu and Aceh (each +10), and Southeast Sulawesi (+9).

Table 1.9. 2014 *What-if* Competitiveness Simulation on Financial, Businesses and Manpower Conditions

	Rank		**Score**	
Province	**Before**	**After**	**Before**	**After**
Aceh	25	15	−0.6762	−0.0550
Bali	17	9	−0.1215	0.3163
Banten	22	11	−0.3739	0.2102
Bengkulu	24	14	−0.6401	0.0162
DI Yogyakarta	13	6	0.1481	0.5593
DKI Jakarta	1	1	3.0912	3.7383
Gorontalo	33	18	−1.4229	−0.2688
Jambi	28	20	−0.8646	−0.3146
West Java	5	4	1.0829	1.6691
Central Java	2	2	1.9709	2.2815
East Java	3	2	1.9106	2.3420
West Kalimantan	8	8	0.3419	0.4484
South Kalimantan	15	12	−0.0642	0.1854
Central Kalimantan	9	6	0.2953	0.6757
East Kalimantan	4	2	1.6325	1.9351
Bangka Belitung Islands	14	11	−0.0252	0.2380
Riau Islands	6	6	0.5307	0.7973
Lampung	26	18	−0.6816	−0.2027
Maluku	23	17	−0.6059	−0.1324
North Maluku	31	27	−1.1722	−0.7911
West Nusa Tenggara	20	14	−0.3124	0.0301
East Nusa Tenggara	29	21	−1.0432	−0.3466
Papua	11	8	0.1943	0.4929
West Papua	12	6	0.1808	0.7093
Riau	7	6	0.5280	0.7181
West Sulawesi	30	23	−1.0802	−0.5816
South Sulawesi	10	6	0.2899	0.5888
Central Sulawesi	27	19	−0.8586	−0.3040
Southeast Sulawesi	32	23	−1.3371	−0.4699
North Sulawesi	16	11	−0.0709	0.2453
West Sumatra	19	14	−0.2855	−0.0313
South Sumatra	18	14	−0.2306	0.0507
North Sumatra	21	14	−0.3303	0.0801

Source: Asia Competitiveness Institute

Quality of Life and Infrastructure Development

In regard to Quality of Life and Infrastructure Development (Table 1.10), these provinces demonstrate the potential to improve significantly: West Kalimantan (+13), West Sulawesi (+12), West Papua (+10), and West Nusa Tenggara (+9).

Table 1.10. 2014 *What-if* Competitiveness Simulation on Quality of Life and Infrastructure Development

	Rank		Score	
Province	**Before**	**After**	**Before**	**After**
Aceh	10	8	0.5340	0.8852
Bali	8	6	0.8412	1.2117
Banten	7	2	0.9396	1.5545
Bengkulu	21	17	−0.4465	−0.0633
DI Yogyakarta	1	1	1.6479	1.9500
DKI Jakarta	3	1	1.5515	2.6290
Gorontalo	27	18	−0.6620	−0.2251
Jambi	19	17	−0.3915	−0.0185
West Java	15	6	0.2935	1.1064
Central Java	13	4	0.5052	1.2233
East Java	4	1	1.2914	1.6832
West Kalimantan	30	17	−1.0744	−0.1746
South Kalimantan	6	4	1.1414	1.4391
Central Kalimantan	17	15	−0.1932	0.3212
East Kalimantan	2	1	1.5912	1.7035
Bangka Belitung Islands	25	17	−0.5751	0.1138
Riau Islands	5	2	1.2437	1.6012
Lampung	22	17	−0.4492	0.0628
Maluku	23	17	−0.4920	0.0635
North Maluku	31	23	−1.1959	−0.5262
West Nusa Tenggara	26	17	−0.6226	0.1962
East Nusa Tenggara	32	26	−1.7266	−0.6768
Papua	33	25	−2.6847	−0.7153
West Papua	28	18	−1.0478	−0.2343
Riau	16	9	0.2667	0.6713
West Sulawesi	29	17	−1.0508	−0.0340
South Sulawesi	9	8	0.5816	0.8586
Central Sulawesi	20	17	−0.4258	0.0431
Southeast Sulawesi	24	17	−0.4970	0.0167
North Sulawesi	12	9	0.5097	0.7118
West Sumatra	11	9	0.5287	0.6555
South Sumatra	18	17	−0.3311	0.2052
North Sumatra	14	9	0.3987	0.7842

Source: Asia Competitiveness Institute

3.3 Analysis of Median and Maximum Competitiveness Webs

To better understand the relative strengths and weaknesses of the top and bottom performing provinces (DKI Jakarta, first, and North Maluku, 33rd), it is useful to compare and contrast their attainment against the median and maximum scores of Indonesia's 33 provinces for 12 sub-environments that make up the four environments.

Figure 1.7 shows the scores plot of DKI Jakarta (solid line) and North Maluku (round dotted line) for each of the 12 sub-environments vis-à-vis the overall median score for the 33 provinces in Indonesia (dashed line). Being the first in Overall Competitiveness, DKI Jakarta excels in most of the sub-environments except for five

Figure 1.7. 2014 Median Competitiveness Web Analysis: DKI Jakarta and North Maluku

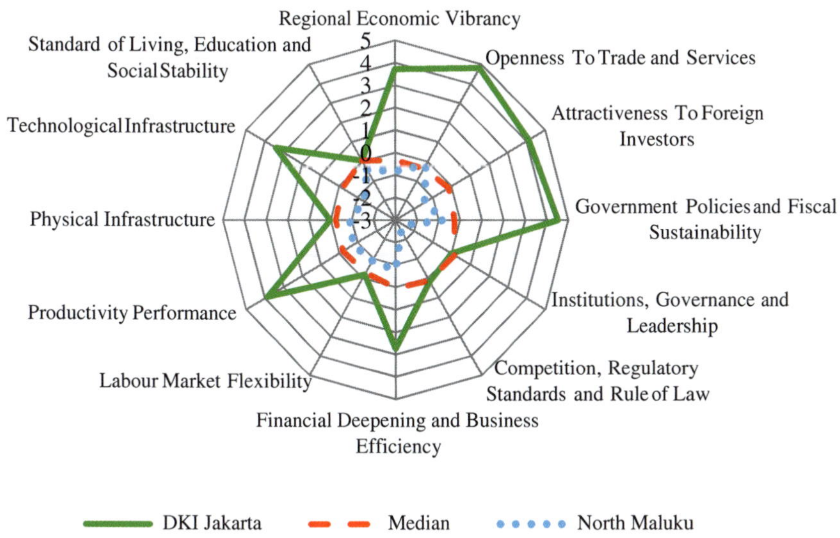

Source: Asia Competitiveness Institute

Figure 1.8. 2014 Maximum Competitiveness Web Analysis: DKI Jakarta and North Maluku

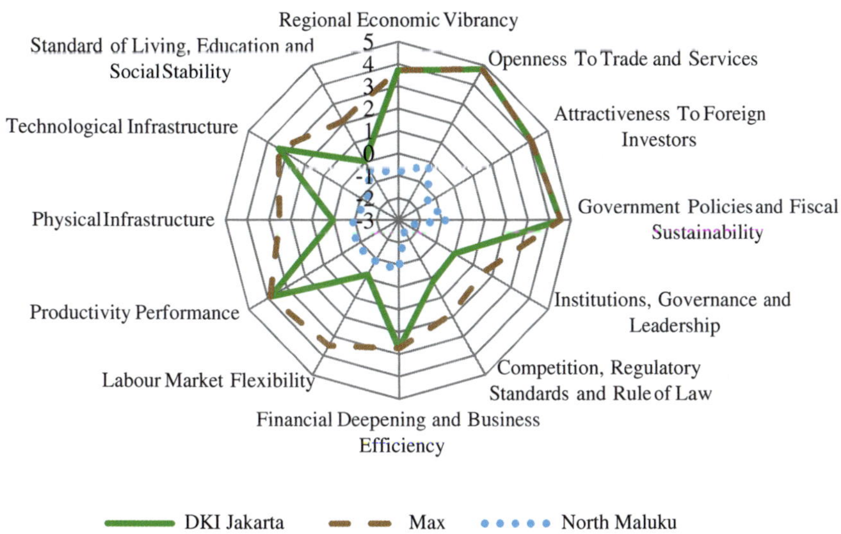

Source: Asia Competitiveness Institute

sub-environments. These include Institutions, Governance and Leadership; Competition, Regulatory Standards and Rule of Law; Labour Market Flexibility; Physical Infrastructure; and Standard of Living, Education and Social Stability. By contrast, the scores for North Maluku are all below the median score.

Maximum Competitiveness Web analysis in Figure 1.8 shows how far the best scores for each sub-environment (dashed line) are, in relation to DKI Jakarta's scores (solid line) and North Maluku's (round dotted line). DKI Jakarta becomes the benchmark, earning the highest scores in seven out of 12 sub-environments. For North Maluku, its scores are all far below the maximum scores with significant gaps in Institutions, Governance and Leadership; and Competition, Regulatory Standards and Rule of Law.

REFERENCES

Bristow, Gillian. *Critical Reflections on Regional Competitiveness: Theory, Policy, and Practice*. New York: Routledge, 2010.

Camagni, Roberto. "On the Concept of Territorial Competitiveness: Sound or Misleading?" *Urban Studies* Vol. 39, No. 13 (2002): 2395–2411.

Cooper, Andrew, and Jongryn Mo. "Middle Power Leadership and the Evolution of the G20." *Global Summitry Journal* Vol. 1 (2013): 1–14.

Coordinating Ministry for Economic Affairs. *Master Plan for Acceleration and Expansion of Indonesia's Economic Development 2011–2025 (MP3EI).* Jakarta: Coordinating Ministry for Economic Affairs, 2011.

Geweke, John. "Measurement of linear dependence and feedback between multiple time series." *Journal of the American Statistical Association* Vol. 77, No. 378 (1982): 304–313.

International Institute for Management Development (IMD). *IMD World Competitiveness Yearbook.* Lausanne: IMD, 2014.

Kitson, Michael, Ronald Leonard Martin, and Peter Tyler. "Regional Competitiveness: An Elusive Yet Key Concept?" *Regional Studies* Vol. 38, No. 9 (2004): 999–1000.

Krugman, Paul. "Competitiveness: a dangerous obsession." *Foreign Affairs* Vol. 73 (1994): 28–44.

Porter, Michael. *Competitive Strategy.* New York: Free Press, 1980.

Tan, Khee Giap, Linda Low, Tan Kong Yam, and Kartik Rao. *Annual Analysis of Competitiveness, Simulation Studies and Development Perspective for 35 States and Federal Territories of India: 2000–2010.* Singapore: World Scientific, 2013.

Tan, Khee Giap, Linda Low, Tan Kong Yam, and Lim Lijuan Amanda. *Annual Analysis of Competitiveness, Development Strategies and Public Policies on ASEAN-10: 2000–2010.* Singapore: Pearson, 2013.

Tan, Khee Giap, and Mulya Amri. "Subnational Competitiveness and National Performance: Analysis and Simulation for Indonesia." *Journal of Centrum Cathedra (JCC): The Business and Economics Research Journal* Vol. 6, No. 2 (2013): 173–192.

Tan, Khee Giap, Mulya Amri, Linda Low, and Tan Kong Yam. *Competitiveness Analysis and Development Strategies for 33 Indonesian Provinces.* Singapore: World Scientific, 2013.

Tan, Khee Giap, Yuan Randong, Sangiita Yoong Wei Cher, and Yang Mu. *Annual Analysis of Competitiveness, Simulation Studies and Development Perspective for 34 Greater China Economies: 2000–2010.* Singapore: World Scientific, 2013.

Weingast, Barry R. "The Economic Role of Political Institutions: Market-Preserving Federalism and Economic Development." *Journal of Law, Economics, & Organisation* Vol. 11, No. 1 (1995): 1–31.

World Economic Forum (WEF). *The Global Competitiveness Report 2013–2014.* Geneva: WEF, 2014.

Chapter 2

2014 Inaugural Regional Competitiveness Ranking and Development Strategies for Indonesia: The Regional Policy Perspective

1. INTRODUCTION

1.1 Motivation, Objectives and Expected Contributions

Indonesia has the potential to further develop and gain its rightful place not only in the Association of Southeast Asian Nations (ASEAN) but also in the world. In fact, the World Bank's International Comparison Programme ranks Indonesia in the Top 10 largest economy, with Gross Domestic Product (GDP), purchasing power parity of 2.06 trillion US Dollar and contribution of 2.3% share of world GDP in 2011.[1]

To maintain the current growth trajectory and further accelerate it, Indonesia can find useful leads from the Asia Competitiveness Institute's (ACI) 2014 Competitiveness Ranking and Simulation Study for 33 Indonesian provinces in Chapter 1.[2] Beyond provincial ranking, the ACI moves forward to cluster the 33 provinces into six regions, in alignment with the Master Plan for Acceleration and Expansion of Indonesia's Economic Development 2011-2025 (MP3EI).[3]

There are several reasons why regional competitiveness is a natural progression from the initial focus on provinces. First, regional analysis is needed to spur regional growth, spreading growth centres across the country. This is in pursuit of spearheading regional competitiveness and balanced national development, which eventually boosts national competitiveness as a whole.[4] Indonesia's western region — mainly Java and Sumatra — is commonly regarded as more developed than the eastern region. This overconcentration has its own spatial shortcomings as seen from overcapacity in selected transportation nodes, and raises issues related to quality of life as sustainability aspect is neglected. This can be seen from DKI Jakarta's relatively low score for Quality of Life and Infrastructure Development despite its strong financial capacity to do better in this aspect. If the gap is not narrowed, the less developed regions become relatively more backward with rudimentary infrastructure that undermines their ultimate potential.

Second, with maturity of growth and development, the clustering approach[5] that groups the provinces based on shared characteristics allows each region to leverage on economies of scale and network effects from working together as a team. Connectivity across provinces in proximity requires regional efforts to provide streamlined infrastructure to ensure seamless distribution of goods and services. The ACI's inaugural competitiveness

---

[1] World Bank, *Purchasing Power Parities and Real Expenditures of World Economies: Summary of Results and Findings of the 2011 International Comparison Program* (Washington: World Bank Publications, 2014), 35.

[2] Studies on sub-national competitiveness have gained tractions among policymakers and academics due to its practical relevance. Relevant literature include: M.E. Porter, "The Economic Performance of Regions," *Regional Studies* 37:6–7 (2003): 549–578; M. Kitson, Ron Martin, and Peter Tyler, "Regional Competitiveness: An Elusive Yet Key Concept?" *Regional Studies* 38:9 (2004): 991–999; and Christian Ketels, "Recent Research on Competitiveness and Clusters: What Are the Implications for Regional Policy?" *Cambridge Journal of Regions, Economy and Society* 6 (2013): 269–284.

[3] Coordinating Ministry for Economic Affairs, *Master Plan for Acceleration and Expansion of Indonesia's Economic Development 2011–2025 (MP3EI)* (Jakarta: Coordinating Ministry for Economic Affairs, 2011).

[4] Organisation for Economic Cooperation and Development (OECD), *Regional Development Policy Trends in OECD Member Countries* (OECD Publishing, 2010) explains in greater details the paradigm shift of regional development policy.

[5] The notion of cluster is initially introduced at firm level context. Cluster provides access to resources, technologies, and markets. For more details, see M.J. Enright, "The Globalisation of Competition and the Location of Competitive Advantage: Policies Towards Regional Clustering," in *The Globalisation of Multinational Enterprise Activity and Economic Development*, ed. N. Hood, and S. Young (London: MacMillan, 2000), 303–331; M.E. Porter, "Location, Competition, and Economic Development: Local Clusters in a Global Economy," *Economic Development Quarterly* Vol. 14, No. 1 (2000): 15–34; and M.E. Porter, *On Competition* (Boston MA: Harvard Business School, 1998).

analysis on 33 Indonesian provinces has identified the need for analysis based on "clusters of provinces" on top of the current analysis done at provincial level.[6] Further economic interdependency among members of the group creates incentives to align their goals and become a solid economic entity, benefitting from agglomeration effects. Similar cluster initiative has been adopted in other countries, for example the Pearl River Delta in China as a cluster for manufacturing and trade that covers Guangdong Province, as well as Special Administrative Regions of Hong Kong and Macau.

Third, regional classification shifts the focus on development away from specific provinces. The strong legacy of top-down administration in the past has created an imbalance in development that benefitted only the capital and surrounding provinces. This is obvious from the provincial ranking analysis that accords DKI Jakarta's exorbitantly high scores in almost all aspects of competitiveness. Its significant distance with subsequent provinces signals a heavy reliance on DKI Jakarta as a driver of competitiveness. The competitiveness of neighbouring provinces — for instance West Java, East Java, and Central Java — are elevated by this fact as shown by their high position in the Top 10. However, the multiplier or spillover effects can go further with more potential competitive clusters.

In that essence, the ACI's analysis at regional level will enable mapping of regional competitiveness and identifying of policy actions to rectify the weaknesses while leveraging the strengths. The regional framework, as identified by the MP3EI, is drilled down into greater details. Section 2 complements the methodology described in Chapter 1 by expanding on details about aggregation to create regional scoring. Section 3 shows snapshots of the ACI's Overall Competitiveness ranking and its environments. On top of the quantitative spread based on regional scoring, geographic and sub-environment spread are also provided. The latter identifies the drivers behind each region's competitiveness that can be used as learning tools for each other.

Quintessentially, the regional framework for competitiveness in Indonesia for each region in Chapter 3 to 8 provides development strategies based on the ACI's empirical competitiveness results, taking into account the MP3EI for Indonesia as a whole and drilling them into the six regions. The ACI as a neutral think-tank offers novel perspectives and independent assessment to improve the implementation of regional policy in the context of regional-based growth.

1.2 Master Plan for Acceleration and Expansion of Indonesia's Economic Development (MP3EI)

The MP3EI is a working document that will be progressively fine-tuned across time, complementing the existing national and provincial development plans. In light of achieving the aspiration to post per capita GDP of 14,250-15,500 US Dollar by 2025, the MP3EI takes a 'not business as usual' approach to accelerate and expand the economic development in Indonesia. It follows five central tenets:[7]

1. Increase productivity and value-adding on natural resource management through the expansion and creation of a sustainable upstream and downstream activity chain;
2. Focus on diverse and inclusive economic development, which connects corridors with other regions to develop opportunities based on local potential and specialisation;
3. Synergise sectorial and regional development to enhance national, regional, and global comparative and competitive advantages;
4. Integrate economic development between transportation and logistics, as well as communications and information systems to open regional access;
5. Provide fiscal and non-fiscal incentives, ease of regulation, licensing, and optimum public services from central and local governments to support the development.

[6] Tan Khee Giap *et al.*, *Competitiveness Analysis and Development Strategies for 33 Indonesian Provinces* (Singapore: World Scientific Publishing, 2013), 12. Subsequent journal article can be found in Tan Khee Giap and Mulya Amri, "Subnational Competitiveness and National Performance: Analysis and Simulation for Indonesia," *Journal of Centrum Cathedra (JCC): The Business and Economics Research Journal* Vol. 6, No. 2 (2013):173–192.

[7] Coordinating Ministry for Economic Affairs, *Master Plan for Acceleration and Expansion of Indonesia's Economic Development (MP3EI).*

The MP3EI acknowledges the urgency to create new economic centres outside the existing ones that are based mainly in Java. It is aimed to realise the vision of self-sufficient, advanced, just, and prosperous Indonesia. Obviously, all layers of government play an important role to spearhead and drive related parties to align the implementation of the MP3EI with the regional plans.

With big ambition to position Indonesia as the world's main food supplier, as well as centre for agriculture, fishery, natural resources, and global logistics by 2025, the MP3EI is supported by three pillars. The first is the development of economic potential for six economic corridors by establishing centres of development, industry clusters, and Special Economic Zones (SEZs) based on advanced commodities resources. The focus of the development is classified into eight main programmes — agriculture, fishery, mining, energy, manufacturing, telecommunication, tourism, and development of strategic areas with a total of 22 main economic activities. The thematic details and provincial composition of six economic corridors are presented in Table 2.1, while Figure 2.1 visualises the location of each corridor in a map.

Table 2.1. Theme and Composition of Six Economic Corridors

Sumatra Economic Corridor
"Centre for production and processing of natural resources and the nation's energy reserves"
Aceh, North Sumatra, West Sumatra, Riau, Riau Islands, Bangka Belitung Islands, Jambi, Bengkulu, South Sumatra, and Lampung

Java Economic Corridor
"Driver for national industry and service provision"
Banten, DKI Jakarta, West Java, Central Java, DI Yogyakarta, and East Java

Kalimantan Economic Corridor
"Centre for production and processing of national mining and energy reserves"
West Kalimantan, Central Kalimantan, South Kalimantan, and East Kalimantan

Sulawesi Economic Corridor
"Centre for production and processing of national agriculture, plantation, fishery, oil and gas, and mining"
North Sulawesi, Central Sulawesi, Gorontalo, West Sulawesi, Southeast Sulawesi, and South Sulawesi

Bali-Nusa Tenggara Economic Corridor
"Gateway for tourism and national food support"
Bali, West Nusa Tenggara, and East Nusa Tenggara

Maluku-Papua Economic Corridor
"Centre for development of food, fisheries, energy, and national mining"
Maluku, North Maluku, Papua, and West Papua

Source: Coordinating Ministry for Economic Affairs of Indonesia, 2011

Figure 2.1. Map of Six Economic Corridors

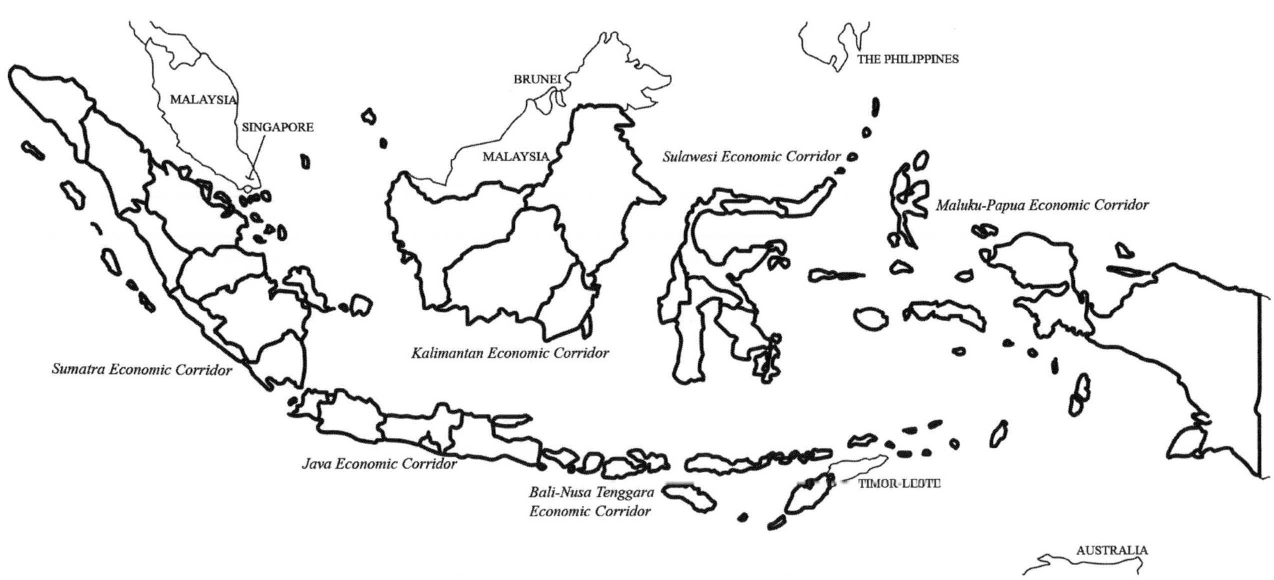

Source: Asia Competitiveness Institute

The second pillar is the strengthening of national connectivity across extensive stretch of Indonesian archipelago. The MP3EI proposes various key infrastructure projects and oversees their implementation. An array of efforts to attract active participation from private sector and debottleneck all possible hindrances at the implementation stage is pursued through various policies and regulation reforms. It is crucial to achieve seamless and efficient local connectivity, both within and between islands, and global connectivity for international trade. And lastly, the strengthening of human resources, and national science and technology capability as the third pillar, as Indonesia is envisioned to move up the value-added chain and stay on track to eventually become an innovation-based economy.

All in all, the MP3EI aims to accelerate and expand economic development in Indonesia that is more inclusive and distributed across Indonesia. As a proof to a shift from Java-centric to broader development, the growth of Java is pegged against national medium-term development plan. This allows other corridors to produce higher growth rate under the implementation of the MP3EI. Besides, based on groundbreaking plan in 2014 from Coordinating Ministry for Economic Affairs, the highest investment value for real sector and infrastructure is dedicated for projects located in Kalimantan and Sumatra economic corridors, respectively.

During 2014 presidential campaign, the incoming President Joko Widodo highlighted the visible regional imbalance that led to wide price discrepancy between Java and Papua. Connectivity and logistic bottlenecks were touted as one of the main reasons hampering development in the eastern part of Indonesia. Moving forward, the president has set a goal of 7% annual growth and the new government has identified key infrastructure projects to support such growth. Projects related to improvement in logistics and energy infrastructure are as the following:[8]

1. *Maritime*: development of 24 new seaports and 60 crossing ports, increasing the number of vessels (pioneer cargo, transport vessels, pioneer crossing vessels, and patrol ships), and revitalisation of shipyard industry.
2. *Air transport*: development of 15 new airports and air cargo facilities in six locations and increasing the number of pioneer airplanes.
3. *Road*: development of 2,650 km of new roads and 1,000 km of new toll roads, and rehabilitation of 46,770 km of existing roads.
4. *Railway*: development of new tracks in Java, Sumatra, Sulawesi, and Kalimantan that include 2,159 km inter-urban railways and 1,099 km urban railways.
5. *Urban transport*: development of Bus Rapid Transit (BRT) in 29 cities and Mass Rapid Transit (MRT) in six metropolis and 17 large cities.
6. *Electricity*: target of 96.6% electrification by 2019 and development of power plants with total capacity of 35,000 MW.
7. *Irrigation system*: development of 33 new dams and 30 hydropower plants, and expansion of 1 million ha and rehabilitation of existing irrigation system.
8. *Fuel production*: construction of new oil refineries of 2 × 300,000 barrels and expansion of existing refineries in Cilacap and Balongan.

The president further delineated his maritime axis doctrine during the East Asia Summit in Naypyitaw, Myanmar on November 13, 2014. The doctrine is centred on five underlying pillars:[9]

1. Revival of Indonesia's maritime culture as the archipelagic geography shapes the identity and livelihood of the people.
2. Better management of Indonesia's oceans and fisheries by developing fishing industry and maritime-based food sovereignty and security.

---

[8] Luky Eko Wuryanto, "Accelerating Infrastructure Development Programmes and Expected Roles of AIIB" (paper presented at 2014 Annual Asia Competitiveness Institute Conference on "Competitiveness Analysis of 112 Asian Economies, Asia Economic Connectivity, Liveable Cities Index for 100 Greater China Cities and Cost of Living Index for Expatriates and Ordinary Residents", Singapore, November 26–27, 2014).

[9] Adelle Neary, "Jokowi Spells Out Vision for Indonesia's Global Maritime Nexus," *Centre for Strategic and International Studies: Southeast Asia from Scott Circle* Vol. V, No. 24 (November 2014): 1–4.

3. Improvement of port infrastructure, shipping industry, and maritime tourism to support maritime economy.
4. Through maritime diplomacy, Indonesia will work together with relevant stakeholders to eliminate conflicts arising from illegal fishing, breaches of sovereignty, territorial disputes, piracy, and marine pollution.
5. Bolstering maritime defences to support its maritime sovereignty and wealth in order to ensure safety of navigation and maritime security.

2. RESEARCH METHODOLOGY

The construction of the competitiveness ranking by region follows the same methodology used for the provincial competitiveness ranking mentioned in Chapter 1, once the appropriate dataset for indicators at the regional-level is ready.[10] Because each region consists of a few provinces, the main problem to be solved in order to extend the ranking analysis from provincial to regional level is data aggregation.

Many of the indicators used for the provincial ranking can be directly aggregated to obtain the indicator values for a region by summing across all the constituent provinces in that region, as long as those indicators are based on absolute quantities, such as 1.1.01 Gross Regional Domestic Product (GRDP) and 4.1.01 Population.

For those indicators that are defined as ratios, they can be computed according to their definition by firstly aggregating the absolute quantities upon which they are defined (e.g. aggregating the denominator and numerator first). As an illustration, below are three examples for data aggregation to derive the regional indicator values. The first example is for indicator 1.1.01 GRDP. Since it is based on absolute quantity, the regional value can be obtained by summing across all the provinces within this region. The second example is for indicator 2.1.03 Tax Revenue/Government Revenue. According to its definition, it is calculated as the ratio between tax revenue and government revenue for a particular region. Since both the numerator and denominator are absolute quantities, they are firstly aggregated across all the provinces within the region to obtain the regional values. The ratio is then computed from these obtained values, hence, arriving at the regional value for indicator 2.1.03 Tax Revenue/Government Revenue. The third example is when the calculation is average-weighted at the regional level by population of the province. This applies to indicators collected from ACI survey and also from indicators that are calculated as percentage of households at original source, as provided in the following example for indicator 4.2.01 Telephone Ownership.

Approach 1: 1.1.01 GRDP; Unit: Million Rupiah, 2000 Constant Prices

For Region A with *n* provinces at time *t*,

$$GRDP_{A,t} = \sum_{i=1}^{n} \text{Real } GRDP_{i,t}$$

Approach 2: 2.1.03 Tax Revenue/Government Revenue; Unit: Ratio of Tax Revenue to Government Revenue

For Region A with *n* provinces at time *t*,

$$Tax\ Revenue/Government\ Revenue_{A,t} = \frac{\sum_{i=1}^{n} Tax\ Revenue_{i,t}}{\sum_{i=1}^{n} Government\ Revenue_{i,t}} \times 100$$

[10] For Indonesian provincial analysis, the ACI used a total of 104 indicators that cover 33 provinces. North Kalimantan, the newly created province in 2012, is not yet included pending availability of data. At the national level as with the rest of ASEAN economies, with more data available, a total of 127 indicators were used for Indonesia as a whole.

Approach 3: 4.2.01 Telephone Ownership; Unit: Percentage of Households

For Region A with *n* provinces at time *t*,

$$Telephone\ Ownership_{A,t} = \sum_{i=1}^{n}\left(Telephone\ Ownership_{i,t} \times \frac{Population_{i,t}}{\sum_{i=1}^{n} Population_{i,t}}\right)$$

For a complete list of indicators used for the regional competitiveness analysis, please refer to Appendix 1. For algorithm to compute the competitiveness ranking, please refer to Appendix 2. For explanatory notes on how to derive regional indicator data from provincial data, please refer to Appendix 3. Once the data aggregation is completed for all relevant indicators, the competitiveness ranking analysis is performed by following the computational procedure.

3. ANALYSIS OF ACI'S REGIONAL COMPETITIVENESS RANKING

This section presents the findings based on competitiveness ranking and score of regions. It consists of Overall Competitiveness and its four environments — Macroeconomic Stability, Government and Institutional Setting, Financial, Businesses and Manpower Conditions, and Quality of Life and Infrastructure Development. It also contains median and maximum competitiveness web analysis based on 12 sub-environments.

Similar to the methodology applied in the provincial ranking, Overall Competitiveness is derived from four environments and each environment is an aggregation of three sub-environments. The ACI adopts six regional classifications as suggested by the MP3EI. These are Sumatra Region, Java Region, Kalimantan Region, Sulawesi Region, Bali-Nusa Tenggara Region, and Maluku-Papua Region.

3.1 Competitiveness Ranking of Six Regions — Rank and Score by Environment[11]

Quantitative Spread — Overall Competitiveness

Table 2.2 presents the ranking and standardised score for Overall Competitiveness. Echoing the finding from provincial analysis, Java Region leads the pack with a substantial score of 1.7233. This is not surprising as there are five out of six provinces from Java Region in the Top 10. Kalimantan Region trails Java Region in second position with a score of almost one-third of Java (0.6511). The average performing regions are Sulawesi at third and Sumatra at fourth, with scores hovering around zero (–0.0392 and –0.0741, respectively).

The spread between Java Region at the top and Maluku-Papua Region at the bottom is not as dramatic as seen in the provincial ranking between DKI Jakarta (first) and North Maluku (33rd). In fact, it is relatively symmetric as the scores are not highly skewed upwards. In spite of that, significant difference in terms of score exists

Table 2.2. 2014 Overall Competitiveness: Ranking and Score

Rank	Region	Score
1	Java Region	1.7233
2	Kalimantan Region	0.6511
3	Sulawesi Region	–0.0392
4	Sumatra Region	–0.0741
5	Bali–Nusa Tenggara Region	–0.9839
6	Maluku–Papua Region	–1.2772

Source: Asia Competitiveness Institute

[11] Results for the 2014 competitiveness study are based on official data in 2011 and survey data collected in 2013. Conventionally due to collation, compilation, and publication of official data, such a lag of data before reaching end-users is acceptable.

Figure 2.2. 2014 Map of Overall Competitiveness Ranking

Source: Asia Competitiveness Institute

between the average performing regions, Sulawesi and Sumatra, and the last two regions, Bali-Nusa Tenggara and Maluku-Papua (–0.9839 and –1.2772, respectively).

Geographic Spread — Overall Competitiveness

Figure 2.2 illustrates the composition of regions based on their respective competitiveness scores. Different colours, from darker to softer tone, are used to denote their competitiveness level.

The geographic map for Overall Competitiveness in Figure 2.2 reveals a striking pattern that although Java Region still holds the top position, the non-western part of Indonesia, Kalimantan Region, emerges as the runner-up. Sumatra Region, which is often coined as Java Region's peer as the engine of the development in the western part of Indonesia, sits at fourth place, one position below Sulawesi Region. Mediocre performance of provinces in Sumatra Region coupled by three provinces in the Bottom 10 contributes to the region's relatively weak competitiveness.

Quantitative Spread — Macroeconomic Stability

Table 2.3 further perpetuates the disparity between the western part of Indonesia, as represented by Java Region and Sumatra Region, and its eastern counterpart. The major policy reforms in 1980s that bred export-oriented industrialisation were mainly concentrated in Java.[12] This, in turn, contributed to the Java Region's remarkable achievement in overall growth and most macroeconomic indicators.

Despite domination of western regions, a wide gap exists between Java Region's exceptional score of 2.046 and Sumatra Region's near average score of 0.1112. The gap in this context is higher than that of the Overall Competitiveness (Table 2.2) between Java Region and Kalimantan Region. Chapter 4 further iterates the historical advantage of Java Region as the epicentre of economic activities in Indonesia. Without doubts, this attracts

[12] Hal Hill, B.P. Resosudarmo, and Yogi Vidyattama, "Economic Geography of Indonesia: Location, Connectivity, and Resources," in *Reshaping Economic Geography in East Asia*, ed. Yukon Huang and A. M. Bocchi (Washington DC: World Bank Publications, 2008), 115–134.

Table 2.3. 2014 Macroeconomic Stability: Ranking and Score

Rank	Region	Score
1	Java Region	2.0461
2	Sumatra Region	0.1112
3	Kalimantan Region	0.0350
4	Sulawesi Region	–0.3896
5	Maluku–Papua Region	–0.7943
6	Bali–Nusa Tenggara Region	–1.0085

Source: Asia Competitiveness Institute

Figure 2.3. 2014 Macroeconomic Stability Sub-Environment

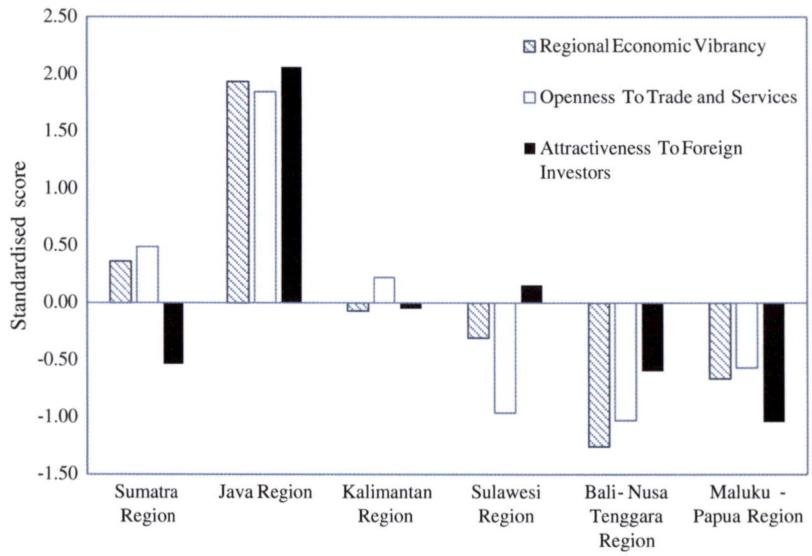

Source: Asia Competitiveness Institute

early investment into the region, targeted at improvements in hard and soft infrastructure. As a whole, Java Region has benefitted from the legacy that allows the region to ramp up its competitiveness posture.

Kalimantan Region secures the third position as an average performing region at 0.0350. With Java Region pulling up the standardised score, the average score is higher than the median score, which is significantly negative (–0.1773), as derived from the mid-value between the third and fourth position. Regions at the far eastern part of Indonesia are still falling behind, with Maluku-Papua Region at fifth and Bali-Nusa Tenggara Region at sixth.

Sub-Environment Spread — Macroeconomic Stability

To understand the driver behind each region's ranking and score in Macroeconomic Stability, the score of its sub-environments is revealed in Figure 2.3.

At the first position, Java Region consistently excels in all aspects. With Java as a home for the most urbanised and industrialised cities and burgeoning middle income class, Java Region attains the highest score in Attractiveness to Foreign Investors (2.062).

For the bottom-performing region, Maluku-Papua's Achilles heel is in Attractiveness to Foreign Investors (–1.041) as proven by its relatively low investment, both from domestic and foreign direct investment. The MP3EI also highlighted that this situation is due to high investment risk, low business certainty, and inadequate infrastructure.

Quantitative Spread — Government and Institutional Setting

Despite Java Region's dominance in the Overall Competitiveness (Table 2.2) and Macroeconomic Stability (Table 2.3), the disparity in scores between Java Region and other economic regions is not highly prevalent in Government and Institutional Setting. In Table 2.4, Sulawesi Region's score (0.7733) in the second position is roughly half of Java Region. The difference between Sulawesi Region and subsequent region, Kalimantan at third, is marginal. Committed government and supportive institutional setting are important components to strengthen the impetus for higher competitiveness.

With regions including Java, Sulawesi, and Kalimantan's above-average score, the median for this environment is positive or higher than average. Additionally, the spread for this environment is rather symmetrical, stretching from Java Region (1.4124) at the top position and Maluku-Papua Region (–1.4937) at the bottom.

Sub-Environment Spread — Government and Institutional Setting

Figure 2.4 provides a snapshot of varying performances for each sub-environment. Java Region's top position is greatly enhanced by its superior Government Policies and Fiscal Sustainability. Although the other two sub-environments are still above average, their scores are much lower. By contrast, Sulawesi Region's strengths are in Institutions, Governance and Leadership and Competition, Regulatory Standards and Rule of Law, which score above Java Region. The strong contributions of these two sub-environments are also the catalyst for Kalimantan Region's position at the third.

Table 2.4. 2014 Government and Institutional Setting: Ranking and Score

Rank	Region	Score
1	Java Region	1.4124
2	Sulawesi Region	0.7733
3	Kalimantan Region	0.5582
4	Sumatra Region	–0.4219
5	Bali–Nusa Tenggara Region	–0.8284
6	Maluku–Papua Region	–1.4937

Source: Asia Competitiveness Institute

Figure 2.4. 2014 Government and Institutional Setting Sub-Environment

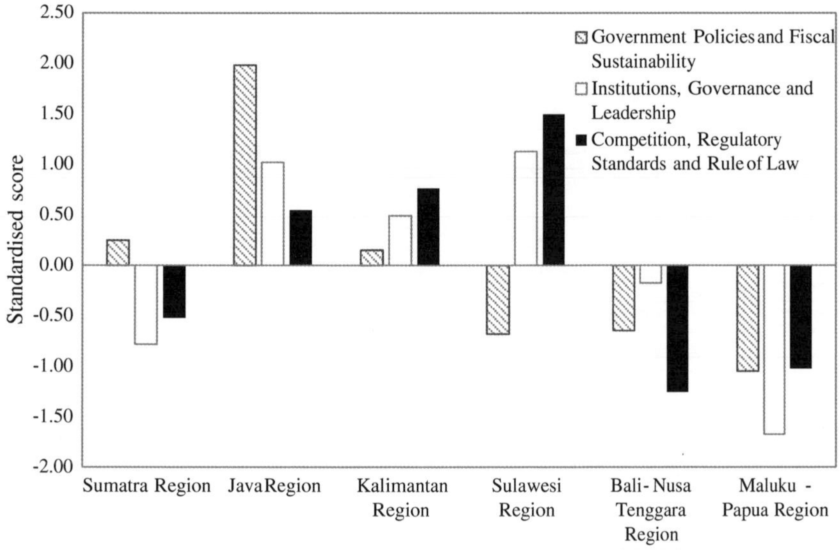

Source: Asia Competitiveness Institute

Sumatra Region's above average performance only lies in its Government Policies and Fiscal Sustainability while poor Competition, Regulatory Standards and Rule of Law sub-environment is the bottleneck for the competitiveness in Bali-Nusa Tenggara Region. Lastly, all sub-environments are almost proportionately low for Maluku-Papua Region with Institutions, Governance and Leadership recording the lowest score.

Quantitative Spread — Financial, Businesses and Manpower Conditions

Based on Table 2.5, Java Region is consistently at number one. The gap between Java Region and Kalimantan Region in Financial, Businesses and Manpower Conditions is rather narrow as compared to that of Overall Competitiveness and Macroeconomic Stability (Table 2.2 and Table 2.3). Nevertheless, the significant difference appears between Kalimantan Region and the following region, Maluku-Papua at third. The ranking defies the dichotomy between west versus east, as Kalimantan and Maluku-Papua are ahead of the Sumatra Region, which is part of the 'west' grouping together with Java Region.

Sub-Environment Spread — Financial, Businesses and Manpower Conditions

Figure 2.5 depicts both commonalities and unevenness of contributions from three sub-environments that make up Financial, Businesses and Manpower Conditions score for each region. For Java Region, its score in Labour Market Flexibility tops the chart (2.1337), which makes it the only region that reports positive score for this sub-environment. The notable strengths come from Java Region's extensive pool of labour force and massive employment opportunities. Despite rising minimum wage requirement in DKI Jakarta, the wage rate in East Java

Table 2.5. 2014 Financial, Businesses and Manpower Conditions: Ranking and Score

Rank	Region	Score
1	Java Region	1.6700
2	Kalimantan Region	1.0027
3	Maluku–Papua Region	–0.3552
4	Sumatra Region	–0.3940
5	Sulawesi Region	–0.7693
6	Bali–Nusa Tenggara Region	–1.1543

Source: Asia Competitiveness Institute

Figure 2.5. 2014 Financial, Businesses and Manpower Conditions Sub-Environment

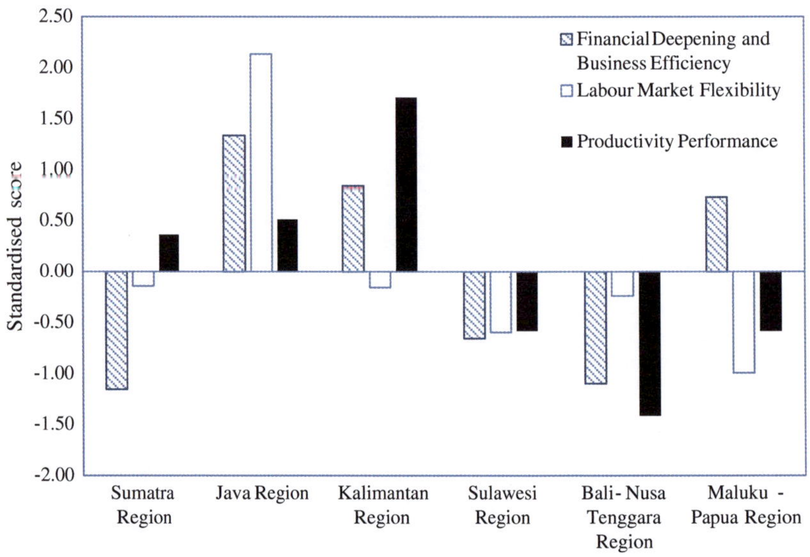

Source: Asia Competitiveness Institute

and Central Java are still competitive. Kalimantan Region boasts its second position from leading the Productivity Performance. On the other hand, Maluku-Papua Region is characterised by the above average Financial Deepening and Business Efficiency. The laggard in this context, Bali-Nusa Tenggara Region, is riddled with poor Productivity Performance and Financial Deepening and Business Efficiency.

Quantitative Spread — Quality of Life and Infrastructure Development

In Table 2.6, Java Region maintains its position as the leader of the group albeit with lower standardised score (1.0603). This implies Java Region's struggles to keep the balance between its well-above average economic-related environments (Macroeconomic Stability and Financial, Businesses and Manpower Conditions) and the needs to ensure excellent quality of life and development for its people. Java Region's score is fairly close to the second place, Kalimantan Region, scoring 0.7425.

The fact that there are four regions with positive standardised scores signals the relatively distributed achievement in Quality of Life and Infrastructure Development across the country. Nevertheless, the disparity still exists with regard to the region at far eastern part of Indonesia, Maluku-Papua Region, with markedly low score at −1.9438.

Sub-Environment Spread — Quality of Life and Infrastructure Development

Unlike Figures 2.3–2.5, there are more instances of positive scores in Figure 2.6 across regions. It is worth noting that Java Region fares low in Standard of Living, Education and Social Stability. At the indicator level, the

Table 2.6. 2014 Quality of Life and Infrastructure Development: Ranking and Score

Rank	Region	Score
1	Java Region	1.0603
2	Kalimantan Region	0.7425
3	Sumatra Region	0.4385
4	Sulawesi Region	0.2448
5	Bali–Nusa Tenggara Region	−0.5423
6	Maluku–Papua Region	−1.9438

Source: Asia Competitiveness Institute

Figure 2.6. 2014 Quality of Life and Infrastructure Development Sub-Environment

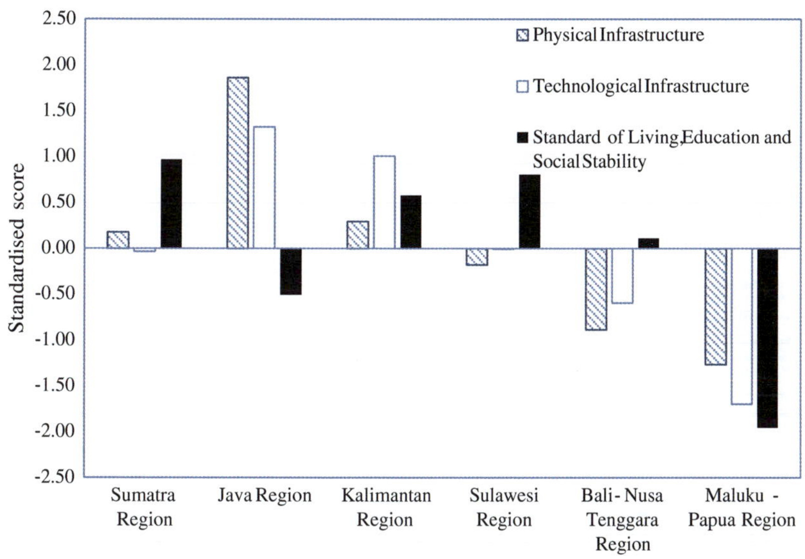

Source: Asia Competitiveness Institute

areas of concern for Java Region include its relatively poor environmental quality and excessive crowd in public facilities, such as school and health centre, that may adversely affect the quality of basic offerings. Regions such as Sumatra, Sulawesi, and Kalimantan are the leaders for Standard of Living, Education and Social Stability. Policy discussion among regions to promote peer learning can be a good platform for Java to learn from others' success. Bali-Nusa Tenggara Region's poor performance is characterised by poor physical and technological infrastructure. Building up intra-regional competitiveness will make Indonesia, as a whole, more competitive. A wide disparity between Bali (eighth) and the other two provinces, West Nusa Tenggara (26th) and East Nusa Tenggara (32nd), serves as a reminder for more even growth within the region. Lastly, Maluku-Papua Region performs poorly in all sub-environments.

3.2 Analysis of Median and Maximum Competitiveness Webs

To further understand the relative strengths and weaknesses of the top performing region (Java, first) and bottom performing region (Maluku–Papua, sixth), it is useful to compare and contrast the 12 sub-environments that make up the four environments with the median and maximum scores of six regions. Figure 2.7 plots the scores of Java Region (solid line) and Maluku–Papua Region (round dotted line) for each of the 12 sub-environments vis-à-vis the overall median score for the six regions in Indonesia (dash line). Being the top in Overall Competitiveness, Java Region excels in most of the sub-environments, except for Standard of Living, Education and Social Stability, which is below the median. By contrast, the scores for Maluku–Papua Region are mostly below the median with an exception of Financial Deepening and Business Efficiency. This sub-environment is, in fact, Maluku–Papua Region's strength, as the score is only slightly behind Java Region, highlighting the important role of private sector in ramping up its competitiveness.

The Maximum Competitiveness Web Analysis in Figure 2.8 shows how far the best scores for each sub-environment (dashed line) are, in relation to the Java Region's scores (solid line) and Maluku–Papua Region's (round dotted line). Java Region becomes the benchmark, earning the highest scores in eight out of 12 sub-environments. For Maluku–Papua Region, its scores are mostly far below the maximum scores, except for Financial Deepening and Business Efficiency which is already fairly close to the maximum score. The gaps are especially large for Labour Market Flexibility; Physical Infrastructure; and Attractiveness to Foreign Investors.

Figure 2.7. 2014 Median Competitiveness Web Analysis: Java Region and Maluku-Papua Region

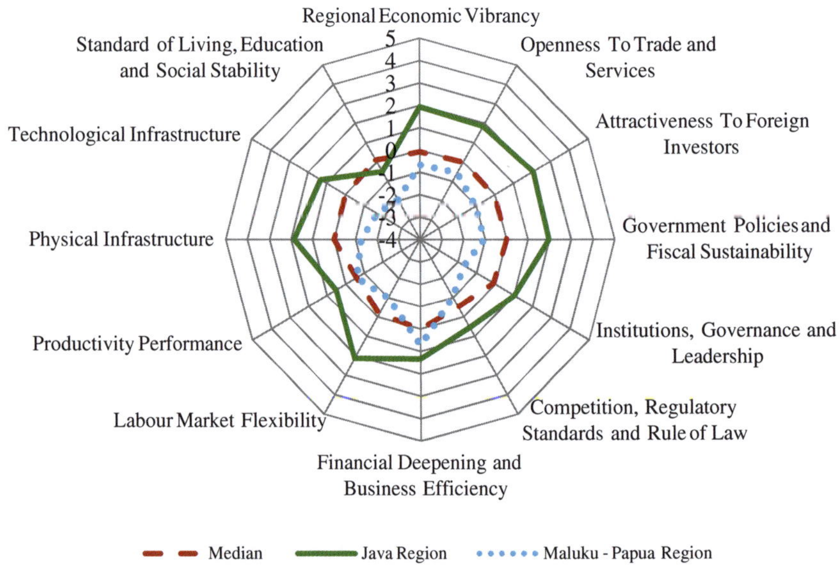

Source: Asia Competitiveness Institute

Figure 2.8. 2014 Maximum Competitiveness Web Analysis: Java Region and Maluku-Papua Region

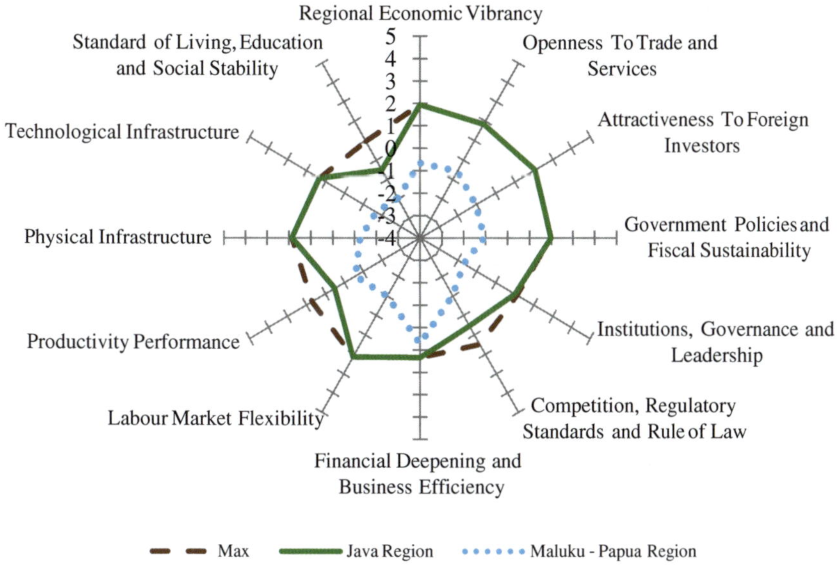

Source: Asia Competitiveness Institute

4. REGIONAL POLICY IMPLICATIONS

The competitiveness analysis and development strategies for six regions in Indonesia underscore the importance of 'regional' approach in paving the development agenda. There are many learning opportunities and experiences from inter-regional friendly rivalry to pull up Indonesia as a whole.

At a glance, some oddities are perceived in terms of conventional economic development theory. Spatial geography may imply that proximity is a natural advantage for spillover economic development. However, our regional competitiveness findings seem to be contradicting. Java Region and Kalimantan Region, which are ranked as top and second position, respectively, are not immediate neighbours. On the other hand, Java Region and Sumatra Region, which are neighbouring enough to build a bridge over, are ranked far apart as the top and fourth position, respectively.

The paradigm shift observed in the formulation of regional policy — evolving from top-down policy interventions often targeted at lagging areas — into much broader policies designed to improve regional competitiveness could well be the new approach forward.[13] Solutions to some perennial issues, such as lack of infrastructure and connectivity, require cross-provincial collaboration. After all, regional challenges require regional solutions. The MP3EI, initiated by Coordinating Ministry for Economic Affairs, has assumed the role of 'joining all the dots' given the complexities in governing multiple layers of government and cross-sectorial initiatives. With alignment between the detailed plan that is tailored to province-specific characteristic, as stipulated in the Provincial Medium-Term Development Plan (RPJMD), and the MP3EI, the concerted efforts are taking place to ensure that Indonesia is on the right trajectory for sustainable growth. The following provides policy briefs to specific areas that require further attention for the six regions in general. Specific development strategies for each region will be elaborated in Chapters 3–8.

4.1 Accelerate Productivity Growth and Sustainable Development

It is logical for Indonesia to spearhead its industrialisation as part of its development plan. Opportunities are abundant with China's eroding competitiveness due to rising wages, especially in the eastern provinces along

[13] OECD, *Regional Development Policy Trends in OECD Member Countries*.

the coast, that allow Indonesia to regain its comparative advantage in labour-intensive export sector. In this context, Indonesia has to further improve its labour productivity growth, which still remains relatively low as compared to other countries. Improvement in the quality of labour, as well as incorporating science and technology and Research and Development (R&D) into the production process, is thus important. This does not only apply to manufacturing per se, but also agricultural sector, in order to further unleash Indonesia's potential to be the food basket for the ASEAN and the world.[14] Further actions for reforms include technological adoption for farm — e.g. machinery, R&D for high yield seedling, supports for farmers, financial access and training, enhancement for extension services to improve the logistics and water management schemes, and improvement on broader agricultural policy governance.[15] Most capital-intensive manufacturing sites, for instance automotive and Fast Moving Consumer Goods (FMCG), are mainly located in Java although they have also been growing in other regions. Similar to how automotive sector benefits from agglomeration in Java Island, such success can also be shared in other initiatives to expand processing industry from raw materials in other regions, such as oleo-chemical from vast palm oil production in Sumatra and cocoa in Sulawesi. More manufacturing clusters, as critical sources of employment creation, should be identified, planned, and set up across other regions.

Along the line of spearheading the growth of these sectors, environmental sustainability should not be neglected. Law enforcement for forest management and legislation on environmental protection are keys to safeguard Indonesia's massive tract of rainforest and control pollution level. Continuous rigorous environmental impact assessment (AMDAL) should also be in place, not only at the onset of the project, but also throughout the implementation and operations.

4.2 Strong Commitment and Continuity in Infrastructure Development

The MP3EI provides a momentum for accelerating infrastructure development across Indonesia. The list of projects, although not exhaustive, is very comprehensive, covering not only conventional land transportation (i.e. road) but also railway for passengers and freight transport, airport, seaport, power and energy, and information and communications technology (ICT). Infrastructure projects are generally for long-term development and require significant amount of investment. The MP3EI is an essential platform in optimising concerted efforts from all related stakeholders that stretch from all layers of government, state-owned enterprises (SOEs), and private sector.

For Indonesia to benefit from the trademark of national connectivity, political will from the government is crucial. Infrastructure projects tend to span across multiple periods where government leaders are constantly changing. Continuity should be upheld despite the persistence temptations to change, rebrand, or even terminate the legacy projects. Democracy and decentralisation should not be a bottleneck for unity in achieving national connectivity vision, if Indonesia stays 'Locally Integrated, Globally Connected'. This is even more pertinent for balancing regional development that will increase Indonesia's competitiveness as a whole. The newly elected President Joko Widodo envisaged Indonesia to be the world's maritime axis. During his presidential campaign, he proposed an ambitious plan of maritime toll road, a sea lane that will be regularly served by cargo ships between western and eastern parts of the country. This initiative can tackle the high logistics transportation cost and wide price difference between the west and east that makes the latter becomes less competitive. The integrated connectivity across lands and seas is essential to promote more diversified and competitive economy across Indonesia.

Land issues constitute a huge stumbling block in infrastructure development which requires long–term commitment for reform. The law on land acquisition has to be further improved. Recognition and protection of customary land rights (*ulayat* rights) should also be taken into account to avoid conflicts that often undermine the livelihoods of smallholders and indigenous population. Financial commitment to infrastructure development also needs to be put in place. The fuel subsidy cut is a step forward to reallocate the budget for

[14] See ACI's furthering studies on agricultural productivity for Indonesian provinces, as briefly elaborated in Chapter 10.

[15] OECD, *OECD Review of Agricultural Policies: Indonesia 2012* (OECD Publishing, 2012), 19–40.

infrastructure development and other pro-poor assistance. Involvement from private sector through Public Private Partnership (PPP), as well as efficient capital market, is equally important as an alternative source of funding. Indonesia should tap into potential infrastructure funding, for instance, the Asian Infrastructure Investment Bank (AIIB).

4.3 Strengthen Human Capital Development

Indonesia should strive harder to improve the quality of human capital to benefit from the existing demographic dividend. The majority of the policies are directed towards access and enrolment, which are still relevant, but focusing solely on these brings some risks, especially with Indonesia moving towards higher value-added sector which requires labour force with more sophisticated skillset. Education policy should be more holistic to go beyond improving the 'quantity', to also account for 'quality' and promote lifelong learning as technology is progressing rapidly. The human capital investment should start at the early stage, from early childhood education and elementary school, to ensure that everyone is equipped with foundation that helps them to develop cognitive and life skills at later stage. At secondary level, it is necessary to improve not only quality but also relevance in terms of curricula, and specific and practical knowledge. Vocational secondary school should be more strategic in designing demand-driven curriculum with systematic industry input and forging stronger consultation mechanisms with industry and government.

University's role should also be strengthened to enhance its capacity and capability to produce graduates that are skilful and 'work ready' with strong competencies in both hard and soft skills. Improvement in university-industry link, through internship or apprenticeship programme, is a key to bridge school to work transition. Additionally, they can establish closer R&D initiatives to spur innovation. As each region is endowed with specific natural resources, the curriculum can then be further catered towards those main economic activities, particularly to enhance downstream industries. For example, forestry centre of educational and training excellence to be developed in Kalimantan, palm oil in Sumatra, and fishery in Maluku-Papua.

Multiple pathways for skill development should not stop at formal level. Government can leverage on its extensive network of vocational training centres (BLKs) and also other non-formal education initiatives targeted for youth, such as Para Professional Course (KPP) and Education for Youth Employment (EYE). The role of private sector in providing training is also crucial in laying the ground for lifelong learning. Professional executive training programme could also be conducted with local and international experts sharing their expertise to enhance governance.

Java Region is still way ahead of other regions in terms of capacity and capability in moulding the talent pipeline. As Indonesia envisions broader development that encompasses all six regions, there is a need to spearhead the improvement in quantity and quality of education across Indonesia. While other regions can learn from Java's success, Java still has to advance to bring up its standards to follow international best practices.

The role of teachers is integral in Indonesia's success in moulding its human capital. The recent law on minimum qualification for teachers is appreciated amidst no rigorous evidence yet over improvement in the students' performance. It is imperative for government to adopt multi-pronged strategies starting from recruitment of highly qualified individual, quality improvement in pre-service teacher education, provision for in-service professional development, and assessment linked to competencies and student performance.

4.4 Changing Pattern of Economic Geography

Conducting competitiveness analysis at supra-provincial level allows us to see economic activities beyond the formal administrative boundaries of provinces. Thus, we are able to see economic agglomerations that transcend districts, provinces, or even regions. For example, the economic and geographic sphere of Jakarta Metropolitan Region overlaps three provinces: DKI Jakarta, West Java, and Banten. Similarly, the cities of Banjarmasin in South Kalimantan and Palangkaraya in Central Kalimantan share the same flat plain on the south side of Kalimantan, and substantial movements and connections between the two cities are taking place.

In analysing the "where" of the economic development, the 2009 World Development Report calls our attention to three factors: density, distance, and division.[16] First, density refers to economies of scale. It reminds us that development does not distribute itself evenly across space, but does so by clustering in certain places and capitalising on the scale economies of clusters. Second, distance refers to movement. It reminds us that for development to take place, movement of people and goods — especially within and between the clusters — must be facilitated. This calls for serious attention to aspects related to connectivity and logistics infrastructure. Third, division refers to ease of conducting trade. It reminds us that movement of goods and people between places should be allowed and encouraged by streamlined, consistent, and fair regulations across these different places.

The third aspect (division) is typically relevant at the country level, where trade regulations may vary from country to country. However, the first two (density and distance) remain critical for sub-national competitiveness analysis. For future analysis, it would be beneficial to look into more details at urban agglomerations (metropolitan areas) across Indonesia, as well as how movement of goods and people between these centres are facilitated.

REFERENCES

Coordinating Ministry for Economic Affairs. *Master Plan for Acceleration and Expansion of Indonesia's Economic Development 2011–2025 (MP3EI)*. Jakarta: Coordinating Ministry for Economic Affairs, 2011.

Enright, M.J. "The Globalisation of Competition and the Location of Competitive Advantage: Policies Towards Regional Clustering." In *The Globalisation of Multinational Enterprise Activity and Economic Development*, ed. by N. Hood, and S. Young, 303–331. London: MacMillan, 2000.

Hill, Hal, B.P. Resosudarmo, and Yogi Vidyattama. "Economic Geography of Indonesia: Location, Connectivity, and Resources." In *Reshaping Economic Geography in East Asia*, ed. by Yukon Huang and A.M. Bocchi, 115–134. Washington DC: World Bank Publications, 2008.

Ketels, Christian. "Recent Research on Competitiveness and Clusters: What Are the Implications for Regional Policy?" *Cambridge Journal of Regions, Economy and Society* Vol. 6 (2013): 269–284.

Kitson, M., Ron Martin, and Peter Tyler. "Regional Competitiveness: An Elusive Yet Key Concept?" *Regional Studies* Vol. 38, No. 9 (2004): 991–999.

Neary, Adelle. "Jokowi Spells Out Vision for Indonesia's Global Maritime Nexus." *Centre for Strategic and International Studies: Southeast Asia from Scott Circle* Vol. V, No. 24 (November 2014): 1–4.

Organisation for Economic Cooperation and Development (OECD). *OECD Review of Agricultural Policies: Indonesia 2012*. OECD Publishing, 2012.

Organisation for Economic Cooperation and Development (OECD). *Regional Development Policy Trends in OECD Member Countries*. OECD Publishing, 2010.

Porter, M.E. "Location, Competition, and Economic Development: Local Clusters in a Global Economy." *Economic Development Quarterly* Vol. 14, No. 1 (2000): 15–34.

Porter, M.E. *On Competition*. Boston MA: Harvard Business School, 1998.

Porter, M.E. "The Economic Performance of Regions." *Regional Studies* Vol. 37, No. 6–7 (2003): 549–578.

Tan, Khee Giap, and Mulya Amri. "Subnational Competitiveness and National Performance: Analysis and Simulation for Indonesia." *Journal of Centrum Cathedra (JCC): The Business and Economics Research Journal* Vol. 6, No. 2 (2013): 173–192.

Tan, Khee Giap, Mulya Amri, Linda Low, and Tan Kong Yam. *Competitiveness Analysis and Development Strategies for 33 Indonesian Provinces*. Singapore: World Scientific, 2013.

World Bank. *Purchasing Power Parities and Real Expenditures of World Economies: Summary of Results and Findings of the 2011 International Comparison Program*. Washington DC: World Bank Publications, 2014.

---

[16] World Bank, *World Development Report 2009: Reshaping Economic Geography* (Washington: World Bank Publications, 2009), 48-121.

World Bank. *World Development Report 2009: Reshaping Economic Geography*. Washington DC: World Bank Publications, 2009.

Wuryanto, Luky Eko. "Accelerating Infrastructure Development Programmes and Expected Roles of AIIB." Paper presented at 2014 Annual Asia Competitiveness Institute Conference on "Competitiveness Analysis of 112 Asian Economies, Asia Economic Connectivity, Liveable Cities Index for 100 Greater China Cities and Cost of Living Index for Expatriates and Ordinary Residents", Singapore, November 26–27, 2014.

Discussant Notes: Competitiveness Ranking, Simulation Study and Development Strategies for 33 Provinces and Six Regions in Indonesia

Dr Luky Eko Wuryanto
Deputy Minister for Infrastructure and Regional Development
Coordinating Ministry for Economic Affairs, Republic of Indonesia

1. BACKGROUND: POSITIONING THE STUDY WITH ON-GOING POLICY EXERCISE

Since 2011, Indonesian Government has promulgated the Master Plan for Acceleration and Expansion of Indonesia's Economic Development up to 2025 (MP3EI). The main goal of the MP3EI is to boost investment as the main driver for economic growth and to formulate an implementable roadmap for a more balanced economic posture as a prerequisite for becoming a more competitive and more resilient economy.

The main spirit of the the MP3EI is an economic transformation to reshape and simultaneously restructure the economic posture to grow faster by empowering unleashed potentials in more optimal manner. To many observers, including some from Indonesians, the MP3EI is considered an ambitious agenda. It may be arguably correct; however, as a government official, I must say that the country does not have any other options rather than to embark on this agenda if it is to become a successful victor in the increasingly competitive international arena.

Currently, as observed in Figure 1, the economic disparity is immense. The economic centres in Java are substantially dominant as to the ones at the outer islands. This pattern has been in place for more than four decades, even though we could observe slow and uneven decreasing trends lately in reducing Java's dominance. Continuing the current pattern of growth would be environmentally disastrous and would not only endanger Java, but may also have national implications. In addition, national logistics system would also be inefficient, hence weakening national competitiveness and resilience. Therefore, there is a justified need to unload Java's burden by creating new economic centres outside Java, relying on the development of regionally strong economic potential that varies across Indonesia.

On the other hand, there is another trend in urban population dispersion. For the last five years, the growth of small and medium–sized cities outside Java has been consistently higher than those of medium to large cities in Java. The trend is much more obvious in Sumatra. For other islands, we could also easily observe high growth of urban population in South Kalimantan and East Kalimantan, North Sulawesi and South Sulawesi, Bali and West Nusa Tenggara, or even more to the eastern part of Indonesia, such as in Maluku, and also in West Papua, such as Sorong and Manokwari.

Increasing population at some urban concentration areas outside Java creates the emergence of middle-class and affluent consumers MACs (Figure 2). Those population class demand better quality of life surrounding their domiciles. Therefore, increasing presence of various economic activities is inevitable. To create sustainable and competitive local economic activities, Indonesia must depend on its strong potential that is enhanced locally or regionally. Industrial clusters should be established, supported by all types of related infrastructure for increased efficiency in connectivity (roads, ports, airports, fibre optics, and also energy supplies). Those industrial clusters should also be equipped with facilities to promote locals' excellence in human resources.

Figure 1. Posture of Indonesia's Economic Landscape (2010)

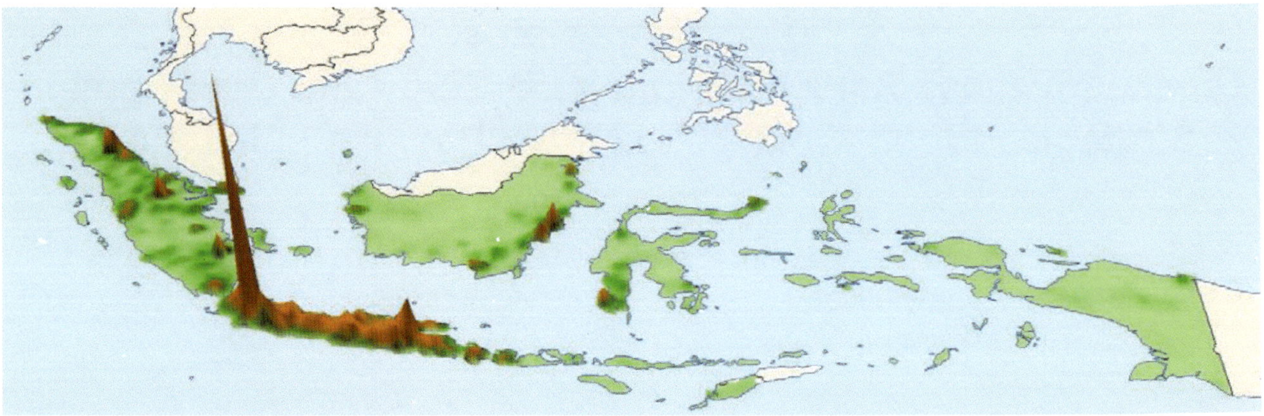

Source: Coordinating Ministry for Economic Affairs, Indonesia

Figure 2. Regional Dispersion of Middle-class and Affluent Consumer (MAC)

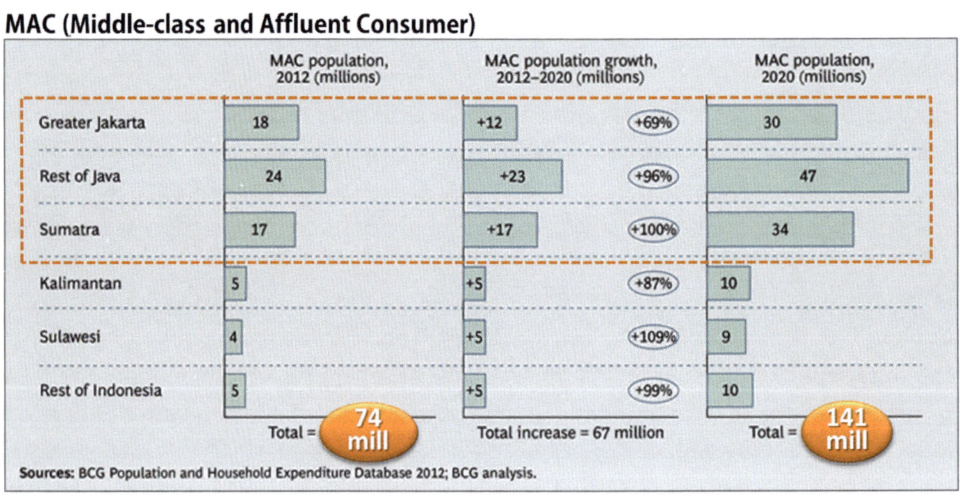

Source: Boston Consulting Group

This is the economic transformation that is embedded in the MP3EI. For instance, to create new economic centres that will systematically reduce Java's dominance, special attention is given to the development and acceleration of eastern Indonesia since most of its untapped natural resources are abundant yet still somehow intact. From geo-economic standpoint, the success to develop this part of the country is very strategic as its dynamic has multiplications for regional economics of Southeast Asia.

Ensuing the plan to revive the Maritime Silk Route for the 21st century, as outlined by China's President Xi Jinping in front of the Indonesian Parliament in October 2013, the effort to accelerate the economic transformation for the eastern part of the country has been put in a higher stake. The success is a must. In addition, the process must also make sure that local communities' welfare will not worsen.

Considering the remoteness of the eastern part of Indonesia, new regional economic centres must be smartly chosen on strategic or relatively accessible locations. Within this context, the roles of Kalimantan and Sulawesi are of utmost importance as the gate for economic dispersion to the east. In addition, a rather different approach must also be employed in order to better integrate the economy from logistics point of view (Figure 3). Enhancement of sea transportation system and armada is the way to go. It becomes the vision of the new government under President Joko Widodo.

Figure 3. National Backbone of Logistics Connectivity

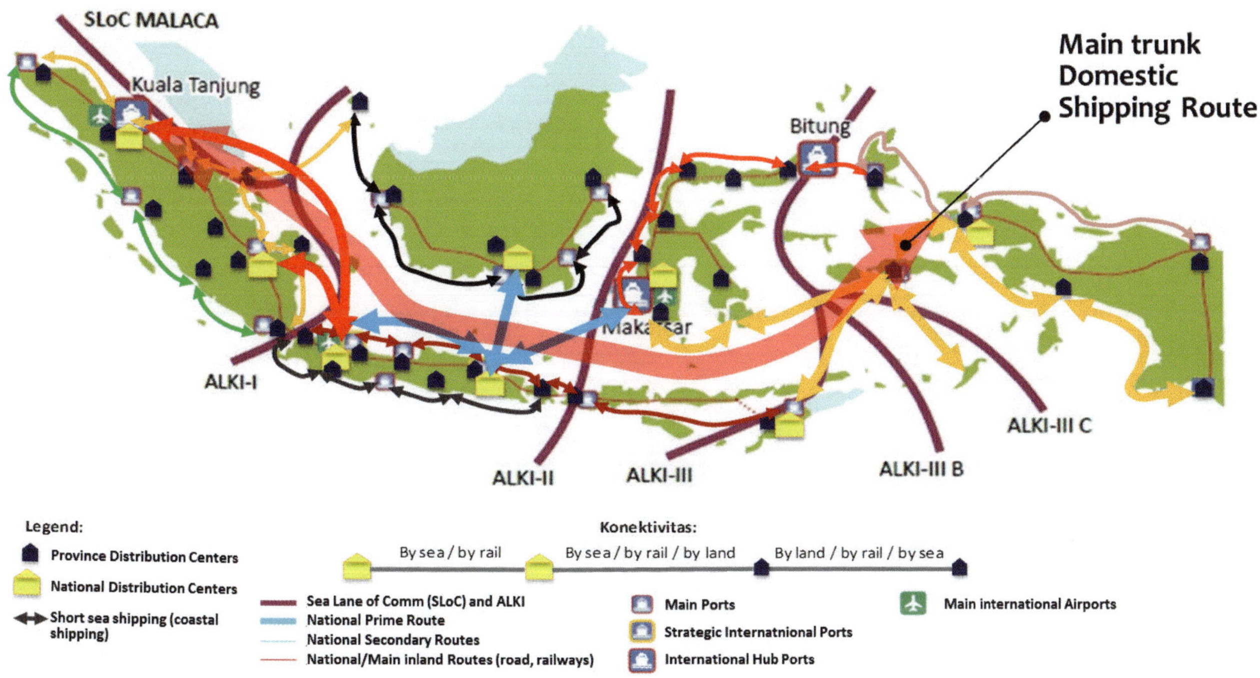

Note: ALKI, *Alur Laut Kepulauan Indonesia*, refers to Indonesia's Archipelagic Sea Lanes
Source: Coordinating Ministry for Economic Affairs, Indonesia

2. REMARKS AND COMMENTS

This is an excellent work and timely for inspiring stronger national policies that should be based more on regional development strategy due to wide differences among regions.

The unit of analysis at provincial level (as opposed to district/city level) has given significant contribution to Indonesian literature and is proven to be much more sensible for recommendation purposes, especially when it comes to economic development policies.

Along with the dynamics of our governance structure that has evolved under decentralisation since 2000, this international perspective will positively boost "higher responsibility" of not only the central government but also provincial government to strategically develop more competitiveness policies.

From methodology standpoint, with the application of 104 indicators, the study provides ample ingredients for many kinds of analysis compared to the previous one. And that is not only for inter-provincial comparison purpose, but also to provide specific information for individual province (or region) analysis. To be applied for more specific policy analysis purposes, I look forward to the Asia Competitiveness Institute (ACI) to develop further cooperation with the interested provincial governments to assist and improve the efficiency of their policy in enhancing regional competitiveness strategic formulation.

Some indicators, inevitably, will have medium to long-term impacts (e.g. improvement on infrastructure or human capacity). Therefore, longer time span comparisons or analyses are more appropriate and more reliable for policy recommendations.

For some of the readers that are familiar with the monitoring of the MP3EI implementation for the last three years, there are some interesting results as shown in Figure 4, as follows:

- At the provincial level, some observations are in fact very much aligned with the data observed in the MP3EI implementation during the period of 2011–2014, especially when we look at some of the achievements that are represented by the amount of ground-breaking (GB) projects at some provinces in Java, Sumatra, or Kalimantan. With the exception of the amount of GB projects in some provinces in Java that are obviously still the highest, some provinces in Kalimantan do have better performance compared to provinces in Java and Sumatra.

Figure 4. Ground-breaking MP3EI's Project until 2nd Quarter of 2014

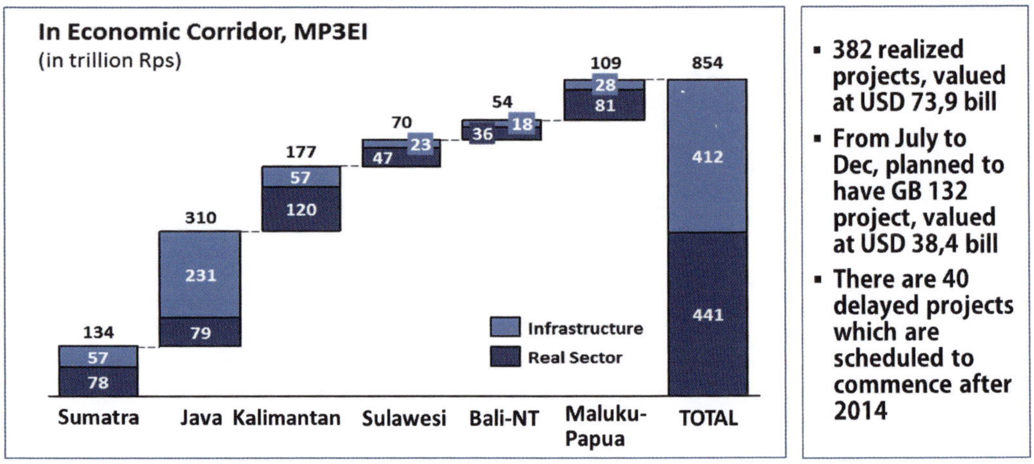

Source: MP3EI National Secretariat

- At regional (economic corridor) level, the competitiveness ranking among them definitely justifies the spirit of the MP3EI. The major goal to accelerate and expand the economic transformation to the eastern part of Indonesia has been echoed by the relatively strong competitive performance of many provincial governments, notably in Kalimantan (headed by East Kalimantan) and Sulawesi (headed by South Sulawesi).
- With maturing infrastructure capacity, Sumatra Economic Corridor is still the logical alternative investment destination after Java in the near future. However, with even larger variety of potentials in the eastern part of Indonesia, some of the provinces in Kalimantan and Sulawesi will also soon become the strong economic centres to lead the development of eastern Indonesia.
- In light of the implementation of the ASEAN Economic Community (AEC), consistency in boosting infrastructure development, including energy readiness, and acceleration of local human resources development are the most crucial strategies for the eastern region (as well as the nation) to have the maximum benefit on reaping the coming opportunities.

I observe that the ACI has now become a credible international entity to provide comprehensive regional economic analysis to many neighbouring countries, especially in Southeast Asia. For greater roles in the future, these are some final notes to be considered based on Indonesian government structure:

- Based on what I observed, the recommendations have been comprehensively formulated to address necessary steps to be taken forward by the regional government to essentially enhance their provincial as well as regional competitiveness. Within this aspect, the need for rigorous infrastructure (presumably includes energy sector) development and human resource enhancement are clearly imperative.
- Many of the development responsibilities are not under provincial government responsibilities only. This suggests that future studies should also map and recommend an optimal role for the central government to support regional governments in creating initiatives to develop infrastructure and human resources. These initiatives will allow an enabling environment to complement regional or local governments in joint efforts to enhance their competitiveness.
- What I am offering as a suggestion is that in drawing up conclusion and proposing prescriptive policy measures to improve regional competitiveness, we should not interpret the existing regional policy measures as solely a result within the domains of regional governments' responsibility, but should also be understood as a result of the national policies. Indonesia has embarked on improving the role of central government in enhancing a sound institutional and legal framework to support and better assist regional governments. The spirit is in simplifying many regulations and procedures as well as licensing process. In regulatory aspect, within three years span, more than 50 regulations have been improved to support the acceleration of investment driven by the MP3EI. Those include improvement at law level, government regulations level, presidential decree level, and ministerial decree level.

Chapter 3
Competitiveness Analysis on the Sumatra Region

Aceh, North Sumatra, West Sumatra, Riau, Riau Islands, Jambi, Bengkulu, South Sumatra, Bangka Belitung Islands, and Lampung

1. INTRODUCTION

1.1 Background and Notes

Figure 3.1 shows the provinces in Sumatra Region as defined by the Master Plan for Acceleration and Expansion of Indonesia's Economic Development 2011–2025 (MP3EI).[1] The 10 provinces with their respective capital cities are Aceh (Banda Aceh), North Sumatra (Medan), West Sumatra (Padang), Riau (Pekanbaru), Riau Islands (Tanjung Pinang), Jambi (Jambi), Bengkulu (Bengkulu), South Sumatra (Palembang), Bangka Belitung Islands (Pangkal Pinang), and Lampung (Bandar Lampung). Batam, Bintan, and Karimun in Riau Islands designated as a Special Economic Zone (SEZ) are part of Indonesia-Malaysia-Singapore Growth Triangle.[2] Sei Mangkei SEZ in North Sumatra, where Unilever's oleo-chemical factory is located, will further enhance economic growth in Sumatra Region.

Geographically, Sumatra is located at the western part of Indonesia which directly faces the Bay of Bengal in the north, the Malacca Strait in the east, the Sunda Strait in the south, and the Indian Ocean in the west. Its strategic location can be further leveraged to connect Indonesia with the rest of the world.

In Figure 3.1, inset map (top right) shows the competitiveness ranking by the Asia Competitiveness Institute (ACI) using the traffic light scheme with green representing the Top 10 provinces, followed by the 13 middle-ranking provinces in yellow and the remaining provinces with lower competitiveness in red. Only Riau is part of the Top 10 while others are scattered in the Middle 13 and Bottom 10 groups.[3]

Sumatra is the second largest region in Indonesia with 480,793.28 km^2 of land area, approximately 25.16% of Indonesia. It is an archipelagic region with 5,277 islands. As of 2011, Sumatra Region was home to almost 52 million people, which accounted for 22% of Indonesia's population. Major ethnic groups in Sumatra include Acehnese, Batak, Minangkabau, Malay, and Tionghoa.

Topographically, the mountain chain of Bukit Barisan is located at the western part of the island, stretching from the northwest to the southeast. Along the chain, there are several active volcanoes such as Geureudong in Aceh, Sinabung in North Sumatra, Marapi and Talang in West Sumatra, Kaba in Bengkulu, and Kerinci at the borders of South Sumatra and Jambi. Sumatra also hosts the world's largest volcanic lake in the world, Lake Toba in North Sumatra, measuring 100 km long, 30 km wide and up to 505 m deep.

The MP3EI designated Sumatra as the "Centre for Production and Processing of Natural Resources and as the Nation's Energy Reserves". The main economic commodities identified in the MP3EI are palm oil, rubber, coal, shipping industry, and steel. This corridor encapsulates 11 economic centres: Banda Aceh, Medan, Pekanbaru, Jambi, Palembang, Tanjung Pinang, Pangkal Pinang, Padang, Bandar Lampung, Bengkulu, and Serang. Serang is a part of Banten in Java Island and is not physically located in Sumatra. Its inclusion in Sumatra's economic centres is due to the fact that the MP3EI has made Sunda Strait Bridge as one of the strategic projects in

---

[1] Coordinating Ministry for Economic Affairs, *Master Plan for Acceleration and Expansion of Indonesia's Economic Development 2011–2025 (MP3EI)* (Jakarta: Coordinating Ministry for Economic Affairs, 2011).

[2] Ooi Giok-Ling, "The Indonesia-Malaysia-Singapore Growth Triangle: Sub-Regional Economic Cooperation and Integration," *GeoJournal* Vol. 36, No. 4 (August 1995): 337–344.

[3] See Tan Khee Giap *et al.*, *Competitiveness Analysis and Development Strategies for 33 Indonesian provinces* (Singapore: World Scientific, 2013) and Tan Khee Giap and Mulya Amri, "Subnational Competitiveness and National Performance: Analysis and Simulation for Indonesia," *Journal of Centrum Cathedra (JCC): The Business and Economics Research Journal* Vol. 6, No. 2 (2013): 173–192 that mark the first attempt to rank provinces based on their competitiveness level.

Figure 3.1. Map of Sumatra Region

Source: Asia Competitiveness Institute

connecting Sumatra and Java islands. Nevertheless, the new government under President Joko Widodo called for a halt to such mega project as it could instigate more imbalanced regional development and was not aligned with the maritime vision to forge improvement in maritime infrastructure.

In terms of economic size, Sumatra plays a strategic role as Indonesia's second largest economic contributor after Java. Sumatra consistently contributed to more than 20% of Indonesia's Gross Domestic Product (GDP) in 2000–2012. Sumatra's strategic location along prominent international shipping lane, Malacca Strait, offers great opportunities to enhance its role in international trade.

Table 3.1 shows the basic economic indicators of Sumatra Region where both primary and tertiary sectors provided rather equal contributions of 35.71% and 36.48%, respectively, to Gross Regional Domestic Product (GRDP) in 2011. The region also boasted a lower poverty rate and higher Human Development Index (HDI) in 2011 as compared to 2006.

1.2 Major Sectors and Activities

Sumatra Region is endowed with rich resources, ranging from agricultural to mining commodities (Table 3.2). One of the region's top commodities is palm oil. Together with Malaysia, Indonesia contributed to 85% of world-wide palm oil production with 23.9 million tonnes of production in 2011.[4] Of the two, Indonesia has a bigger potential in palm oil production due to its vast land size. At the national level, according to the MP3EI, Sumatra and Kalimantan produce 96% of Indonesia's palm oil. Indonesia is also the largest thermal coal exporter in the world, overtaking Australia, with about 26% of the world's export. There are over 52.4 billion tonnes of coal reserves in Sumatra Island, 90% of which are concentrated in South Sumatra. The region is also home to 8% of Indonesia's laterite iron ore reserves, which are found in Bengkulu, West Sumatra, and Riau Islands. At the provincial level, Aceh is rich with natural gas, while oil is produced in North Sumatra, Riau, and South Sumatra.

In terms of shipping and transport, the MP3EI states that the east coast of Sumatra is a vibrant shipping passage with no fewer than 300 ships passing through per day; out of which, 50 of them are classified as Very Large Crude Carrier (VLCC), plying from the Arabian Gulf and carrying oil to the eastern part of Asia. To capture this enormous potential, the region is designated to develop the shipyard industry, both shipbuilding and ship repair, as shipping traffic increases. Some strategic locations for developing this industry are Karimun Island in Riau

[4] "Infocomm Commodity Profile Palm Oil," United Nations Conference on Trade and Development (UNCTAD), retrieved on July 25, 2014, <http://www.unctad.info/en/Infocomm/AACP-Products/Palm-oil/>.

Table 3.1. Sumatra Region: Basic Economic Indicators

A. Population	**2006**	**2011**
Total population	47,184,520	51,553,628
% urban	34.90	39.12
B. Area		**2011**
Km^2		480,793.28
% equivalent to country		25.16
C. Gross Regional Domestic Product (GRDP)	**2006**	**2011**
Rupiah (million)	389,067,100	497,177,000
Rupiah (million) without oil & gas	311,680,282	424,005,200
Rupiah (million) without oil & gas & mineral	307,938,080	418,633,368
D. Economic composition, as % GRDP	**2006**	**2011**
Primary sector	40.28	35.71
Secondary sector	27.02	27.80
Tertiary sector	32.69	36.48
E. GRDP per capita	**2006**	**2011**
Rupiah (million)	8.25	9.64
Rupiah (million) without oil & gas	6.61	8.22
Rupiah (million) without oil & gas & mineral	6.53	8.12
F. Poverty Rate	**2006**	**2011**
% of population	17.55	12.21
G. Human Development Index	**2006**	**2011**
Index	71.47	73.90

GRDP based on 2000 Constant Price
Source: Asia Competitiveness Institute using data from Indonesia Statistical Yearbook

Table 3.2. Major Products and Activities

Primary	Rice, cassava, sweet potato, vegetables, fruits, fishery, palm oil, rubber, cacao, coffee, coal, oil, and natural gas
Secondary	Processing industry for agricultural products, shipyard, fertiliser, and steel
Tertiary	Tourism, hotel, transport and communication, and trade

Source: Asia Competitiveness Institute

Islands, Belawan Seaport and Kuala Tanjung Seaport in North Sumatra. The development of Sumatra's shipyard industry is expected to support the shipyard industry in Java Region.

With Sumatra's iron ore potential, emphasis to further develop it into a full-fledged steel industry is a natural progression for moving up the value chain and accelerating downstream activities. Several private companies in iron processing, such as Gunung Garuda Group and PT Gainet International Indonesia, have been operating in North Sumatra and West Sumatra, respectively. Indonesia's steel consumption is expected to grow due to burgeoning middle class and buoyant economy. This is in line with the MP3EI theme to make Sumatra not only as the industrial centre, but also the hub for processing natural resources.

Although tourism is not listed as the main economic activity in the MP3EI, Sumatra Region is home to notable tourism destinations such as Lake Toba, Samosir Island, and scenic beaches in Bintan Island. In addition, several provinces in Sumatra Region have hosted international events, such as the 26th Southeast Asian Games in 2011 and the third Islamic Solidarity Games in 2013 in South Sumatra. Tour de Singkarak is an annual international road bicycle racing event held in West Sumatra and is part of the UCI Asia Tour. International events generate revenues for hotels, restaurants, and other service sectors, rendering the tertiary sector as the highest contributor to GRDP at 36.48% in 2011. Thus, joining the dots to form strategic clusters within Sumatra Region is a right move for both economies of scale and scope.

1.3 Infrastructure Provision

Major cities in Sumatra are connected through the West Route, Middle Route, and East Route land infrastructure. The West Route passes through West Sumatra, Bengkulu, and Lampung, while the Middle Route links North Sumatra, West Sumatra, Jambi, South Sumatra, and Lampung. The East Route is through Aceh, North Sumatra, Riau, Jambi, South Sumatra, and Lampung.

Roads form the primary mode of land transportation due to relatively underdeveloped railway track. For the northern part of Sumatra, the railways connect Medan and Tebing Tinggi in North Sumatra, mostly transporting palm oil. Further down in the central part of the island, there is West Sumatra with only train service connecting Sawahlunto, Padang, and Padang Pariaman, built in the Dutch colonial period. These tracks are mainly used as tourist attractions. In the southern part of Sumatra, the train service connects Bandar Lampung and Palembang.

There are seven international airports in Sumatra Region, namely, Hang Nadim International Airport in Batam (Riau Islands), Sultan Iskandar Muda International Airport in Banda Aceh (Aceh), Kuala Namu International Airport in Medan (North Sumatra), Minangkabau International Airport in Padang (West Sumatra), Sultan Syarif Kasim II International Airport in Pekanbaru (Riau), Sultan Mahmud Badaruddin II International Airport in Palembang (South Sumatra), and Raja Haji Fisabilillah International Airport in Tanjung Pinang (Riau Islands). Additionally, there are 29 domestic airports across Sumatra. As the demand for air transportation grows, several airports are expanded to increase their capacity. Kuala Namu International Airport, for example, replaced the old Polonia Airport which has helped to increase the capacity from 900,000 to 8.3 million passengers per year since July 2013. Phase II expansion plans to increase the capacity to 16 million, and eventually to more than 20 million by 2023 in Phase III.

The three main ports to facilitate sea transport are Belawan in Medan (North Sumatra), Teluk Bayur in Padang (West Sumatra), and Bakauheni in Lampung. In early 2013, Belawan Port handled up to 1.2 million twenty-foot equivalent units (TEUs) per year. With gradual expansion, its capacity is raised to 2 million TEUs per year. Teluk Bayur Port is the busiest port in the western part of Sumatra with plans for major renovation to modernise operation. Bakauheni, located at the southern end of Sumatra Island, is an important hub between Sumatra and Java. The average time for traveling to Merak Port in Banten is around 2–3 hours.

The MP3EI has further assigned Kuala Tanjung Port as an alternative international shipping hub connecting Indonesia with the rest of the world. Other than the three main ports in Sumatra, there are also Tanjung Balai Karimun Port in Riau Islands, Tanjung Api-Api Port in South Sumatra, Tanjung Pandan Port in Bangka Belitung Islands, and other ports that support passenger and cargo traffic.

2. RELATIVE COMPETITIVENESS OF REGIONS

The competitiveness framework for the region follows the same approach with the provincial competitiveness, as explained in Chapter 1 in greater detail. Further explanation on the aggregation of individual province's indicators into regional scores can be found in Chapter 2.

2.1 Competitiveness Ranking of Six Regions — Rank and Score by Environment[5]

Table 3.3. 2014 Overall Competitiveness: Ranking and Score

Rank	Region	Score
1	Java Region	1.7233
2	Kalimantan Region	0.6511
3	Sulawesi Region	–0.0392
4	*Sumatra Region*	*–0.0741*
5	Bali–Nusa Tenggara Region	–0.9839
6	Maluku–Papua Region	–1.2772

Source: Asia Competitiveness Institute

Despite a general presumption that puts Sumatra as the second most developed island in Indonesia after Java, Table 3.3 shows that in reality, Sumatra Region is only ranked fourth in the Overall Competitiveness analysis. Its score (–0.0741), which is below Sulawesi Region (–0.0392) and above Bali–Nusa Tenggara Region (–0.9839), requires improvement.

The difference in scores between Sumatra Region and Sulawesi Region is relatively narrow compared to the difference between Sumatra Region and Bali–Nusa Tenggara Region at the fifth position. This implies that Sumatra Region can easily take over Sulawesi Region's position, but it is harder for Bali–Nusa Tenggara Region to overtake Sumatra Region.

At provincial level, Riau at the ninth position is the sole Sumatra province in the Top 10 most competitive provinces. Riau Islands (11th), Aceh (13th), South Sumatra (16th), West Sumatra (17th), North Sumatra (19th), and Bangka Belitung Islands (20th) are in the Middle 13 group, while Lampung (24th), Jambi (27th), and Bengkulu (30th) are at the Bottom 10. These relatively low ranks contribute to its overall position in the fourth place. This means that well-planned and comprehensive strategies that combine the potentials of all provinces will increase the competitiveness score for Sumatra Region.

Table 3.4. 2014 Macroeconomic Stability: Ranking and Score

Rank	Region	Score
1	Java Region	2.0461
2	*Sumatra Region*	*0.1112*
3	Kalimantan Region	0.0350
4	Sulawesi Region	–0.3896
5	Maluku–Papua Region	–0.7943
6	Bali–Nusa Tenggara Region	–1.0085

Source: Asia Competitiveness Institute

For Macroeconomic Stability, presented in Table 3.4, Sumatra Region is ranked second, scoring 0.1112. This is the strongest of four environments for Sumatra Region. Sumatra Region places below Java Region and above Kalimantan Region. To overtake Java Region, Sumatra Region needs to narrow the difference in score by 1.9349.

Three provinces sit comfortably in the Top 10 of the provincial ranking. They are Riau Islands (fifth), Riau (eighth), and North Sumatra (ninth). Other provinces still need to improve their competitiveness score in this environment to pull up the overall score for Sumatra Region. They include South Sumatra (12th), Bangka Belitung Islands (19th), Jambi (20th), West Sumatra (26th), Aceh (28th), Lampung (29th), and Bengkulu (31st). Leveraging a strategic cluster of activities is a logical way to pull up these positions.

[5] Results for the 2014 competitiveness study are based on official data in 2011 and survey data collected in 2013. Conventionally due to collation, compilation, and publication of official data, such a lag of data before reaching end-users is acceptable.

Table 3.5. 2014 Government and Institutional Setting: Ranking and Score

Rank	Region	Score
1	Java Region	1.4124
2	Sulawesi Region	0.7733
3	Kalimantan Region	0.5582
4	*Sumatra Region*	*–0.4219*
5	Bali–Nusa Tenggara Region	–0.8284
6	Maluku–Papua Region	–1.4937

Source: Asia Competitiveness Institute

For Government and Institutional Setting, as seen in Table 3.5, Sumatra Region is fourth in rank with a score of –0.4219. Sumatra is in between Kalimantan Region (0.5582) and Bali–Nusa Tenggara Region (–0.8284). The difference in scores between Sumatra Region and Kalimantan Region is wider compared to that of Sumatra Region and Bali–Nusa Tenggara Region.

Aceh, ranked ninth in the provincial ranking, is the only province from Sumatra Region that is in the Top 10 for this environment. Four provinces are in the Middle 13 while five others are in the Bottom 10, with Riau Islands ranked at 31st.

Table 3.6. 2014 Financial, Businesses and Manpower Conditions: Ranking and Score

Rank	Region	Score
1	Java Region	1.6700
2	Kalimantan Region	1.0027
3	Maluku–Papua Region	–0.3552
4	*Sumatra Region*	*–0.3940*
5	Sulawesi Region	–0.7693
6	Bali–Nusa Tenggara Region	–1.1543

Source: Asia Competitiveness Institute

For Financial, Businesses and Manpower Conditions (Table 3.6), Sumatra Region holds fourth place with a score of –0.3940, just below Maluku–Papua Region (–0.3552) and above Sulawesi Region (–0.7693).

Sumatra Region's score in this environment is closer to Maluku–Papua Region's score with a difference of 0.0388. This shows that Sumatra Region can easily overtake Maluku–Papua Region, currently ranked at the third. Riau Islands and Riau are the only two provinces from Sumatra Region in the Top 10 of the provincial ranking, at sixth and seventh, respectively. Jambi is the last province in this environment, placing 28th.

Table 3.7. 2014 Quality of Life and Infrastructure Development: Ranking and Score

Rank	Region	Score
1	Java Region	1.0603
2	Kalimantan Region	0.7425
3	*Sumatra Region*	*0.4385*
4	Sulawesi Region	0.2448
5	Bali–Nusa Tenggara Region	–0.5423
6	Maluku–Papua Region	–1.9438

Source: Asia Competitiveness Institute

For the Quality of Life and Infrastructure Development, as shown in Table 3.7, Sumatra Region is at the third place, scoring 0.4385. Its score is in the positive range, reflecting above average performance. Nevertheless, Sumatra Region should not be complacent as Sulawesi Region trails closely at the fourth place.

Riau Islands and Aceh are at fifth and 10th place, respectively, while Bangka Belitung Islands, at 25th, is the only province in the Bottom 10 in provincial ranking.

2.2 Analysis of Median and Maximum Competitiveness Webs

To better understand Sumatra Region's relative strengths and weaknesses, it is useful to compare and contrast its attainment against the median and the maximum scores of Indonesia's six regions for the 12 sub-environments. The median competitiveness web plots Sumatra Region's attained scores for each of the 12 sub-environments.

In Figure 3.2, the median scores for six Indonesian regions are shown in the dashed line while the scores for Sumatra Region are in solid line.

Sumatra's Overall Competitiveness ranking is among the medium range of the six regions. Some of the sub-environments where Sumatra scores relatively higher than the median are Regional Economic Vibrancy; Openness to Trade and Services; Government Policies and Fiscal Sustainability; Productivity Performance; Physical Infrastructure; and Standard of Living, Education and Social Stability. Sumatra's strong performance in sub-environments under Macroeconomic Stability environment is consistent with its stellar achievement in securing second position in Table 3.4. For Labour Market Flexibility, its score is only slightly above the median, while the scores for the remaining sub-environments are lower than the median. For example, Financial Deepening and Business Efficiency is far below the national median at –1.1560. Other areas that can be improved are Competition, Regulatory Standards and Rule of Law; Technological Infrastructure; Institutions, Governance and Leadership; and Attractiveness to Foreign Investors.

The maximum competitiveness web in Figure 3.3 shows how far the best score for each sub-environment is, in relation to Sumatra Region's score. The maximum scores for the six regions are shown in the dashed line while the scores for Sumatra Region are shown in the solid line.

Sumatra attains the maximum score in Standard of Living, Education and Social Stability. Relatively narrow gaps exist for seven out of 12 sub-environments, namely, Technological Infrastructure; Physical Infrastructure; Productivity Performance; Institutions, Governance and Leadership; Government Policies and Fiscal Sustainability; Openness to Trade and Services; and Regional Economic Vibrancy.

Figure 3.2. 2014 Median Competitiveness Web Analysis for Sumatra Region

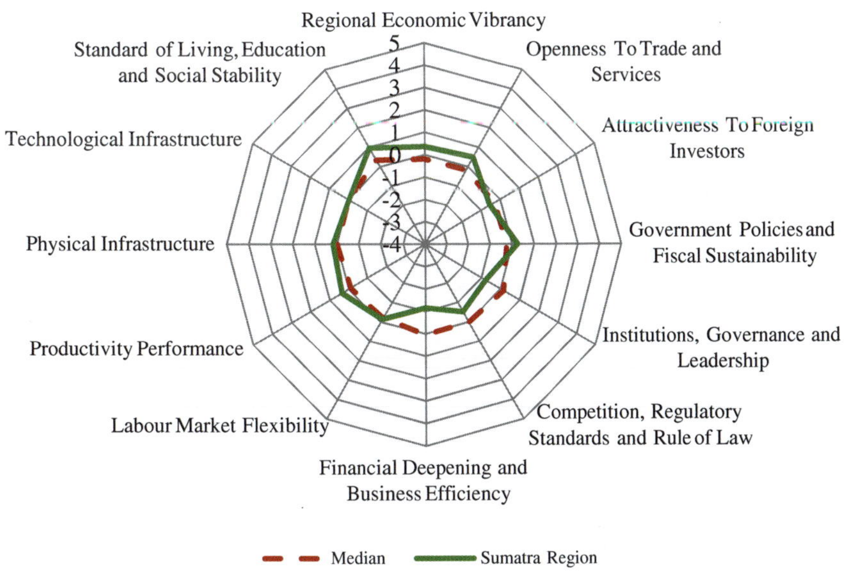

Source: Asia Competitiveness Institute

Figure 3.3. 2014 Maximum Competitiveness Web Analysis for Sumatra Region

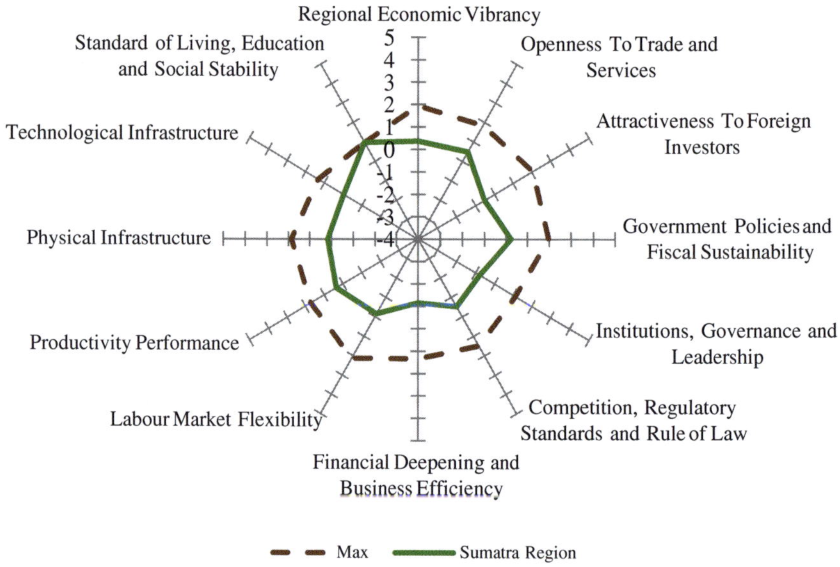

Source: Asia Competitiveness Institute

On the other hand, Sumatra has wider gaps with the maximum score in four sub-environments. These are Labour Market Flexibility; Financial Deepening and Business Efficiency; Competition, Regulatory Standards and Rule of Law; and Attractiveness to Foreign Investors.

2.3 Analysis of Strengths and Weaknesses

Tables 3.8 and 3.9 respectively show the strongest and weakest indicators for Sumatra Region. Table 3.8 shows the region's top 20%, or 21 strongest indicators out of a total of 104 indicators, in descending order. Table 3.9 shows the top 20% of weakest indicators in ascending order.[6]

As seen in Table 3.8, the top three strengths for Sumatra Region are Gini Ratio (#1); Mean Years of Schooling (#2); and Length of Paved Roads (#3) from the Quality of Life and Infrastructure Development. Indicators from this environment dominate the top 20%, with a total of 15 out of 21 indicators. Education sector becomes a strong point for Sumatra Region, as seen with the favourable ranks for enrolment rate in primary school (#15), junior high school (#11), and senior high school (#5). In regard to student-teacher ratio, Sumatra is leading for junior high school (#17) and senior high school (#20).

The next source of strength for Sumatra Region comes from Macroeconomic Stability environment with four indicators, namely, GRDP of Primary Industry (#4); Exports (#8); Exports for Non-Oil and Gas (#10); and Openness to Trade (#19).

[6]These 21 strongest and 21 weakest indicators are obtained by sorting all of the 104 indicators' scores that the region received, from the highest to the lowest. Those that appear at the top 21 are identified as the region's strengths, and those that appear at the bottom 21 are identified as the region's weaknesses. The comparison is done relatively among the indicator scores of said region, without comparing to the indicator scores of other regions.

Table 3.8. 2014 Top 20% Strongest Indicators List for Sumatra Region

Rank	20% Strongest Indicator	Score	Environment
1	Gini Ratio	1.8602	QLID
2	Mean Years of Schooling	1.6571	QLID
3	Length of Paved Roads	1.3557	QLID
4	GRDP of Primary Industry	1.3511	MS
5	School Enrollment Rate (Senior High)	1.3379	QLID
6	Human Development Index	1.1572	QLID
7	Adult Illiteracy Rate	1.1448	QLID
8	Exports	1.0105	MS
9	Handphone Ownership	0.8244	QLID
10	Exports, Non-oil & gas	0.8023	MS
11	School Enrollment Rate (Junior High)	0.7279	QLID
12	Life Expectancy at Birth	0.7273	QLID
13	Employment in Primary Industry	0.7133	FBMC
14	Environmental Quality Index	0.5781	QLID
15	School Enrollment Rate (Primary)	0.5536	QLID
16	Fiscal Balance	0.5309	GIS
17	Student-Teacher Ratio (Junior High)	0.5009	QLID
18	Cargo at Inter-island Seaport	0.4898	QLID
19	Openness To Trade	0.4748	MS
20	Student-Teacher Ratio (Senior High)	0.4530	QLID
21	Registered Motor Vehicles	0.4463	QLID

Note: MS = Macroeconomic Stability; GIS = Government and Institutional Setting; FBMC = Financial, Businesses and Manpower Conditions; QLID = Quality of Life and Infrastructure Development
Source: Asia Competitiveness Institute

Table 3.9 shows that Sumatra's 20% weakest indicators are mostly from the Government and Institutional Setting environment (eight out of 21 indicators). This shows that the governance in Sumatra Region needs major improvement. Those weak indicators include Government Inclusiveness and Accountability (#84); Provincial Governing Capacity (#86); and Government Efficiency (#87). Other indicators worth noting are the existence of the two indicators related to corruption, Lack of Corruption (#94) from ACI's perception survey and Corruption Perception Index (#96) from Transparency International.

Nevertheless, indicators from Quality of Life and Infrastructure Development; and Financial, Businesses and Manpower Conditions environments also feature prominently in the top 20% weakest indicators with both contributing to the same proportion (six out of 21 indicators). Despite Quality of Life and Infrastructure Development indicators dominating the strength of Sumatra Region, some of them are concurrently listed as its weaknesses, with Urban Population Growth (#104) as the weakest indicator. Other top 20% weakest indicators for Sumatra Region are Firms' Strategy (#103); Firms' Innovation (#102); and Labour Participation Rate (#101), which are part of Financial, Businesses and Manpower Conditions environment.

Table 3.9. 2014 Top 20% Weakest Indicators List for Sumatra Region

Rank	20% Weakest Indicator	Score	Environment
84	Government Inclusiveness and Accountability	–0.4825	GIS
85	Firms' Equipment Capacity	–0.4900	FBMC
86	Provincial Governing Capacity	–0.5388	GIS
87	Government Efficiency	–0.5472	GIS
88	Regulatory Governance	–0.5678	GIS
89	Internet Access at Office	–0.5680	QLID
90	Laptop Computer Ownership	–0.5829	QLID
91	Non-Performing Loans per Total Bank Loans	–0.6024	FBMC
92	Coordination of Local Governments	–0.6586	GIS
93	Firms' Human Resource Capacity	–0.7193	FBMC
94	Lack of Corruption	–0.7394	GIS
95	Population Per Medical Worker	–0.7482	QLID
96	Corruption Perception Index	–0.8102	GIS
97	Investment Promotion and Management	–0.8991	MS
98	Government Progress & Expectation	–0.9111	GIS
99	Households with pipe water services	–0.9449	QLID
100	Population Per Health Facility	–1.0734	QLID
101	Labour Force Participation Rate	–1.0849	FBMC
102	Firms' Innovation	–1.1486	FBMC
103	Firms' Strategy	–1.3514	FBMC
104	Urban Population Growth	–1.3916	QLID

Note: MS = Macroeconomic Stability; GIS = Government and Institutional Setting; FBMC = Financial, Businesses and Manpower Conditions; QLID = Quality of Life and Infrastructure Development
Source: Asia Competitiveness Institute

3. POLICY THEMES AND DEVELOPMENT STRATEGIES

3.1 Official Policies[7]

Under the MP3EI, Sumatra Region is designated as the centre for production and processing of natural resources and as the nation's energy reserve. The main economic activities in the MP3EI stretch from extraction of raw materials to processing of key commodities such as palm oil, rubber, coal, and development of shipping and steel industries.

Looking at each key commodity, there is a limitation to further expand palm oil plantation due to environmental issues that include slash and burn practice, leading to haze seen in Singapore and Malaysia. Several provinces have indicated the need for conserving mature plantations in their Provincial Medium-Term Development Plan (RPJMD). Therefore, as identified in the MP3EI, the focus shifts to the intensification programme to improve productivity, for instance, by improving seed quality, and developing better milling, refinery, and downstream industries in palm oil, as well as rubber sector.

[7]At national level, Indonesia's development plan is documented in the 2005–2025 National Long-Term Development Plan (RPJPN 2005–2025). It was in the second phase of implementation under the 2010–2014 National Medium-Term Development Plan (RPJMN 2010–2014). Provincial governments must take into account the RPJMN 2010–2014 when formulating or adjusting their respective Provincial Medium-Term Development Plan (RPJMD) to reach national development targets. The MP3EI is not intended to replace RPJMN or the ongoing national and provincial development plans. It is a complementary working document for the above-mentioned development plans, aimed at accelerating and expanding economic development in Indonesia.

Strategies to enhance coal production also emphasise the importance of standardisation of law and regulation. Moreover, some provinces have also noted improvement in distribution networks for transporting coal, quality of human resources, and corporate governance for investment in coal mining as part of their strategies.

Geographically, Sumatra Region is anticipated to be an alternative international hub on the western part of Indonesia, with Kuala Tanjung Port in North Sumatra. For road connectivity, Trans-Sumatra Highway, with a length of 2,732 km, is expected to connect the island from Banda Aceh in the north to Bandar Lampung in the south and will be part of Asian Highway Network Route.

Each province has its own RPJMD that fits its unique characteristics.[8] Aceh's vision in the RPJMD 2012–2017 revolves around its aspiration to create a prosperous, just, and independent province based on Law on the Governing of Aceh as a commitment to the Helsinki Agreement that ended previous conflict. Aceh's government also prioritises several strategies to revitalise local agriculture and agro-industry.

For North Sumatra, its policy is directed at development of potential sectors such as agriculture, forestry, processing industry, and tourism. Infrastructure development is also one of the key policies, as seen in its efforts to complete Kuala Namu International Airport construction, develop seaports, and ensure adequate clean water and electricity supply to support growth. The regional development plan underscores improvement in vocational track and training to increase productivity level. Similarly, Riau affirms the importance of growing human resources capability to integrate upstream and downstream industries for both agricultural and mining activities.

West Sumatra has an enormous potential to be the nation's energy reserves due to its vast hydro and geothermal reserves for power generation. In its medium-term plan (RPJMD 2010–2015), West Sumatra reiterates the need to create high quality human resources and develop the processing industry, trade, small and medium-sized enterprises (SMEs) and cooperatives.

Jambi places infrastructure development as its first mission in its RPJMD 2010–2015. It encompasses improvement in energy, electricity, clean water, irrigation network, education, and health infrastructure. All economic activities related to natural resources should be conducted based on spatial plan. Strong focus on infrastructure is also echoed in Bangka Belitung's RPJMD 2012–2017. This includes the development of supporting infrastructures that are crucial for attracting investment, such as airports, seaports, industrial sites, electricity, and communication. Riau Islands, as an archipelagic province, puts more emphasis on strategies to leverage its maritime potential. Batam, Bintan, and Karimun SEZ, which hosts information technology, consumer electronics, engineering, and ship building multinational companies (MNCs), are still the drivers for investment in the province.

In its RPJMD 2011–2015, Bengkulu highlights its vision to be an advanced and prosperous province, as indicated by the improvement in the HDI and GRDP per capita and the decline in poverty and unemployment level. On the other hand, South Sumatra's vision is to create a prosperous and advanced province with an educated and cultured society. It also emphasises a comprehensive, coordinated, effective, and efficient formulation of strategies and policies. In terms of economic activities, South Sumatra is endowed with fertile paddy fields and natural resources that render the province suitable for being both energy and food supplier. For Lampung, infrastructure development is one of its key missions in the RPJMD 2010–2014. It lists development of Sunda Strait Bridge as one of its major programmes, highlighting further the alignment between the MP3EI and the provincial government. Nevertheless, further adjustment is inevitable as President Joko Widodo decided to stop this megaproject.

Sumatra's vulnerable location to natural disasters makes disaster mitigation, preparedness, and resiliency efforts as part of the provinces' RPJMD. The region also indicates environmental preservation as its priority to ensure sustainable development. In terms of common goals, the aspiration to move up the value chain is a common thread underlined in the RPJMD of each province. To attain that, the provinces in Sumatra Region have placed greater importance in improving quality of human capital to ensure sufficient skilled workforce for processing industry.

---

[8] Provincial Development and Planning Agency, *Medium-Term Development Plan (RPJMD) of various provinces across various time spans.*

3.2 Development Strategies

The development strategies for Sumatra revolve around leveraging its strengths and improving its weaknesses as indicated in the ACI's analysis, and applying those to accelerate the attainment of optimal growth in identified sectors as envisioned in the MP3EI.

Based on the top 20% strongest indicators for Sumatra Region, education-related indicators dominate the list. With relatively high mean years of schooling, low illiteracy rate, excellent enrolment rates, and favourable student-teacher ratio, the region seems to be on a right track in ensuring adequate pool of skilled workforce. Nevertheless, this does not mean the region can be lulled into complacency. In fact, Sumatra has to leverage on this strong foundation to boost its vocational sector as the region aspires to grow and feed into its processing industries. For palm oil, as the focus is shifted from plantation to refinery and downstream activities — including distillation, production of oleo-chemical and biofuel — that are more capital-intensive, technology-savvy workforce is required. Similar demand for technical workers is also applicable for growing the steel and shipping construction industries. This integration of upstream and downstream activities will generate the chain of production and value adding that eventually increases the dollar revenue from export.

To solve the perennial issue of low productivity in palm oil and rubber, instituting regular training schemes for farmers, as simple as training them to set optimal spacing, is instrumental as sizeable area of land are owned by smallholders. Additionally, research into superior quality seedlings for both palm oil and rubber should also be intensified as a means to boost productivity in plantation sector in the long run.

Because Sumatra's emphasis is centred on extraction and processing industries, environmental sustainability should not be neglected. By witnessing the concurrent health hazard and economic loss from the infamous slash and burn practices and the resulting haze issue, both the regional and central governments should work together with the private sector to strengthen the regulation and enforcement processes to stop this practice. Regulation has to be put in place to enforce the effective implementation of law, particularly relating to the use of forest reserves for economic activities by both big corporations and smallholders. Public education for all stakeholders is needed as this perennial issue requires a change in the mindset to prioritise long–term sustainability instead of harmful short–term gain.

Private sector-led initiatives can also be supported beyond Corporate Social Responsibility (CSR) programmes. International programmes, such as United Nations Initiative for Reducing Emissions from Deforestation and Forest Degradation (UN-REDD), are crucial to address global warming by reducing deforestation and emissions through reforestation and afforestation projects.

Connectivity is indeed another key to Sumatra's development strategies. On top of its extensive length of paved roads, other infrastructure projects should further enhance inter-provincial and inter-island connectivity. Even road improvements to expedite the distribution of agricultural products are very much needed. This is crucial especially for palm oil as the quality of fresh fruit bunch declines within 48 hours after picking. Railway track is vital for coal transportation from the inland to the port as it is more efficient than road transport. Sumatra's strategic location along the Malacca Strait underlines the importance of seaports as the main mode of transportation for delivering the key products. Several expansion projects for seaports have been identified in the MP3EI for the following ports — Dumai Port and Pekanbaru Port (Riau), Panjang Port (Lampung), Belawan Port and Kuala Tanjung Port (North Sumatra), and Tanjung Api-Api Port (South Sumatra). With better infrastructure, the opportunity is wide open for the region to benefit from the implementation of the ASEAN Economic Community (AEC) in 2015.[9]

Among the 10 provinces in Sumatra Region, Aceh is the only province in the Top 10 provincial ranking for Government and Institutional Setting environment. The region is at fourth place with a negative score, which

[9]The AEC is envisaged to transform the ASEAN in 2015 into a region with free movement of goods, services, investment, and skilled labour. It is expected that this regional economic integration will further enhance trade and Foreign Direct Investment (FDI) in the region. See, for example, Sanchita Basu Das *et al.*, ed., *The ASEAN Economic Community: A Work In Progress* (Singapore: Institute of Southeast Asian Studies and Asian Development Bank, 2013) and Gary Rynhart and Jae-Hee Chang, *The Road to ASEAN Economic Community 2015: The challenges and opportunities for enterprises and their representative organisations* (Geneva: International Labour Office, 2014) for greater details.

means that its performance remains below national average. Eight of the 21 weakest indicators (Table 3.9) are from this environment. These include Government Inclusiveness and Accountability; Provincial Governing Capacity; Government Efficiency; Regulatory Governance; Coordination of Local Governments; Lack of Corruption; Government Progress and Expectation and Corruption Perception Index. This is alarming and calls for improvement in the public sector.

Good governance is crucial in order to attract investments to Sumatra. On top of increasing commitment to good governance, coordination among agencies and local governments, harmonisation of laws, transparency, and clarity of regulation are also important in creating conducive business environment. All layers of governments — provincial, city, and district levels — should work together to streamline the regulations pertinent to attracting businesses.

Related to cost, time, and administrative requirements to deal with permits, the government can build on information and communications technology (ICT) that not only improves the efficiency, transparency, and accountability, but also as a tool to prevent corruption. This is even more relevant in the context of Indonesia as an archipelagic nation.

Successful implementation of e-government hinges upon government's sincere commitment in tackling the issues at hand and enhancing its capability to build the system and prepare the human resources to run the programme, as well as to maintain this initiative as a continuous process. Additionally, activities to promote, train, and increase the awareness of citizens to adopt the e-government initiatives should be put in place. Peer learning from other provinces, districts, or cities that have been noted with advanced e-government platform can be a first step when mapping out the strategic and implementation plan. In line with the move towards e-governance, One Stop Integrated Service initiative or in local term, *Pelayanan Terpadu Satu Pintu,* should be further enhanced and evaluated in terms of its effectiveness. This is essential for attracting investors to Sumatra. With the MP3EI in tandem, prioritisation of key sectors and infrastructure development coupled with improved governance further pave the way for Sumatra to reach its utmost potentials and fulfil its expectation as the centre of production and processing of natural resources as well as the nation's energy reserves.

REFERENCES

Coordinating Ministry for Economic Affairs. *Master Plan for Acceleration and Expansion of Indonesia's Economic Development 2011–2025 (MP3EI).* Jakarta: Coordinating Ministry for Economic Affairs, 2011.

Das, Sanchita Basu, Jayant Menon, Rodolfo C. Severino, and Omkar Lal Shrestha, ed. *The ASEAN Economic Community: A Work In Progress*. Singapore: Institute of Southeast Asian Studies and Asian Development Bank, 2013.

Ooi, Giok-Ling. "The Indonesia–Malaysia–Singapore Growth Triangle: Sub-Regional Economic Cooperation and Integration." *GeoJournal* Vol. 36, No. 4 (August 1995): 337–344.

Provincial Development and Planning Agency. *Medium-Term Development Plan (RPJMD) of various provinces across various time spans.*

Rynhart, Gary, and Jae-Hee Chang. *The Road to ASEAN Economic Community 2015: The challenges and opportunities for enterprises and their representative organisations.* Geneva: International Labour Office, 2014.

Tan, Khee Giap, and Mulya Amri. "Subnational Competitiveness and National Performance: Analysis and Simulation for Indonesia." *Journal of Centrum Cathedra (JCC): The Business and Economics Research Journal* Vol. 6, No. 2 (2013):173–192.

Tan, Khee Giap, Mulya Amri, Linda Low, and Tan Kong Yam. *Competitiveness Analysis and Development Strategies for 33 Indonesian Provinces*. Singapore: World Scientific, 2013.

United Nations Conference on Trade and Development (UNCTAD). "Infocomm Commodity Profile Palm Oil." Retrieved on July 25, 2014. <http://www.unctad.info/en/Infocomm/AACP-Products/Palm-oil/>.

Chapter 4
Competitiveness Analysis on the Java Region

Banten, DKI Jakarta, West Java, Central Java, DI Yogyakarta, and East Java

1. INTRODUCTION

1.1 Background and Notes

Figure 4.1 shows the provinces in Java Region as defined by the Master Plan for Acceleration and Expansion of Indonesia's Economic Development 2011–2025 (MP3EI).[1] The six provinces and their respective capital cities are Banten (Serang), DKI Jakarta (Jakarta), West Java (Bandung), Central Java (Semarang), DI Yogyakarta (Yogyakarta), and East Java (Surabaya). Java Island is surrounded by Java Sea in the north, Sunda Strait in the west, Indian Ocean in the south, and Bali Strait in the east.

In Figure 4.1, inset map (top right) shows the competitiveness ranking of Java Region by the Asia Competitiveness Institute (ACI) using the traffic light scheme with green representing the Top 10 provinces, followed by 13 middle-ranking provinces in yellow, and the remaining provinces with lower competitiveness in red. Almost all provinces in Java Region are part of the Top 10, except for Banten at the 12th position. DKI Jakarta leads the pack, followed by East Java as the runner-up.[2]

Java Island is the nucleus of economic vibrancy in Indonesia. The region has dominated Indonesia's Gross Domestic Product (GDP) for the past decades. Despite central government's efforts to share Java's success, the region still contributed to 58.9% of country's GDP in 2012.

Located at the southern end of the archipelago, Java Island carries strong legacy as a centre of development since the Majapahit Kingdom during the 13th to 16th centuries. Java has over 138 million inhabitants, a home to nearly 60% of the total population in Indonesia.

The region holds two biggest metropolitan areas. The Greater Jakarta Area or *Jabodetabek* consists of Jakarta, Bogor, Depok, Tangerang, and Bekasi. The other one is *Gerbangkertosusila* that includes Gresik, Bangkalan, Mojokerto, Surabaya, Sidoarjo, and Lamongan. Yogyakarta is particularly well known as the cultural capital of Indonesia.

As the biggest economic contributor, Java Island is the most advanced region in terms of economic activities. It has several leading manufacturing industries such as footwear, textile, automotive, food and beverage for domestic consumption and exports. According to the Indonesia's Investment Coordinating Board (BKPM), Java accounts for more than half of the country's domestic and foreign investments as it is viewed to have the most conducive investment climate by investors. Starting and doing business in Java are relatively straightforward, as it boasts relatively advanced infrastructure, affordable and relatively skilled labour force, and accessibility to imported materials via Tanjung Priok Port.

However, being the centre of the economy also has other repercussions. As the 'land of hope' for people around the country, in-migration from the other islands is very high, and thus Java Island today is overpopulated.[3] During the Soeharto regime, a cross-country transmigration scheme was implemented with the intention to ease

[1] Coordinating Ministry for Economic Affairs, *Master Plan for Acceleration and Expansion of Indonesia's Economic Development 2011–2025 (MP3EI)* (Jakarta: Coordinating Ministry for Economic Affairs, 2011).

[2] See Tan Khee Giap *et al.*, *Competitiveness Analysis and Development Strategies for 33 Indonesian provinces* (Singapore: World Scientific, 2013) and Tan Khee Giap and Mulya Amri, "Subnational Competitiveness and National Performance: Analysis and Simulation for Indonesia," *Journal of Centrum Cathedra (JCC): The Business and Economics Research Journal* Vol. 6, No. 2 (2013): 173–192 that mark the first attempt to rank provinces based on their competitiveness level.

[3] Especially for DKI Jakarta with consistent in-migration of people, estimated at 250,000 annually based on World Bank, "Annex 5: Jakarta Case Study," in *Climate Change, Disaster Risk and the Urban Poor*, ed. Judy L. Baker (Washington DC: World Bank, 2012), 199–215.

Figure 4.1. Map of Java Region

Source: Asia Competitiveness Institute

the overpopulation issue. However, the programme received a lot of criticism over its implementation and even triggered land issues and ethnic conflicts.

As Java becomes more industrialised, much of the agricultural land is converted into commercial land to build factories as well as residences. The industrialisation and urbanisation resulted in the lost of approximately 42,000 ha irrigated land in Java during 1991 to 2000.[4] The phenomenon has led to lower rice production in the region. Industrialisation has also affected the quality of water and air. The infamous polluted river Citarum in West Java is a proof of poor industrialisation management that discounts environmental sustainability.

Due to Java's obvious economic characteristic as a powerhouse, the MP3EI designates the Java Economic Corridor as "The Driver for National Industry and Service Provision". The economic activities are concentrated in manufacturing value-added products such as textile, food and beverage, transportation, and defence equipment. However, Java has several issues that may hamper its vision for economic development. Inadequate infrastructure and disparity among and within provinces are prevalent. Another risk arises from conflict with labour unions in important industries in Java.

To improve both economic development and competitiveness in Java, better infrastructure is paramount to create conducive business environment. Ensuring that environmental preservation goes hand in hand with industrialisation is also crucial. This can be achieved by comprehensive urban and city planning that includes rigorous environmental impact assessment.

Table 4.1 shows how Java Region's urbanisation rate had increased from 50.73% in 2006 to 58.60% in 2011. The shift towards city-based economy is also reflected in its relatively high shares of tertiary and secondary sectors in Gross Regional Domestic Product (GRDP), at 52.06% and 36.48%, respectively.

1.2 Major Sectors and Activities

Both Table 4.1 and Table 4.2 show that agricultural sector still plays a role, albeit small, in Java's economy. The primary sector, such as agriculture, livestock, forestry, and fishery, is mostly dominated by East Java, Central Java, and West Java, accounting for 11.46% of the GRDP. Despite the diminishing contribution of primary sector to GRDP, Java remains the biggest rice producer in the country, producing over 52.39% of national rice

[4] Sudar D. Atmanto, "Persaingan dan Pemanfaatan Sumber Daya Air dan Lahan," *Irigasi Pertanian* Vol. VII, No. 22 (1995).

Table 4.1. Java Region: Basic Economic Indicators

A. Population	**2006**	**2011**
Total population	130,184,204	138,083,615
% urban	50.73	58.60
B. Area		**2011**
Km^2		129, 438.28
% equivalent to country		6.77
C. Gross Regional Domestic Product (GRDP)	**2006**	**2011**
Rupiah (million)	1,071,135,538	1,446,836,500
Rupiah (million) without oil & gas	1,050,791,811	1,424,203,900
Rupiah (million) without oil & gas & mineral	1,050,185,787	1,423,062,387
D. Economic composition, as % GRDP	**2006**	**2011**
Primary sector	12.09	11.46
Secondary sector	38.56	36.48
Tertiary sector	49.36	52.06
E. GRDP per capita	**2006**	**2011**
Rupiah (million)	8.23	10.48
Rupiah (million) without oil & gas	8.07	10.31
Rupiah (million) without oil & gas & mineral	8.07	10.31
F. Poverty Rate	**2006**	**2011**
% of population	17.35	12.10
G. Human Development Index	**2006**	**2011**
Index	70.41	72.95

GRDP based on 2000 Constant Price
Source: Asia Competitiveness Institute using data from Indonesia Statistical Yearbook

Table 4.2. Major Products and Activities

Primary	Rice, corn, peanut, soybean, coconut, cocoa, coffee, tea, fishery, copper, oil, and gas
Secondary	Food and beverages, textile, transport equipment, steel, petrochemicals, cement, leather works, woodcraft, and ceramic
Tertiary	Information and communications technology (ICT), tourism, financial services, media, and trade

Source: Asia Competitiveness Institute

output in 2012. Java accounts for 42.35% of the total wetland areas in the country and most of the paddy fields are located in West Java, Central Java, and East Java. Thus, it is important for Java to not only focus on industrialisation, but also increase its agriculture productivity.

The secondary sector contributed to 36.48% of the GRDP in 2011. It is dominated by manufacturing industries that are located in West Java, Central Java, and East Java. Garments, textiles, industrial components, and handicraft accounted for 41.97% of its GRDP in 2011. Those industries were located in clusters near DKI Jakarta such as Bekasi and Cikarang. Banten's industries produce a wide range of commodities from metals, petrochemicals to footwear, food, and clothing. There are at least 19 industrial zones in this province, most of which are located in Tangerang city.[5]

[5] Such nationwide industrial clusters across provinces are relevant for Indonesia's overall competitiveness. Immense effects of agglomeration and concentration for economies of scale and scope enable provinces to complement and supplement each other, while they compete cohesively to challenge each other in the ACI's unique methodology of competitiveness ranking.

Two other provinces that dominate manufacturing sector are Central Java and East Java. Garment and cigarette industries are mostly found in Central Java while East Java has more diverse industries such as textile, machinery, transportation, food and beverage, and cigarette. The headquarters of ship-builder PT PAL and train-maker PT INKA are also located in this province.

Java receives significant contributions from trade, hotel, restaurant, finance, real estate, and business services as Indonesia's major cities are located in this region. Greater Jakarta Area, which consists of districts/cities in DKI Jakarta, Banten, and West Java, is a centre for the nation's trade and financial activities. Tourism is also thriving in Java, which is home to 10 national tourism destinations. With relatively more educated population, Java has a potential to be the backbone of creative and service industries.

1.3 Infrastructure Provision

Ironically, Java is still riddled by poor infrastructure. Problems do not only exist in the capital city, DKI Jakarta, with its perennial traffic jam, but also in the connectivity among provinces in the region. The airports and seaports are deemed not able to keep up with the rising economic growth. As a result, overcapacity and overcrowded infrastructure lead to a higher production cost. Similar problems also appear in the case of electricity where the power supply fails to meet the demand growth.

Logistics and human transportations are currently relying heavily on roads and railway tracks. Java's northern coast highway, or known as *Pantura*, is the main access to transport both human and freight throughout Java. However, lack of supervision that gives way to overloaded vehicles affect the quality of the road. Each year, the government allocates approximately 1.8 trillion Rupiah to repair the damaged roads. Some 36 trillion Rupiah worth of roadwork is dedicated to build the Trans-Java toll road — a project of 615 km-long road connecting DKI Jakarta to Surabaya — in a bid to reduce traffic congestion. It is due to be completed in 2017, postponed from its previous target of 2015 due to land acquisition issues.

Railway is another alternative transportation within Java. Currently, train remains under the management of state-owned enterprise (SOE), PT KAI, that provides train services within DKI Jakarta (known as Commuter Line) as well as across provinces. The vein of railway track that connects Tanjung Priok International Seaport to Surabaya is, however, dominated by passenger trains. Freight transportation is only limited to transporting gasoline, cement, and fertiliser. To increase the efficiency of freight transportation, the government is building 727 km double–track railway that connects Jakarta to Surabaya. With the project, the government targets to increase the loads from the current 160 TEUs (twenty foot equivalent units) with five trips per day to 500 TEUs with 15 trips per day.[6]

Two main national airports are located in this region, namely Soekarno-Hatta International Airport (Banten) and Juanda International Airport (Surabaya). Other airports that serve international flights are Adisucipto (Yogyakarta), Husein Sastranegara (Bandung), Adisumarmo (Solo), Achmad Yani (Semarang), and Halim Perdanakusuma (Jakarta).

Soekarno–Hatta International Airport, however, can only accommodate 22 million passengers per year, while the actual numbers of domestic and international passengers are already surpassing 50 million. Thus, PT Angkasa Pura II — another SOE that manages the airport — decided to convert another airport in DKI Jakarta, Halim Perdanakusuma, from military and private aircraft usage to commercial airport in early 2014. In the future, the government also plans to expand Soekarno-Hatta International Airport, albeit difficulties regarding land acquisition in Tangerang district that has hampered the proposal. The expansion of new Terminal 3 was

---

[6] Erlangga Djumena, "Rel Ganda Selesai Jakarta-Surabaya Lebih Cepat 3 Jam", *Kompas,* March 27, 2014, retrieved on June 24, 2014, <http://bisniskeuangan.kompas.com/read/2014/03/27/0924327/Rel.Ganda.Selesai.Jakarta-Surabaya.Lebih.Cepat.3.Jam>.

targeted to finish by 2014. Changi International Airport in Singapore and Incheon International Airport in South Korea are used as models to expand the airport.

For seaport infrastructure, Java Region has two busiest seaports in Indonesia, Tanjung Priok and Tanjung Perak. The seaports serve international cargo mainly for export and import activities. According to Pelindo II, Tanjung Priok Port serves two-third of Indonesia's international trade. However, high logistic costs and longer waiting time for containers continue to become a burden. The length of waiting time has deteriorated, from 4.8 days in 2010 to 6.4 days in 2013. This results in significantly higher logistic costs for the industry and eventually higher final price for the consumer.[7]

For infrastructure in the provinces, DKI Jakarta is ill-reputed for its traffic congestion. According to Jakarta Local Government data in 2010, private vehicle ownership grew at 9.5% and was expected to rise.[8] The length of paved roads, however, has only increased by 1.3%, and hence, traffic congestion is unavoidable. The congestion costs the economy approximately $3 billion per year.[9] TransJakarta and Commuter Line are two main mass public transportations in Jakarta while Mass Rapid Transit (MRT) construction is still ongoing. Similar MRT plan will also be developed in Bandung, Surabaya, and Semarang under President Joko Widodo's leadership.

Although electrification rate in Java remains the highest when compared to other regions, balancing the power demand is a huge challenge. According to PT PLN, the state-owned electricity company, electrification ratio in Java is 78%, above the national rate of 73%.[10] The capacity delivered with the installed power plant units in the region is as much as 25,787.45 MW (78.38% of the nation's total capacity). To meet the growing demand in power supply, the construction of a 2,000 MW coal-fired power plant project in Batang, Central Java was proposed. The project, however, has been put on hold due to land acquisition negotiations. If the project continues to be delayed, Java could face up to 30% power deficit by 2017. The current supply may not be adequate for any instances of emergencies. Should one of the power plants experiences trouble, no back-up is present to mitigate blackouts in the capital city. One notable widespread blackout in Java and Bali occurred in 2005 due to power disruption.

Another challenge in Java is the water management stemming from bad environmental practices and poor industrial waste management in some cities. The most obvious case is in the capital city DKI Jakarta, where floods — both from seasonal rainfall and rising sea level — have become a chronic problem in the history of the city. Although DKI Jakarta has west and east flood canals, the yearly flooding still persists. Rising sea level also often triggers floods in northern DKI Jakarta. Flood has also become an important issue in Semarang and Surabaya.

2. RELATIVE COMPETITIVENESS OF REGIONS

The competitiveness framework for the region follows the same approach with the provincial competitiveness, as explained in Chapter 1 in greater detail. Further explanation on the aggregation of individual province's indicators into regional scores can be found in Chapter 2.

---

[7] World Bank, "Moving Cargo Faster in Indonesia Main Sea Port," February 19, 2014, retrieved on June 24, 2014, <http://www.worldbank.org/in/news/feature/2014/02/19/moving-cargo-faster-in-indonesia-main-sea-port>.

[8] Jakarta Local Government, "Jakarta Urban Transport Problems and Their Environmental Impacts", retrieved on June 24, 2014, <http://www.ui.ac.id/download/apru-awi/jakarta-local-goverment.pdf>.

[9] "Traffic Jams Cost Jakarta 3b Annually", *The Jakarta Post,* February 10, 2011, retrieved on June 24, 2014, <http://www.thejakartapost.com/news/2011/02/10/traffic-jams-cost-jakarta-3b-annually.html>.

[10] PT PLN, *Statistik PLN 2012* (Jakarta: PLN, 2012).

2.1 Competitiveness Ranking of Six Regions — Rank and Score by Environment[11]

Table 4.3. 2014 Overall Competitiveness: Ranking and Score

Rank	Region	Score
1	*Java Region*	*1.7233*
2	Kalimantan Region	0.6511
3	Sulawesi Region	–0.0392
4	Sumatra Region	–0.0741
5	Bali–Nusa Tenggara Region	–0.9839
6	Maluku–Papua Region	–1.2772

Source: Asia Competitiveness Institute

For Overall Competitiveness, as shown in Table 4.3, Java is ranked first and noted as the most competitive region in Indonesia.

With a standardised score of 1.7233, Java is far above other regions. A huge gap exists between Java and Kalimantan in the second position (0.6511). This is not surprising as five out of the six provinces in Java Region are among the Top 10 of Overall Competitiveness for the 33 provinces. Its standardised scores in most indicators are also exceptionally high. DKI Jakarta attains the highest rank, while Banten is ranked 12th.

Table 4.4. 2014 Macroeconomic Stability: Ranking and Score

Rank	Region	Score
1	*Java Region*	*2.0461*
2	Sumatra Region	0.1112
3	Kalimantan Region	0.0350
4	Sulawesi Region	–0.3896
5	Maluku–Papua Region	–0.7943
6	Bali–Nusa Tenggara Region	–1.0085

Source: Asia Competitiveness Institute

For Macroeconomic Stability (Table 4.4), Java is still ranked first. Its standardised score of 2.0461 is far above Sumatra Region (0.1112). Although Java's strength in macroeconomic condition is not surprising, the gaps with the other regions can be narrowed for the country to achieve a balanced Macroeconomic Stability across the board.

As the centre of business and administration, Java Region has considerably high economic vibrancy and attractiveness to foreign investors. Looking at the individual performance of each province, DKI Jakarta, East Java, and West Java are in the top three while Banten and Central Java are part of the Top 10.

Table 4.5. 2014 Government and Institutional Setting: Ranking and Score

Rank	Region	Score
1	*Java Region*	*1.4124*
2	Sulawesi Region	0.7733
3	Kalimantan Region	0.5582
4	Sumatra Region	–0.4219
5	Bali–Nusa Tenggara Region	–0.8284
6	Maluku–Papua Region	–1.4937

Source: Asia Competitiveness Institute

As seen in Table 4.5, Java Region is consistently ranked first for Government and Institutional Setting. With a standardised score of 1.4124, Java shows substantially higher performance than other regions in Indonesia. Its score is almost twice of Sulawesi Region's at the second place (0.7733). Five out of the six provinces in Java Region are part of the Top 10 for this environment.

Strong leaderships from authoritative figures, such as Basuki Tjahaja Purnama in DKI Jakarta, Ridwan Kamil in Bandung (West Java), Tri Rismarini in Surabaya (East Java), and Ganjar Pranowo in Central Java, have resulted in impressive improvements in many areas. On the other hand, a series of high-profile corruption cases found in Banten has pulled down its rank to 23rd.

[11] Results for the 2014 competitiveness study are based on official data in 2011 and survey data collected in 2013. Conventionally due to collation, compilation, and publication of official data, such a lag of data before reaching end-users is acceptable.

Table 4.6. 2014 Financial, Businesses and Manpower Conditions: Ranking and Score

Rank	Region	Score
1	*Java Region*	*1.6700*
2	Kalimantan Region	1.0027
3	Maluku–Papua Region	–0.3552
4	Sumatra Region	–0.3940
5	Sulawesi Region	–0.7693
6	Bali–Nusa Tenggara Region	–1.1543

Source: Asia Competitiveness Institute

For Financial, Businesses and Manpower Conditions (Table 4.6), Java Region is at the top. With a standardised score of 1.6700, the gap between Java and Kalimantan is not exceptionally high as often found in other environments.

As the centre of the nation's financial services, it is natural for Java to lead the pack in this context. It requires exhaustive efforts for other regions seeking to overtake Java's position. DKI Jakarta, Central Java, East Java, and West Java are among the top five nationally while Banten performs poorly with the position at 22nd.

Table 4.7. 2014 Quality of Life and Infrastructure Development: Ranking and Score

Rank	Region	Score
1	*Java Region*	*1.0603*
2	Kalimantan Region	0.7425
3	Sumatra Region	0.4385
4	Sulawesi Region	0.2448
5	Bali–Nusa Tenggara Region	–0.5423
6	Maluku–Papua Region	–1.9438

Source: Asia Competitiveness Institute

As shown in Table 4.7, Java Region remains at the first place for Quality of Life and Infrastructure Development. For this environment, the spread of standardised score is relatively more even with narrower gap between Java and subsequent regions. Kalimantan closely trails Java with 0.7425, followed by Sumatra (0.4385), and Sulawesi (0.2448).

In terms of physical infrastructure, Java Region has benefitted from the legacy of having been the centre of colonial administration and the seat of power and development in New Order Era led by then President Soeharto.

2.2 Analysis of Median and Maximum Competitiveness Webs

To better understand Java's relative strengths and weaknesses, it is useful to compare and contrast its attainment against the median and the maximum scores of Indonesia's six regions for the 12 sub-environments. The median competitiveness web plots Java's attained scores for each of the 12 sub-environments.

In Figure 4.2, the median scores for six Indonesian regions are shown in the dashed line, while the scores for Java Region are shown in the solid line.

Java Region performs exceptionally well, far above the median value, in Physical Infrastructure; Labour Market Flexibility; Government Policies and Fiscal Sustainability; Attractiveness to Foreign Investors; Openness to Trade and Services; and Regional Economic Vibrancy.

Despite its stellar performance in Overall Competitiveness, Java Region scores rather poorly, below the median, in terms of Standard of Living, Education and Social Stability sub-environment. At indicator level, its score is particularly low in Environmental Quality Index due to higher emissions that contribute to pollution and susceptibility to natural disasters. This implies that policymakers have to prioritise their economic agenda towards force majeure improvement when enhancing the standard of living for their citizens.

The maximum competitiveness web (Figure 4.3) shows how far the best score for each sub-environment is, in relation to Java Region's score. The maximum scores for the six regions are shown in the dashed line, while the scores for Java are shown in the solid line.

Java sets the bar for the maximum score in most of the sub-environments. It has the highest score in Regional Economic Vibrancy; Openness to Trade and Services; Attractiveness to Foreign Investors; Government Policies and Fiscal Sustainability; Financial Deepening and Business Efficiency; Labour Market Flexibility; Physical

Figure 4.2. 2014 Median Competitiveness Web Analysis for Java Region

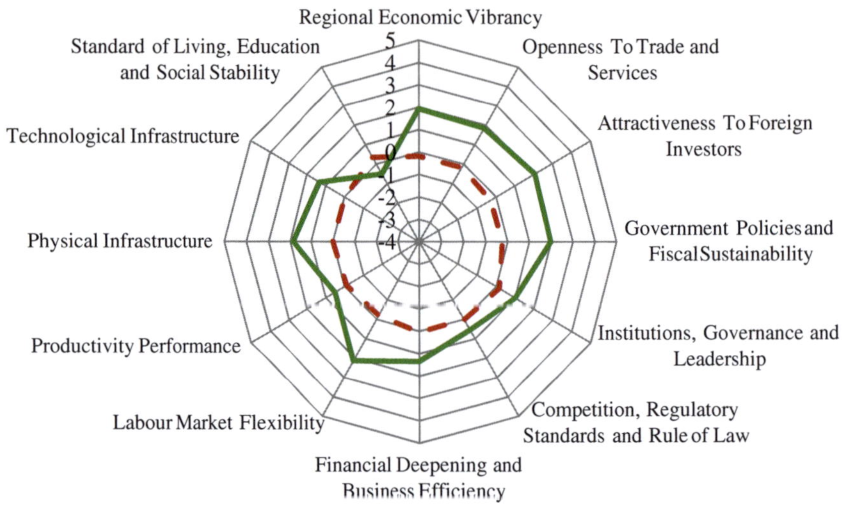

Source: Asia Competitiveness Institute

Figure 4.3. 2014 Maximum Competitiveness Web Analysis for Java Region

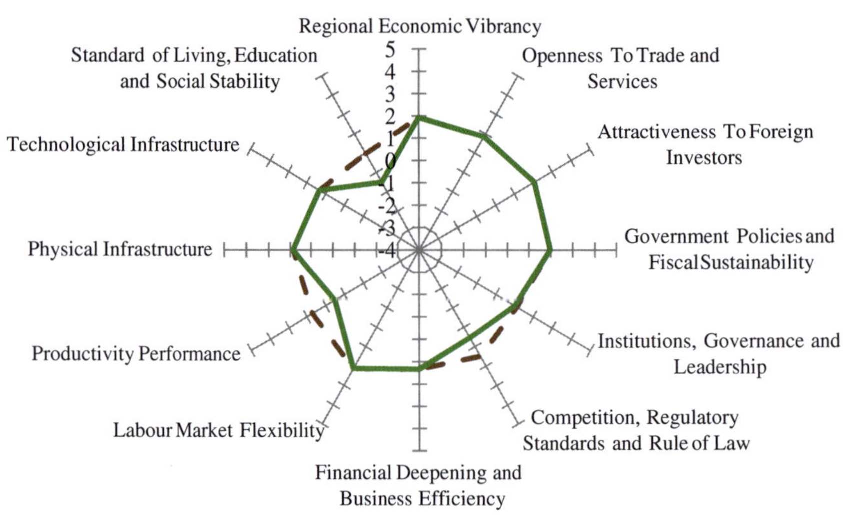

Source: Asia Competitiveness Institute

Infrastructure; and Technological Infrastructure. Its score in Institutions, Governance and Leadership is only slightly below the maximum value.

In sharp contrast, Java Region scores lower than the maximum for Competition, Regulatory Standards and Rule of Law; Productivity Performance; and Standard of Living, Education and Social Stability. It is performing below its potential and can certainly do better.

2.3 Analysis of Strengths and Weaknesses

Tables 4.8 and 4.9 show the strongest and weakest indicators of Java Region, respectively. Table 4.8 shows the region's top 20% or 21 strongest indicators out of a total of 104 indicators, in descending order. Table 4.9 shows, in ascending order, the top 20% of weakest indicators.[12]

Performing at the top of Overall Competitiveness ranking amongst other regions, Java's strength has been largely dominated by two environments, Macroeconomic Stability and Financial, Businesses and Manpower Conditions. The top 20% strongest indicators under Macroeconomic Stability are Foreign Direct Investment (FDI) (#1), Imports Non-Oil and Gas (#4), Imports (#6), GRDP of Tertiary Industry (#7), GRDP of Secondary Industry (#10), GRDP Non-Oil and Gas (#12), Domestic Direct Investment (#13), GRDP (#16), and Gross Domestic Fixed Capital Formation (#18). There are seven indicators from Financial, Businesses and Manpower Conditions — Bank Deposit (#2), Bank Loans (#3), Employment in Secondary Industry (#5), Employment in Tertiary Industry (#11), Labour Force (#14), Employment (#15), and Number of Bank Branches/Offices (#19).

Table 4.8. 2014 Top 20% Strongest Indicators List for Java Region

Rank	20% Strongest Indicator	Score	Environment
1	Foreign Direct Investment, Last 3 Year Average	2.2283	MS
2	Bank Deposits	2.2204	FBMC
3	Bank Loans	2.2167	FBMC
4	Imports, Non-oil & gas	2.2085	MS
5	Employment in Secondary industry	2.2080	FBMC
6	Imports	2.2066	MS
7	GRDP of Tertiary Industry	2.1884	MS
8	Tax Revenue	2.1738	GIS
9	Passengers of Domestic Air Traffic	2.1737	QLID
10	GRDP of Secondary Industry	2.1731	MS
11	Employment in Tertiary Industry	2.1611	FBMC
12	GRDP, Non-oil & gas	2.1592	MS
13	Domestic Direct Investment, Last 3 Year Average	2.1559	MS
14	Labour Force	2.1336	FBMC
15	Employment	2.1302	FBMC
16	Gross Regional Domestic Product	2.1283	MS
17	Population	2.1225	QLID
18	Gross Domestic Fixed Capital Formation	2.1219	MS
19	Number of Bank Branches/Offices	2.1117	FBMC
20	Government Expenditure	2.0865	GIS
21	Government Revenue	2.0716	GIS

Note: MS = Macroeconomic Stability; GIS = Government and Institutional Setting; FBMC = Financial, Businesses and Manpower Conditions; QLID = Quality of Life and Infrastructure Development
Source: Asia Competitiveness Institute

[12] These 21 strongest and 21 weakest indicators are obtained by sorting all of the 104 indicators' scores that the region received, from the highest to the lowest. Those that appear at the top 21 are identified as the region's strengths and those that appear at the bottom 21 are identified as the region's weaknesses. The comparison is done relatively among the indicator scores of said region, without comparing to the indicator scores of other regions.

Table 4.9. 2014 Top 20% Weakest Indicators List for Java Region

Rank	20% Weakest Indicator	Score	Environment
84	Secondary Industry Productivity	–0.3011	FBMC
85	Non-Performing Loans per Total Bank Loans	–0.4639	FBMC
86	Student-Teacher Ratio (Primary)	–0.4896	QLID
87	Urban Population Growth	–0.5264	QLID
88	Gini Ratio	–0.5780	QLID
89	Primary Industry Productivity	–0.6249	FBMC
90	Firms' Application of IT	–0.7481	FBMC
91	Households with pipe water services	–0.7720	QLID
92	Population Growth	–0.9621	QLID
93	Population Per Medical Worker	–1.0918	QLID
94	Firms' Equipment Capacity	–1.1280	FBMC
95	Student Teacher Ratio (Junior High)	–1.1371	QLID
96	School Enrollment Rate (Senior High)	–1.2513	QLID
97	Population Per Health Facility	–1.4355	QLID
98	Unemployment Rate	–1.5771	FBMC
99	Population per Number of Bank Branches/Offices	–1.6751	FBMC
100	Registered Motor Vehicles per Km of Paved Road	–1.8648	QLID
101	Environmental Quality Index	–2.0017	QLID
102	Student-Teacher Ratio (Senior High)	–2.1547	QLID
103	Fatalities due to Natural Disaster	–2.1949	QLID
104	Non-Performing Loans	–2.2133	FBMC

Note: MS = Macroeconomic Stability; GIS = Government and Institutional Setting; FBMC = Financial, Businesses and Manpower Conditions; QLID = Quality of Life and Infrastructure Development
Source: Asia Competitiveness Institute

In contrast, 13 indicators under Quality of Life and Infrastructure Development appear in the top 20% weakest indicators. These include low ratio for student-teacher in primary (#86), junior high (#95), and senior high school (#102), low school enrolment rate for senior high school (#96), road congestion (#100), Environmental Quality Index (#101), and Fatalities due to Natural Disaster (#103). Eight relatively weak indicators under Financial, Businesses and Manpower Conditions may hinder Java in maintaining or even improving its competitiveness. These indicators are, Secondary Industry Productivity (#84), Non-Performing Loans Per Total Bank Loans (#85), Primary Industry Productivity (#89), Firms' Application of IT (#90), Firms' Equipment Capacity (#94), Unemployment Rate (#98), Population Per Number of Bank Branches/Offices (#99), and Non-Performing Loans (#104).

3. POLICY THEMES AND DEVELOPMENT STRATEGIES

3.1 Official Policies[13]

The MP3EI has proposed various policies and regulations to pave the way for integrated manufacturing and services industries across Java Island. Some of them are related to improvement in infrastructure connectivity,

[13] At national level, Indonesia's development plan is documented in the 2005–2025 National Long-Term Development Plan (RPJPN 2005–2025). It was in the second phase of implementation under the 2010–2014 National Medium-Term Development Plan (RPJMN 2010–2014). Provincial governments must take into account the RPJMN 2010–2014 when formulating or adjusting their respective Provincial Medium-Term Development Plan (RPJMD) to reach national development targets. The MP3EI is not intended to replace RPJMN or the ongoing national and provincial development plans. It is a complementary working document for the above-mentioned development plans aimed at accelerating and expanding economic development in Indonesia.

power supply, and infrastructure supports for trade hub such as airports and seaports as well as dry ports. For food and beverage industry, the region is designed to be competitive in the global market. For textile industry, the MP3EI aims to create vertical integration between upstream and downstream activities. Transportation equipment industry is also expected to accelerate in particular areas such as Jakarta, Bogor, Bekasi, and Karawang.

In designing clusters of industries, *Jabodetabek* area holds a key role since it accounts for 60% of national import and export activities, in addition to hosting food and beverage, textile, and transportation equipment industries. Bandung and its surrounding areas will become the centre of defence equipment and textile industries. The food and beverage industry will be the main focus for Pasuruan-Malang, *Gerbangkertosusila* Metropolitan, and southern Central Java. In addition to that, shipping and textile industries will also be central to *Gerbangkertosusila* Metropolitan and southern Central Java, respectively.

Each province has its own regional policies that are relatively aligned to the MP3EI vision.[14] Banten's provincial government has identified five priority zones to enhance its economic potential and competitiveness such as industrial zone, tourism zone, agricultural zone, territorial/isolated zone, and growth zone. The province is also committed to a number of strategic infrastructure projects such as new airport in southern Banten, power grids, water resources system, capacity enhancement of Merak Port, and international port development in Bojonegara.

For DKI Jakarta, its strategic policies are centred on boosting its service industry to support manufacturing and investment across the country. It serves as the centre of government and financial activities. Urban planning policies are framed to tackle floods, poverty in slum areas, and traffic congestion, and improve waste management. In terms of infrastructure, to reduce traffic congestion and flooding issues, constructions of MRT and canal infrastructure are in the pipeline.

West Java, according to its RPJMD, will focus on fashion, footwear, industrial component, food and beverage, telematics, and creative industries. The province plans to expand its infrastructure such as building a new international airport in Kertajati, which requires investment of 112.5 million US Dollar.[15]

Central Java will focus on developing infrastructure related to transportation system, roads, and energy to improve its business climate. Located as a hub between two main industrial centres, Jakarta and Surabaya, infrastructure and capacity building in Central Java are crucial. There is a major progress in railway development that connects West Java and East Java, known as the Trans-Java railway project. A number of ongoing power supply projects to support industrial areas are being further developed.

To fast track its journey in industrialisation, East Java has an ambitious plan to build industrial cluster by increasing activities in its Tanjung Perak Port to reach the same level as Tanjung Priok's. According to the MP3EI, East Java is designated as the centre of shipping and food and beverage industries, which is located mostly in Surabaya, Pasuruan, and Malang. A one-stop-service for potential investors has been designed as a platform to boost further investment into the province. In its RPJMD, the provincial government has mentioned a number of programmes such as encouraging small and medium-sized enterprises (SMEs) as an industrial base and reorganising industrial structure for a value chain with upstream-downstream industries. In its latest RPJMD 2014–2019, East Java also sets the development and empowerment of agroindustry in seeding technology, fertilisation, and irrigation system as its priority.

None of the 10 major initiatives and investment planned for the Java Economic Corridor is directly related to DI Yogyakarta. According to its RPJMD, there are primarily three pillars for development, namely, education, culture, and tourism. It is also to build upon the multiple titles representing the strengths of Yogyakarta such as *Kota Pendidikan* (Education City) with its 131 universities/institutes of higher education and 6,700 schools, *Kota Budaya* (Cultural City) with its living heritage, *Kota Perjuangan* (Struggle City) with its history of independence movements against the Dutch, and *Kota Gudeg* (Exotic City), with reference to the city's specialty food.

[14] Provincial Development and Planning Agency, *Medium-Term Development Plan (RPJMD) of various provinces across various time spans.*

[15] Nurmayanti, "Pembangunan Bandara Kertajati Dikebut Buat Pemilu," *Liputan 6,* April 3, 2014, retrieved on June 24, 2014, <http://bisnis.liputan6.com/read/2031766/pembangunan-bandara-kertajati-dikebut-buat-pemilu>.

In tandem, the provincial government also supports the expansion of its marine and fisheries, agriculture, and industry sectors.

According to the Coordinating Ministry for Economic Affairs, the trend of investment realisation in the MP3EI projects is dominated by the government and SOE projects.[16] Therefore, the commitment of provincial government to support investment climate in the industrial sector through its policies is needed in a bid to meet the MP3EI targets. Furthermore, political will from the local government to develop industrialisation and pursue more of the Public Private Partnership (PPP) initiatives is also needed.

One critical issue pertaining to prolonged conflict in land acquisition process remains. The 2012 Land Acquisition Law stipulates that land acquisition is to be prioritised for public facility projects, including road, water dam, airport, seaport, and power plant. Despite the new law, many projects are still being delayed because of the long procedure and negotiation process on land acquisition. Both public and private projects have to go through this stage before the shovel hits the ground, further exacerbating the cost of investment. Further analysis of the problems and possible solutions will be explained in Section 3.2.

3.2 Development Strategies

The ACI's analysis shows that both foreign and domestic investments are amongst the strongest indicators (Table 4.8) in Java Region. It indicates that Java has a favourable environment for investment, which is a good starting point to develop a more advanced economy.

In the MP3EI, Java is designated as the driver for manufacturing and service industries. The region will be set as a benchmark for transitioning from primary to tertiary sector, following the successful cases of Singapore, Shenzhen, and Dubai. Since the region is moving towards a more advanced economic structure, it is important to underline the needs of human capital and technology to spur the economic growth.

In contrast, based on the ACI's findings, education-related indicators, such as student-teacher ratio for primary (#86), junior high (#95), and senior high school (#102) as well as school enrolment rate for senior high school (#96), are among the weakest indicators. A study conducted by the World Bank proves that there is a gap in quantity and quality of labour.[17] Improvement to increase the relevance of secondary and tertiary education to the needs of the manufacturing industry is crucial.

Higher quality of labour, to a certain extent, can mitigate the existing low productivity in secondary sector. Concurrently, it is necessary for the region to shift from labour-intensive to capital-intensive industry by attracting more investment in high-tech sector such as defence equipment and high-end manufacturing products.

In order to successfully assume its role as the driver for national industry and services provision, the region needs to first address the human capital shortage through instituting the 12-year basic education requirement and enlarging the pool of vocational high school (SMK) graduates. As the economic structure is shifting to a more advanced stage, re-training of existing labour force should also take place. This can be done not only through vocational training centres (BLKs) initiated by the government, but also by the private sector through training within firms.

Secondly, in order to attract investment in more advanced industries, incentives for prospective investors, such as lower import tax for sophisticated machinery with advanced technology, should also be considered. Incentives to lower taxation can be an alternative to address the lower investment realisation in industrial sector. It is also important to determine a value chain across the country. For instance, raw materials for rice flour can be grown in Sulawesi and Sumatra islands and corn can be produced in food estates in Papua while subsequent processing takes place in Java Island.

Thirdly, in regard to improving logistics transportation, the government should emphasise on building additional access to connect two main seaports in Java, Tanjung Priok in DKI Jakarta and Tanjung Perak in Surabaya. The government can also optimise railway usage by increasing the frequency of rail freight transport.

---

[16] Coordinating Ministry for Economic Affairs, *MP3EI Development Report* (Jakarta: Coordinating Ministry for Economic Affairs, 2013).

[17] World Bank, *Indonesia Skills Report: Trends in Skills Demand, Gaps, and Supply in Indonesia* (Washington DC: World Bank Publications, 2010).

It bears repeating that issues related to land acquisition remain the main bottleneck in a number of infrastructure projects. Although the law on land acquisition has been approved, it still contains loopholes to be closed. One main constraint is the difference between the land price that is currently determined based on the Sales Value of the Tax Object (NJOP) and the higher price demanded by landlords. The land acquisition committee, formed on project basis, regularly encounters difficulties in determining the land price, as individual negotiation is needed. Community-based negotiation rounds may be a solution to discuss land pricing. In addition to the NJOP, the team may also refer to other alternatives for valuing land compensation such as comparison with surrounding areas' sales prices (as adopted in Malaysia, China, United States, and India) or by accounting intangible cost — including sense of belonging in ethnic areas. The advantages of using the community-based approach are expected to spread the compensation equally without inflicting conflicts. Other solution includes collaboration with the World Bank or Asian Development Bank (ADB) in terms of knowledge sharing about best practices guidelines on land acquisition — both at planning and implementation stages — and for them to evaluate the actual implementation. The method has been successfully implemented in India.[18] Additionally, local government plays a vital role to negotiate the process. Further clarity regarding land issues needs the commitment of the central government in both promulgation and enforcement of streamlined land regulation.

The central government, especially the Ministry of Energy and Mineral Resources, should hasten the development of renewable energy to support the power supply in Java. Java has abundant resources of geothermal energy that can generate considerable power. For example, West Java has a potential capacity in generating 6,000 MW from geothermal power grid. It is important to bear in mind that clean energy must always be prioritised, as it will support long-term sustainable development.

For DKI Jakarta, in particular, its government should pay more attention to traffic congestion. DKI Jakarta government, under Basuki Tjahaja Purnama, has started building a much-needed MRT that is expected to finish in 2018. However, the project is not the only solution to solve the traffic congestion. Building additional railway network across *Jabodetabek* as well as to the airport will increase its connectivity. As the MRT project is funded and supervised by Japan International Cooperation Agency (JICA), DKI Jakarta government may also take Tokyo's railway network as a model to effectively manage its high load of commuters around *Jabodetabek*. Vertical and horizontal coordination across relevant stakeholders are needed in aligning the projects to avoid overlap.

The lack of involvement of DI Yogyakarta in the MP3EI programme does not mean that the province contributes less to the region. The plan to build an industrial zone in Piyungan and Sentolo[19] must be well appreciated. DI Yogyakarta is only involved in manufacturing steel slag for value-added products, but this remains under scrutiny since the Government Regulation No. 18/1999 does not permit the use of steel slag. DI Yogyakarta also has fewer incentives to build manufacturing industries since the province is far from the nearest seaport located in Tanjung Emas, Semarang. Cargo transportation for export is mainly hampered by insufficient road infrastructure that connects Central Java and DI Yogyakarta. Thus, collaboration among the two provincial governments is needed to provide adequate infrastructure to transport products from DI Yogyakarta to Tanjung Emas. Alternatively, building dry port can be implemented at the nearest checkpoint for export activities to address bottlenecks.

REFERENCES

Anugraheni, Ekasanti. "DIY Wacanakan Kawasan Industri 100 Ha di Sentolo." *Tribun News,* October 2, 2013. Retrieved on June 24, 2014. <http://jogja.tribunnews.com/2013/10/02/diy-wacanakan-kawasan-industri-100-ha-di-sentolo>.

Atmanto, Sudar D. "Persaingan dan Pemanfaatan Sumber Daya Air dan Lahan." *Irigasi Pertanian* Vol. VII, No. 22 (1995).

[18] Ashwin Mahalingam and Aditi Vyas, "Comparative Evaluation of Land Acquisition and Compensation Process across the World," *Economic and Political Weekly* Vol. XLVI, No. 32 (2011): 94–102.

[19] Ekasanti Anugraheni, "DIY Wacanakan Kawasan Industri 100 Ha di Sentolo," *Tribun News,* October 2, 2013, retrieved on June 24, 2014, <http://jogja.tribunnews.com/2013/10/02/diy-wacanakan-kawasan-industri-100-ha-di-sentolo>.

Coordinating Ministry for Economic Affairs. *Master Plan for Acceleration and Expansion of Indonesia's Economic Development 2011–2025 (MP3EI).* Jakarta: Coordinating Ministry for Economic Affairs, 2011.

Coordinating Ministry for Economic Affairs. *MP3EI Development Report.* Jakarta: Coordinating Ministry for Economic Affairs, 2013.

Djumena, Erlangga. "Rel Ganda Selesai Jakarta-Surabaya Lebih Cepat 3 Jam." *Kompas,* March 27, 2014. Retrieved on June 24, 2014. <http://bisniskeuangan.kompas.com/read/2014/03/27/0924327/Rel.Ganda.Selesai.Jakarta-Surabaya.Lebih.Cepat.3.Jam>.

Jakarta Local Government. "Jakarta Urban Transport Problems and Their Environmental Impacts." Retrieved on June 24, 2014. <http://www.ui.ac.id/download/apru-awi/jakarta-local-goverment.pdf>.

Mahalingam, Ashwin and Aditi Vyas. "Comparative Evaluation of Land Acquisition and Compensation Process across the World." *Economic and Political Weekly* Vol. XLVI, No. 32 (2011): 94–102.

Nurmayanti. "Pembangunan Bandara Kertajati Dikebut Buat Pemilu." *Liputan 6,* April 3, 2014. Retrieved on June 24, 2014. <http://bisnis.liputan6.com/read/2031766/pembangunan-bandara-kertajati-dikebut-buat-pemilu>.

Provincial Development and Planning Agency. *Medium-Term Development Plan (RPJMD) of various provinces across various time spans.*

PT PLN. *Statistik PLN 2012.* Jakarta: PLN, 2012.

Tan, Khee Giap, and Mulya Amri. "Subnational Competitiveness and National Performance: Analysis and Simulation for Indonesia." *Journal of Centrum Cathedra (JCC): The Business and Economics Research Journal* Vol. 6, No. 2 (2013): 173–192.

Tan, Khee Giap, Mulya Amri, Linda Low, and Tan Kong Yam. *Competitiveness Analysis and Development Strategies for 33 Indonesian Provinces.* Singapore: World Scientific, 2013.

"Traffic Jams Cost Jakarta 3B Annually." *The Jakarta Post,* February 10, 2011. Retrieved on June 24, 2014. <http://www.thejakartapost.com/news/2011/02/10/traffic-jams-cost-jakarta-3b-annually.html>.

World Bank. "Annex 5: Jakarta Case Study." In *Climate Change, Disaster Risk and the Urban Poor*, ed. by Judy L. Baker, 199–215. Washington DC: World Bank Publications, 2012.

World Bank. *Indonesia Skills Report: Trends in Skills Demand, Gaps, and Supply in Indonesia.* Washington DC: World Bank Publications, 2010.

World Bank. "Moving Cargo Faster in Indonesia's Main Sea Port," February 19, 2014. Retrieved on June 24, 2014. <http://www.worldbank.org/in/news/feature/2014/02/19/moving-cargo-faster-in-indonesia-main-sea-port>.

Chapter 5
Competitiveness Analysis on the Kalimantan Region

West Kalimantan, Central Kalimantan, South Kalimantan, and East Kalimantan

1. INTRODUCTION

1.1 Background and Notes

Figure 5.1 shows the provinces in Kalimantan Region as defined by the Master Plan for Acceleration and Expansion of Indonesia's Economic Development 2011–2025 (MP3EI).[1] The five provinces with their respective capital cities are West Kalimantan (Pontianak), Central Kalimantan (Palangkaraya), South Kalimantan (Banjarmasin), East Kalimantan (Samarinda), and the newly created North Kalimantan (Tanjung Selor). North Kalimantan became the country's 34th province in 2012 and is composed of several regencies carved out from East Kalimantan. Balikpapan in East Kalimantan is another major city that is commercially important.

In Figure 5.1, inset map (top right) shows the competitiveness ranking by the Asia Competitiveness Institute (ACI) using the traffic light scheme with green representing the Top 10 provinces, followed by the 13 middle-ranking provinces in yellow, and the rest of the provinces with lower competitiveness in red. North Kalimantan is not yet included due to the absence of data at the time of the study. Two provinces are in the Top 10, with East Kalimantan and South Kalimantan at third and eighth place, respectively. Central Kalimantan and West Kalimantan are ranked at 15th and 18th, respectively.[2]

Kalimantan is Indonesia's largest region with 544,150.07 km^2 of land area, covering 28.48% of Indonesia. The region comprises five provinces, 47 regencies, nine cities, 616 sub-districts, and 7,044 villages. Borneo Island is divided among three countries: Indonesia — which takes up about two-thirds of the island, Malaysia as states of Sabah and Sarawak, and Brunei Darussalam. Kalimantan Region shares borders with Sabah and Sarawak in the north, while to its south lies the Java Island, with Sulawesi and Sumatra on its east and west, respectively.

As of 2011, the population in Kalimantan is approximately 14,062,883 people, with 66% of the population in their productive age (15–64 years). Indigenous Kalimantan ethnic groups, Banjar, Dayak, and Kutai, are prevalent all over the region. There is a significant number of Javanese, Chinese, Malay, Buginese, and other migrants residing in South Kalimantan and East Kalimantan.

Kalimantan is rich with energy and minerals. Nearly 50% of the total Gross Regional Domestic Product (GRDP) is contributed by oil and gas. In the MP3EI, the region is referred as the Kalimantan Economic Corridor and designated as the "Centre for Productivity and Processing of National Mining and Energy Reserves". This is shown in the list of 'fast track' investment plans in the MP3EI, which is concentrated on oil, gas, coal, palm oil, iron ore, steel, bauxite, and timber. The main economic centres of Kalimantan are Pontianak, Palangkaraya, Banjarmasin, and Samarinda, which will be connected with a corridor-wide connectivity lane.

Kalimantan has extensive river networks that serve as transportation networks and eco-tourism attraction. East Kalimantan, the region's richest province, is home to the 920 km-long Mahakam River that flows through the western and eastern parts, and serves as the main transportation route in the province, particularly for transporting crude palm oil (CPO) and coal to the seaport. Barito River is as vital in connecting South Kalimantan to

[1] Coordinating Ministry for Economic Affairs, *Master Plan for Acceleration and Expansion of Indonesia's Economic Development 2011–2025 (MP3EI)* (Jakarta: Coordinating Ministry for Economic Affairs, 2011).

[2] See Tan Khee Giap et al., *Competitiveness Analysis and Development Strategies for 33 Indonesian provinces* (Singapore: World Scientific, 2013) and Tan Khee Giap and Mulya Amri, "Subnational Competitiveness and National Performance: Analysis and Simulation for Indonesia," *Journal of Centrum Cathedra (JCC): The Business and Economics Research Journal* Vol. 6, No. 2 (2013):173–192 that mark the first attempt to rank provinces based on their competitiveness level.

Figure 5.1. Map of Kalimantan Region

Source: Asia Competitiveness Institute

Central Kalimantan, while Kapuas River, the longest river in Indonesia with more than 1,000 km long, is located in West Kalimantan and provides transportation for locals and indigenous population.

Despite its resources, issues, such as declining industrialisation, low productivity, and the lack of capacity to create value-added manufacturing sector from these abundant resources, need to be resolved or they will hinder economic progress. Restructuring and diversification of industries are as needful to avert over-reliance on raw material exports. Downstream processing can spur its under-developed secondary and tertiary sectors.

Such environmental sustainability for economic development needs both the government and the private sector to work hand in hand to build competitiveness for Kalimantan Region. Crucial investment in infrastructure, resource management, and downstream manufacturing are underway. The provinces are looking into connecting with neighbouring countries, such as Malaysia or the Philippines, but firstly, efforts to enhance connectivity across and within provinces form a key priority.

Likewise, improvement in education and skills training programmes should be in tandem for better livelihood. Good governance practices presiding over the development policies need to be strengthened. In turn, this will spill over to improve the quality of life and address the development gap among regions and that of urban-rural divide. Therefore, strong coordination during the planning and implementation processes, both at the national and provincial levels of medium-term plans, needs to move in harmony.

As seen in Table 5.1, Kalimantan Region is heavily reliant on extraction activities as indicated from the significant difference between its total GRDP with and without mining. The primary sector's contribution to the GRDP stood as high as 47.68% in 2011. Revenues from this sector enable Kalimantan to improve the welfare of its people, where poverty rate was lowered from 11.78% in 2006 to 7.01% in 2011.

1.2 Major Sectors and Activities

Table 5.2 reiterates that Kalimantan Region is highly dependent on economic activities in the primary sector. Collectively, nearly half of the region's GRDP is contributed by oil, gas, and mining activities. East Kalimantan and South Kalimantan are rich in coal and palm oil. Timber is found in Central Kalimantan, East Kalimantan, and West Kalimantan. Iron ore is largely extracted in Central Kalimantan and South Kalimantan. West Kalimantan holds the largest bauxite reserve in the country. However, disparity of development within the region exists between provinces that produce oil and gas and those without such hydrocarbons.

Table 5.1. Kalimantan Region: Basic Economic Indicators

A. Population	**2006**	**2011**
Total population	12,408,993	14,062,883
% urban	36.94	41.32
B. Area		**2011**
Km^2		544,150.07
% equivalent to country		28.48
C. Gross Regional Domestic Product (GRDP)	**2006**	**2011**
Rupiah (million)	160,687,207	199,968,400
Rupiah (million) without oil & gas	111,458,112	159,192,800
Rupiah (million) without oil & gas & mineral	89,303,648	114,302,345
D. Economic composition, as % GRDP	**2006**	**2011**
Primary sector	43.40	47.68
Secondary sector	31.65	23.60
Tertiary sector	24.95	28.71
E. GRDP per capita	**2006**	**2011**
Rupiah (million)	12.95	14.22
Rupiah (million) without oil & gas	8.98	11.32
Rupiah (million) without oil & gas & mineral	7.20	8.13
F. Poverty Rate	**2006**	**2011**
% of population	11.78	7.01
G. Human Development Index	**2006**	**2011**
Index	69.75	72.93

GRDP based on 2000 Constant Price
Source: Asia Competitiveness Institute using data from Indonesia Statistical Yearbook

Table 5.2. Major Products and Activities

Primary	Mining (coal, iron ore, bauxite, gold, chromite, diamond, gem stone, quartz sand, phosphate, granite), crude oil, natural gas, plantation (rubber, palm oil, coconut, coffee), fisheries (brackish cultivation, cage cultivation, fishery catch, floating cage cultivation, fresh water pond culture, rice-field cultivation, sea culture), agriculture (rice, corn, banana), stockbreeding (cow, buffalo, goat, horse, sheep), and forestry (timber, rattan)
Secondary	Processing industries, construction, and manufacturing
Tertiary	Tourism, restaurant, trade, and services

Source: Asia Competitiveness Institute

The secondary sector has notably experienced a decline in share of the GRDP since 2006, down to 23.60% in 2011. Creating higher value-added goods in food processing and manufactured goods is thus important and it also diversifies the structure of the economy in this region. East Kalimantan is focusing on various industrial, agricultural, and oleochemical processing facilities in Maloy, tapping into its rich non-renewable resources. Central Kalimantan has a potential in processing various plantation products. South Kalimantan has extensive fishery and forestry products. West Kalimantan's economy is made up of agricultural and consumer goods production activities.

The tertiary sector is driven by a young tourism industry that is growing at a steady rate. Key tourism sites include Berau, Mahakam River Banks, and Derawan Marine Preserve in East Kalimantan. Local floating markets in South Kalimantan and Tanjung Puting National Park in Central Kalimantan are also part of the tourist attractions. Distinctive nature and cultural experiences can be developed further to increase revenues from the tourism industry.

1.3 Infrastructure Provision

Basic infrastructure services, such as roads, electricity, and clean water, are crucial to close the development gap between the rural-urban areas and among provinces. In the Kalimantan Region, intra-provincial connectivity remains hindered by insufficient infrastructure. The sheer distance across provinces and extensive river networks crisscrossing around them contribute to high transportation and logistics costs. Overall, Kalimantan still lags behind in road infrastructure.[3]

Traditionally, infrastructure is a public good as provided by the government. As the private sector gains from better connectivity between all industrial sites by saving both cost and time, the trend of the Public Private Partnership (PPP) in infrastructure projects is growing. Nevertheless, this is still very low compared to the Java Region, implying that incentives can be strategically crafted.[4]

There are currently eight international airports serving the five provinces, together with 27 domestic airports and more regional airports being planned. Central Kalimantan has several airports, including Tjilik Riwut Airport in Palangkaraya, Iskandar Airport in Pangkalan Bun, and H. Asan Airport in Sampit. There are seven airports in West Kalimantan, with one international airport, Supadio Airport in Pontianak. East Kalimantan's main airport, Sepinggan International Airport, is located in Balikpapan and is supported by three other airports. Lastly, three airports serve South Kalimantan, namely Syamsudin Noor International Airport in Banjarmasin, Bersujud Airport in Batulicin, and Stagen Airport in Kotabaru.

Kalimantan Region has several major seaports. South Kalimantan's four seaports are Kotabaru Port, Batulicin Port, North Pulau Laut Coal Terminal Port (NPLCT), and Trisakti Port in Banjarmasin. West Kalimantan has eight seaports: Kendawangan, Ketapang, Merbau-Paloh, Pontianak, Singkawang, Sintete, Telok Air, and Telok Melano. Central Kalimantan has 10 seaports. There are Pangkalan Bun Port along the Kotawaringin River and Sampit Port in the district of East Kotawaringin. These are the major exporting ports to ship off the province's palm oil products. East Kalimantan is rapidly building the capacity of its seaports. As of 2011, it has 15 seaports (domestic and international), including the newly completed TPK Palaran.

Energy supply remains an issue in the region despite its abundance of energy resources. Increasing energy demand and limited capacity of the present power plants frequently cause power interruptions and blackouts. According to the Ministry of Energy and Mineral Resources, electrification rates remain low. They are 45.83% for West Kalimantan, 72.29% for South Kalimantan, 45.22% for Central Kalimantan, and 68.56% for the energy-rich province of East Kalimantan.[5]

The lack of electricity supply has curtailed the potential use of information and communications technology (ICT) to improve the efficiency of bureaucracy. E-government is crucial for communication by all parties, namely the government, businesses, and citizens. Its adoption is mostly found in East Kalimantan, where plans to implement electronic service delivery in issuance of licences, medicine, and microfinance, and standardisation are underway. Connectivity by an integrated policy should be implemented in all provinces, starting with infrastructure to foster e-governance. Technology and information sharing are therefore crucial to advance e-governance.

2. RELATIVE COMPETITIVENESS OF REGIONS

The competitiveness framework for the region follows the same approach with the provincial competitiveness, as explained in Chapter 1 in greater detail. Further explanation on the aggregation of individual province's indicators into regional scores can be found in Chapter 2.

---

[3] Organisation for Economic Cooperation and Development (OECD), "Structural Policy Country Notes: Indonesia," in *Southeast Asian Economic Outlook 2013: With Perspectives on China and India* (OECD Publishing, 2013).

[4] OECD, "Structural Policy Country Notes: Indonesia."

[5] "Rasio Elektrifikasi 14 Provinsi Diatas 60%", Ministry of Energy and Mineral Resources, retrieved on June 25, 2014, <http://www.esdm.go.id/berita/39-listrik/2719-rasio-elektrifikasi-14-provinsi-diatas-60.html>.

2.1 Competitiveness Ranking of Six Regions — Rank and Score by Environment[6]

Table 5.3. 2014 Overall Competitiveness: Ranking and Score

Rank	Region	Score
1	Java Region	1.7233
2	*Kalimantan Region*	*0.6511*
3	Sulawesi Region	–0.0392
4	Sumatra Region	–0.0741
5	Bali–Nusa Tenggara Region	–0.9839
6	Maluku–Papua Region	–1.2772

Source: Asia Competitiveness Institute

As seen in Table 5.3, Kalimantan Region is second to Java Region, scoring 0.6511 for Overall Competitiveness. It is followed by Sulawesi Region, with a score of –0.0392 at third place. The distance of scores between Kalimantan and Sulawesi is relatively wide. However, Java Region still far dominates the Indonesian economy. Given its abundant resources, Kalimantan will need to execute wise management to realise its true potential.

Kalimantan's high competitiveness can be attributed to East Kalimantan and South Kalimantan, which are placed third and eighth, respectively, in the provincial ranking. Central Kalimantan and West Kalimantan are at 15th and 18th place, respectively. This region's competitiveness is being lifted disproportionately by East Kalimantan and South Kalimantan.

Table 5.4. 2014 Macroeconomic Stability: Ranking and Score

Rank	Region	Score
1	Java Region	2.0461
2	Sumatra Region	0.1112
3	*Kalimantan Region*	*0.0350*
4	Sulawesi Region	–0.3896
5	Maluku–Papua Region	–0.7943
6	Bali–Nusa Tenggara Region	–1.0085

Source: Asia Competitiveness Institute

For Macroeconomic Stability (Table 5.4), Kalimantan Region is in third position with a score of 0.0350, following Java Region (first) and Sumatra Region (second). However, in terms of the difference in scores between Sumatra (0.1112) and Kalimantan, it is clear that Kalimantan can easily catch up to Sumatra while it is harder to compete with Java.

Kalimantan Region may not need to worry about being taken over by Sulawesi Region at fourth place. Within the region itself, East Kalimantan and South Kalimantan once again exceeded their peers, by attaining the fourth and 10th position, respectively, in the provincial ranking. These two are among the Top 10 provinces and are better than Central Kalimantan (15th) and West Kalimantan (21st) in this environment. Inter-regional and inter-provincial rivalries are actually one way to learn best practices from each other.

[6] Results for the 2014 competitiveness study are based on official data in 2011 and survey data collected in 2013. Conventionally due to collation, compilation, and publication of official data, such a lag of data before reaching end-users is acceptable.

Table 5.5. 2014 Government and Institutional Setting: Ranking and Score

Rank	Region	Score
1	Java Region	1.4124
2	Sulawesi Region	0.7733
3	*Kalimantan Region*	*0.5582*
4	Sumatra Region	–0.4219
5	Bali–Nusa Tenggara Region	–0.8284
6	Maluku–Papua Region	–1.4937

Source: Asia Competitiveness Institute

For Government and Institutional Setting (Table 5.5), Kalimantan is placed third nationally (0.5582), below Sulawesi Region and above Sumatra Region. This pattern of being at the median or average amongst the six regions does not reflect its true potential, considering Kalimantan's resource endowment. Thus, Kalimantan has to focus on improving its weaknesses to reach its true potential.

Kalimantan Region, in general, performs adequately in this environment. East Kalimantan ranks fourth, while South Kalimantan, West Kalimantan, and Central Kalimantan rank at 11th, 13th, and 19th in the provincial ranking, respectively.

Table 5.6. 2014 Financial, Businesses and Manpower Conditions: Ranking and Score

Rank	Region	Score
1	Java Region	1.6700
2	*Kalimantan Region*	*1.0027*
3	Maluku–Papua Region	–0.3552
4	Sumatra Region	–0.3940
5	Sulawesi Region	–0.7693
6	Bali–Nusa Tenggara Region	–1.1543

Source: Asia Competitiveness Institute

Kalimantan is at the second position for Financial, Businesses and Manpower Conditions (Table 5.6), with a score of 1.0027. Clearly, this is an environment that Kalimantan can further develop to approach the top-scoring Java Region (1.6700).

Across provinces, East Kalimantan still dominates the ranking, sitting at fourth position. Nevertheless, West Kalimantan also achieves a notable eighth position, followed by Central Kalimantan at ninth. This pushes three of the provinces to be in the Top 10 tier, while South Kalimantan ranks 15th in the provincial ranking. The excellent performance of the majority of the provinces contributes to the high competitiveness of Kalimantan Region in this environment.

Table 5.7. 2014 Quality of Life and Infrastructure Development: Ranking and Score

Rank	Region	Score
1	Java Region	1.0603
2	*Kalimantan Region*	*0.7425*
3	Sumatra Region	0.4385
4	Sulawesi Region	0.2448
5	Bali–Nusa Tenggara Region	–0.5423
6	Maluku–Papua Region	–1.9438

Source: Asia Competitiveness Institute

In the Quality of Life and Infrastructure Development environment (Table 5.7), Kalimantan Region once again scores second place below Java Region. This is an important environment for Kalimantan to continuously maintain or improve on to be on par with the top achiever, Java Region. Sumatra Region, at the third position (0.4385), also has the potential to be on the same level or better than Kalimantan if the latter is too complacent.

This environment illustrates the extremities of the region, as East Kalimantan is ranked second and South Kalimantan is placed sixth among the provinces. Central Kalimantan only achieves 17th position and West Kalimantan lags behind at 30th position. Therefore, the score within this environment is heavily skewed by the two provinces — East Kalimantan and South Kalimantan, affecting the regional score. This should not be seen as a reason to be complacent in pushing for greater connectivity between the underdeveloped and more advanced provinces, as there is a great potential waiting to be unleashed from the abundance of Kalimantan resources.

2.2 Analysis of Median and Maximum Competitiveness Webs

To better understand Kalimantan's relative strengths and weaknesses, it is useful to compare and contrast its attainment against the median and the maximum scores of Indonesia's six regions for the 12 sub-environments. The median competitiveness web plots Kalimantan's attained scores for each of the 12 sub-environments.

Kalimantan is ranked second for Overall Competitiveness ranking, which makes it one of the top performing regions. This is reflected in Figure 5.2, where the median competitiveness scores for six Indonesian regions are shown in the dashed line, while the scores for Kalimantan are in solid line.

For the 12 sub-environments, Kalimantan far exceeds the median scores in Productivity Performance and Technological Infrastructure. Its performance in Financial Deepening and Business Efficiency and Competition, Regulatory Standards and Rule of Law are also well ahead of the median scores. Additionally, the remaining sub-environments are still higher than the median scores, albeit by narrow margins. Given Kalimantan's potential, Kalimantan should strive hard to uplift those scores, especially in Labour Market Flexibility, which is at the border of the median score.

The maximum competitiveness web (Figure 5.3) shows how far the best score for each sub-environment is, in relation to Kalimantan Region's score. The maximum scores for the six regions are shown in the dashed line, while the scores for Kalimantan are shown in the solid line.

As illustrated in Figure 5.3, Kalimantan has kept up with the best scores nationally in four out of the 12 sub-environments: Productivity Performance; Technological Infrastructure; Standard of Living, Education and Social Stability; and Financial Deepening and Business Efficiency. Kalimantan in fact achieves the maximum score in Productivity Performance.

Kalimantan still needs to close the gap with the best scores in eight out of the 12 sub-environments, including: Physical Infrastructure; Labour Market Flexibility; Regional Economic Vibrancy; Openness to Trade and Services; Attractiveness to Foreign Investors; Government Policies and Fiscal Sustainability; Institutions, Governance and Leadership; and Competition, Regulatory Standards and Rule of Law. The high scores of the top performing Java Region have set a really high benchmark, which is evident from the scores presented in Table 5.3 to 5.7.

Figure 5.2. 2014 Median Competitiveness Web Analysis for Kalimantan Region

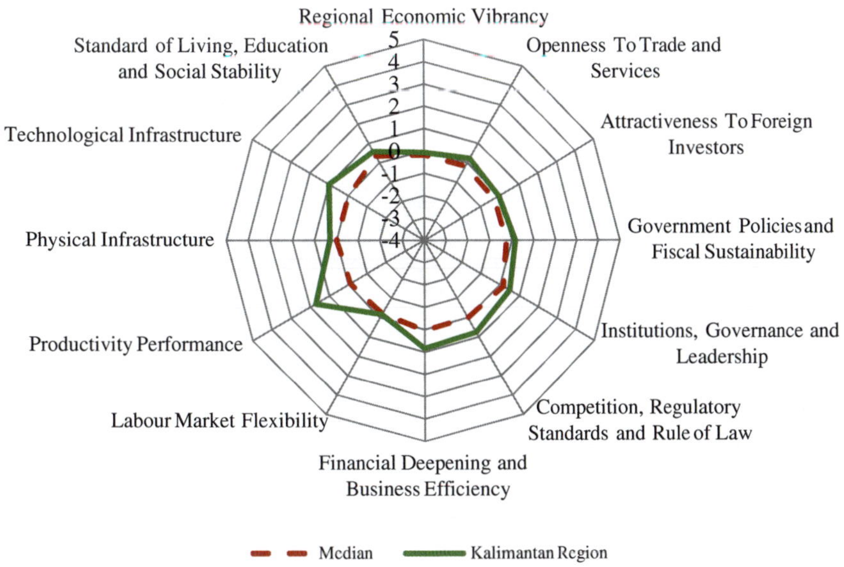

Source: Asia Competitiveness Institute

Figure 5.3. 2014 Maximum Competitiveness Web Analysis for Kalimantan Region

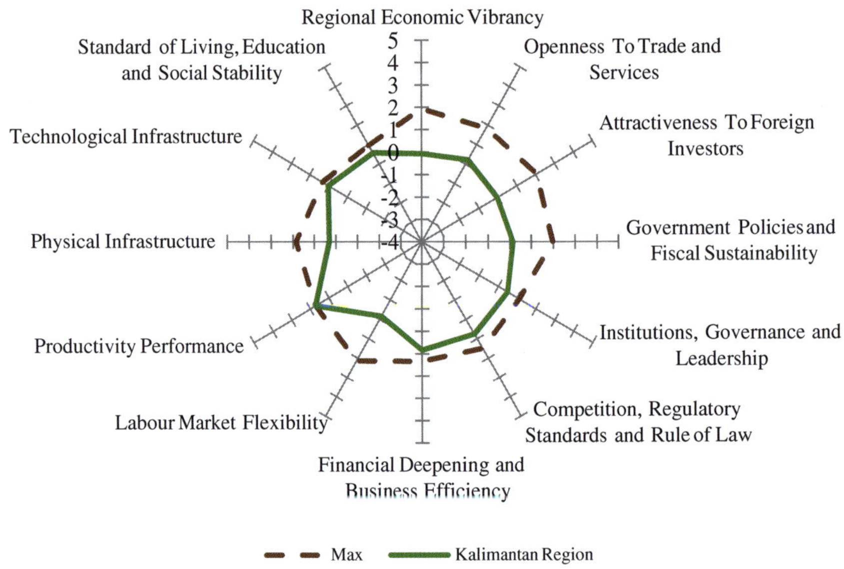

Source: Asia Competitiveness Institute

2.3 Analysis of Strengths and Weaknesses

Tables 5.8 and 5.9 show, respectively, the strongest and weakest indicators of Kalimantan Region. Table 5.8 shows the region's top 20% or 21 strongest indicators out of a total of 104 indicators, in descending order. Table 5.9 shows the top 20% of weakest indicators in ascending order.[7]

In Table 5.8, some indicators from Quality of Life and Infrastructure Development and Financial, Businesses and Manpower Conditions environments dominate Kalimantan's strengths. The top three strengths are Cargo at International Seaport (#1), Primary Industry Productivity (#2), and Laptop Computer Ownership (#3). Including Cargo at Inter-Island Seaport (#4) and Population Per Medical Worker (#5), there are four indicators from the Quality of Life and Infrastructure Development environment in the top five strongest indicators. Other promising strengths are Overall Labour Productivity (#7), Firms' Human Resource Capacity (#11), Secondary Industry Productivity (#12), Overall Labour Productivity, Non-Oil and Gas (#16), and Labour Force Participation Rate (#17). Table 5.8 also reflects strength in Financial, Businesses and Manpower Conditions environment.

[7] These 21 strongest and 21 weakest indicators are obtained by sorting all of the 104 indicators' scores that the region received, from the highest to the lowest. Those that appear at the top 21 are identified as the region's strengths, and those that appear at the bottom 21 are identified as the region's weaknesses. The comparison is done relatively among the indicator scores of said region, without comparing to the indicator scores of other regions.

Table 5.8. 2014 Top 20% Strongest Indicators List for Kalimantan Region

Rank	20% Strongest Indicator	Score	Environment
1	Cargo at International Seaport	2.1070	QLID
2	Primary Industry Productivity	2.0641	FBMC
3	Laptop Computer Ownership	1.8664	QLID
4	Cargo at Inter island Seaport	1.8105	QLID
5	Population Per Medical Worker	1.7882	QLID
6	GRDP Per Capita	1.7539	MS
7	Overall Labour Productivity	1.6708	FBMC
8	Openness To Trade	1.5279	MS
9	Internet Access at Office	1.4754	QLID
10	GRDP Per Capita, Non-oil & gas	1.4686	MS
11	Firms' Human Resource Capacity	1.4662	FBMC
12	Secondary Industry Productivity	1.4430	FBMC
13	Fiscal Balance	1.4192	GIS
14	Households with pipe water services	1.4154	QLID
15	Internet Access in Handphone	1.3885	QLID
16	Overall Labour Productivity, Non-oil & gas	1.3498	FBMC
17	Labour Force Participation Rate	1.3052	FBMC
18	Vibrancy of Competition and Collaboration	1.2840	GIS
19	Population per Number of Bank Branches/Offices	1.1881	FBMC
20	Internet Access at Home	1.1493	QLID
21	Non-Performing Loans per Total Bank Loans	0.9982	FBMC

Note: MS = Macroeconomic Stability; GIS = Government and Institutional Setting; FBMC = Financial, Businesses and Manpower Conditions; QLID = Quality of Life and Infrastructure Development

Source: Asia Competitiveness Institute

Interestingly, indicators from these two environments also dominate the top 20% weaknesses, each contributing eight indicators. Environmental Quality Index (#88), Quality of Education (#92), and Quality of Physical Infrastructure (#104) indicators illustrate some limitation despite strengths noted in Table 5.8. From Financial, Businesses and Manpower Conditions, it should be noted that Employment in Secondary Industry (#91), Employment in Tertiary Industry (#95), Labour Force (#96), and School Enrolment Rate (Senior High) (#102) indicators illustrate the lack of Human Resources Development (HRD) in the region. There are also other crucial weaknesses related to Macroeconomic Stability environment such as Inflation (#103) and GRDP Growth (#90).

Table 5.9. 2014 Top 20% Weakest Indicators List for Kalimantan Region

Rank	20% Weakest Indicator	Score	Environment
84	Gross Domestic Fixed Capital Formation	–0.4562	MS
85	Number of Bank Branches/Offices	–0.4636	FBMC
86	Bank Loans	–0.4702	FBMC
87	GRDP of Tertiary Industry	–0.4771	MS
88	Environmental Quality Index	–0.4887	QLID
89	Imports, Non-oil & gas	–0.4928	MS
90	GRDP Growth	–0.4969	MS
91	Employment in Secondary industry	–0.5256	FBMC
92	Quality of Education	–0.5298	QLID
93	Firms' Strategy	–0.5382	FBMC
94	Registered Motor Vehicles	–0.5415	QLID
95	Employment in Tertiary Industry	–0.5431	FBMC
96	Labour Force	–0.5478	FBMC
97	Employment	–0.5502	FBMC
98	Employment in Primary Industry	–0.5638	FBMC
99	Population	–0.5660	QLID
100	Length of Paved Roads	–0.7042	QLID
101	Passengers of International Air Traffic	–0.7201	QLID
102	School Enrollment Rate (Senior High)	–0.9406	QLID
103	Inflation	–1.2708	MS
104	Quality of Physical Infrastructure	–1.4563	QLID

Note: MS = Macroeconomic Stability; GIS = Government and Institutional Setting; FBMC = Financial, Businesses and Manpower Conditions; QLID = Quality of Life and Infrastructure Development
Source: Asia Competitiveness Institute

3. POLICY THEMES AND DEVELOPMENT STRATEGIES

3.1 Official Policies[8]

Kalimantan is highly endowed with energy resources in the form of oil, gas, and coal. It is thus logical to identify and promote mining, energy, and plantation sectors as priority industries under the MP3EI strategy. Demand for energy continues to increase with rapid economic activities across the country. Therefore, the success of other region's development is actually contingent on Kalimantan's ability to fulfil the demand of expanding national economic growth. Within Kalimantan, monetising its oil-based wealth for economic restructuring and diversification is also wise and forward-looking.

Projects promoting infrastructure improvement and regulatory reforms include attractive oil and gas production sharing contracts and reduction in gas subsidies. Coal production is enhanced through legislative reforms to clear up land permit regulations and tax incentives to encourage more environmentally friendly technology. Major incentive plans are also in place to boost investment in palm oil production and other minerals such as

[8]At national level, Indonesia's development plan is documented in the 2005–2025 National Long-Term Development Plan (RPJPN 2005–2025). It was in the second phase of implementation under the 2010–2014 National Medium-Term Development Plan (RPJMN 2010–2014). Provincial governments must take into account the RPJMN 2010–2014 when formulating or adjusting their respective Provincial Medium-Term Development Plan (RPJMD) to reach national development targets. The MP3EI is not intended to replace RPJMN or the ongoing national and provincial development plans. It is a complementary working document for the abovementioned development plans aimed at accelerating and expanding economic development in Indonesia.

bauxite, iron ore, and timber. Furthermore, the government is encouraging investment in downstream production that can add value to raw exports such as establishing alumina smelters and iron ore processing industry. The New Mining Law, banning the exports of unprocessed minerals, aims to boost domestic processing facilities in order to add value to mining products, thus increasing state revenue.

Aligned with the MP3EI, some infrastructure projects have been identified for Kalimantan Region:

a. Expanding the capacity of two ports in Central Kalimantan, Kumai Port and Pangkalan Bun, to increase exports.
b. Developing the ports to connect the Barito River in Central Kalimantan and Mahakam River in East Kalimantan with planned coal railway system.
c. Establishing non-renewable and renewable energy-based innovation zone model in East Kalimantan.
d. Creating investor-friendly policies to finance alumina smelting industry and other downstream industry from abundant bauxite.
e. Fast tracking investment plan to build commercial scale Industrial Plantation Forest Estates across the island.
f. Implementing the Trans Kalimantan Railway Master Plan, which consists of 10 railway projects in Kalimantan that will be developed under the PPP scheme by 2020. They include Banjarmasin–Pelaihari–Batakan and Tanjung–Martapura–Banjarbaru–Banjarmasin Airport in South Kalimantan, Balikpapan–Samarinda and Tanjung Redeb–Lubuk Tutung in East Kalimantan, and an intra-provincial project to connect Muara Teweh (Central Kalimantan)–Samarinda (East Kalimantan).

As of 2014, there were nearly 136 commitments in infrastructure projects planned for Kalimantan Region, with significant portions funded by both PPP-led initiatives and the private sector.[9] Over 47 projects were in groundbreaking stage in the first quarter of 2014 alone, setting a promising trajectory for the progress of the implementation of MP3EI-guided projects.

The MP3EI similarly outlines the need to also increase the quality of education and provide skills training to upgrade human resources to adapt to new technologies, especially in oil and gas, coal, palm oil, and bauxite industries. However, there is no explicit mention on the human resources plan for timber, which is an equally important industry particularly for the lesser-developed provinces like Central Kalimantan and to some extent, West Kalimantan. Therefore, there is a need to clarify national development plans across other industrial sectors.

Aside from cross-regional connectivity infrastructure, nearly all provinces develop specific comprehensive plans over the next few years that echo the vision outlined by the MP3EI.[10]

The leading province, East Kalimantan faces immediate challenges of managing environmental impact of major resource extraction. Therefore, in the province's Medium-Term Development Plan (RPJMD 2013–2018), East Kalimantan articulated the *Kaltim Green* initiative to maintain sustainability of its environment and welfare of its population when undertaking its economic activities. Additionally, it also plans to address setbacks to competitiveness such as HRD and energy shortages that have been caused by sporadic rapid growth. The province is committed to create better coordination among local governments, build more power plants proportionally to the energy the province requires, and tackle corruption.

On the other hand, West Kalimantan, the more underdeveloped province in this region, needs to increase manufacturing and agricultural competitiveness to attract further investment. In its RPJMD 2013–2018, West Kalimantan seeks to achieve equitable development by reforming the bureaucracy, increasing training of skilled workers, and stabilising the province's large agricultural sector from external and environmental shocks.

Central Kalimantan in its RPJMD 2010–2015 outlines a policy mix to address factors that affect access to health and education, empower small-scale economies, and improve government responsiveness capacity.

[9] Coordinating Ministry for Economic Affairs, "Progress of MP3EI Q1 2014" (PowerPoint presentation, 2014).

[10] Provincial Development and Planning Agency, *Medium-Term Development Plan (RPJMD) of various provinces across various time spans.*

These policies include establishing industrial clusters that can absorb a larger number of workers, increasing quantity and quality of educational and health institutions, integrating transportation, communication, and technology into public policy, and reforming the bureaucracy.

Lastly, South Kalimantan, in its RPJMD 2011–2015, articulates the same desire to address the limitations in access to health and education, foster a more competitive trade and industry-based economy while also managing natural resources more efficiently by strengthening provincial and regional government cooperation. Some of the notable initiatives are fostering the role of industry and the private sector to play a role in shaping the economy, increasing the number of mandatory schooling to 12 years, and compiling information of the province's natural resource habitats.

These plans are logical but the difficult part lies in its execution and implementation with appropriate development strategies, which will be further elaborated in Section 3.2.

3.2. Development Strategies

Kalimantan is the development centre of eastern Indonesia, with significant resources in agriculture, mining, fishery, and plantation sectors. The imperative to prioritise equitable development is even more important since Kalimantan Region is now made up of five provinces, including the newly formed North Kalimantan. Kalimantan's current high competitiveness ranking can be attributed to East Kalimantan and South Kalimantan, which placed third and eighth, respectively, in the provincial ranking of Overall Competitiveness, followed by Central Kalimantan and West Kalimantan placing 15th and 18th, respectively.

Considering the vital function for enhancing the economic competitiveness and social services, spending in infrastructure has been prioritised both in the national development plan and provincial development plans. The National Medium-Term Development Plan (RPJMN) of 2010–2014 indicates that the infrastructure development including road construction has an increasingly important role in improving public welfare and economic growth.[11] Revitalisation of industry, for example, cannot succeed without adequate roads, given the increasingly dominant transportation costs in the cost structure of agricultural and industrial commodities. By connecting major economic centres in Kalimantan, companies that engage in mining, coal in particular, can share the usage of infrastructure to increase production efficiency.

However, road infrastructure is still inadequate especially at the inter-provincial level. The quality and the quantity of major roads remain as part of its crucial weaknesses, as identified in the ACI's analysis in Table 5.9. Kalimantan Highway is a major link connecting Brunei Darussalam, Indonesia, and Malaysia that has a great potential in promoting international cooperation and integration. Adequate road network is crucial in transporting industrial goods and agricultural products, minerals, and petroleum from provincial centres, industrial centres, and plantation areas to shipping ports.

Improving and establishing important linkages across provinces would also facilitate trade and encourage investment and economic growth by increasing access to social services and employment. Government-to-Business nexus and Business-to-Business (B2B) relations should also be able to drive the investment and implementation of new infrastructure, as it is important to all stakeholders. This can occur through sharing of existing and upcoming infrastructure between different industries and sectors.

For the secondary and tertiary sectors, some provinces, such as West Kalimantan, have done better than the others. The focus on agro-business and manufacturing consumer goods is a promising start to create and increase job opportunities that require semi-skilled workforce. This certainly needs to be supported by the aforementioned large-scale investment in education, health, training, and physical infrastructure that will enable the workforce to excel in various goods production. The ACI has identified Kalimantan's seaport capacity as part of the top 20% strongest indicators (Table 5.8). Further development and expansion of the ports, be it air, sea, or river ports, and the cross-Kalimantan roads are thus crucial to the provinces for efficient production of higher value-added goods.

---

[11] Ministry of National Development and Planning Agency, *National Medium-Term Development Plan (RPJMN) 2010–2014* (Jakarta: Ministry of National Development and Planning Agency, 2010).

An important consideration in the implementation of the Kalimantan Region development plans is to uphold environmental sustainability whilst encouraging accelerated industrialisation. Kalimantan has the second largest forest area after Papua and is considered as one of the world's "lungs" with unique features of massive tracts of rainforest and rich biodiversity covering 41 million ha. The region's Environmental Quality Index, which stood at 64.14 in 2011 was already significantly lower than other resource-intensive regions such as Sumatra (72.83) and Papua (71.99).[12] It has further been acknowledged by the ACI's analysis to be one of the top 20% weakest indicators for the region (Table 5.9). Meanwhile, the abundance of nature and rainforest habitats in the unique island of Borneo shows that there is a potential to build tourism attractiveness and investment, which may subsequently affect other service sectors. This long-term potential of ecotourism should be considered as a cross-sectorial issue, especially for those that specifically interact with the rainforests, water sources, and saltwater resources.

This means that major economic industries in the region, such as natural gas, oil, timber, bauxite, coal, and palm oil industries, should consider the impact of resources extraction in relation to environmental degradation. The government has acknowledged the issues by mapping appropriate tracts of production and natural forests, and maximising industrial processes to utilise forest products beyond raw timber exports. There is also a huge market potential for creative value-added products such as fruits, rattan, bamboo, beehive, silk, and eaglewood. To encourage the private sector, incentives that promote environmental protection efforts, such as introducing tax incentives to preserve rainforests or planting eco-friendly mangrove forests, have been suggested by civil society.[13] The high-profile United Nations Initiative for Reducing Emissions from Deforestation and Forest Degradation (UN-REDD+) initiative that aims to protect rainforests in Kalimantan and utilise the global carbon market for the country's advantage can shift policies from extractive to productive arrangements.[14]

As seen from the ACI's analysis, the present economic condition in the Kalimantan Region favours large-scale resource-intensive industries as a result of large Foreign Direct Investment (FDI) in the primary sector, and has subsequently caused a gap between large-scale industries and small and medium-sized enterprises (SMEs). The shortage of skilled labour, the poor quality of education, the present infrastructure and connectivity deficiencies, and the pattern of investment have thus far undermined the development of a more sustainable secondary and tertiary sectors.

Kalimantan Region needs to consider a long-term sustainable plan as outlined in the national and provincial medium-term plans, and not neglect welfare in pursuit of accelerated but unsustainable growth. National, provincial, and local governments have targeted a promising vision for the region. The Coordinating Ministry for Economic Affairs can play a pivotal role in joining the dots for a holistic, integrated, and systemic approach in development strategies. This requires effective communication and policy sequencing among the layers of government. In the end, it is the competitiveness that drives the momentum; the ACI has shown the way from the analysis of 33 Indonesian provinces.

REFERENCES

Coordinating Ministry for Economic Affairs. *Master Plan for Acceleration and Expansion of Indonesia's Economic Development 2011–2025 (MP3EI).* Jakarta: Coordinating Ministry for Economic Affairs, 2011.

Coordinating Ministry for Economic Affairs. "Progress of MP3EI Q1 2014." PowerPoint presentation, 2014.

Mattangkilang, Tunggadewa. "Activists Call Efforts to Save Balikpapan Bay." *The Jakarta Globe,* May 28, 2014. Retrieved on June 25, 2014. <http://www.thejakartaglobe.com/news/activists-call-efforts-save-balikpapan-bay/>.

[12] Environmental Quality Index is part of Quality of Life and Infrastructure Development environment in ACI's Competitiveness Framework, which is an aggregate index of air pollution, water pollution, and forest coverage.

[13] Tunggadewa Mattangkilang, "Activist Call Efforts to Save Balikpapan Bay", *The Jakarta Globe,* May 28, 2014, retrieved on June 25, 2014, <http://www.thejakartaglobe.com/news/activists-call-efforts-save-balikpapan-bay/>.

[14] UN-REDD+, "Indonesia's Green Economy Corridor Initiative", retrieved on August 4, 2014, <http://sustainabledevelopment.un.org/index.php?page=view&type=1006&menu=1348&nr=2229>.

Ministry of Energy and Mineral Resources. "Rasio Elektrifikasi 14 Provinsi Diatas 60%." Retrieved on June 25, 2014. <http://www.esdm.go.id/berita/39-listrik/2719-rasio-elektrifikasi-14-provinsi-diatas-60.html>.

Ministry of National Development and Planning Agency. *National Medium-Term Development Plan (RPJMN) 2010–2014.* Jakarta: Ministry of National Development and Planning Agency, 2010.

Organisation for Economic Cooperation and Development (OECD). "Structural Policy Country Notes: Indonesia." In *Southeast Asian Economic Outlook 2013: With Perspectives on China and India*. OECD Publishing, 2013.

Provincial Development and Planning Agency. *Medium-Term Development Plan (RPJMD) of various provinces across various time spans.*

Tan, Khee Giap, and Mulya Amri. "Subnational Competitiveness and National Performance: Analysis and Simulation for Indonesia." *Journal of Centrum Cathedra (JCC): The Business and Economics Research Journal* Vol. 6, No. 2 (2013):173–192.

Tan, Khee Giap, Mulya Amri, Linda Low, and Tan Kong Yam. *Competitiveness Analysis and Development Strategies for 33 Indonesian Provinces*. Singapore: World Scientific, 2013.

UN-REDD+. "Indonesia's Green Economy Corridor Initiative." Retrieved on August 4, 2014. <http://sustainabledevelopment.un.org/index.php?page=view&type=1006&menu=1348&nr=2229>.

Chapter 6
Competitiveness Analysis on the Sulawesi Region

South Sulawesi, Central Sulawesi, Southeast Sulawesi, North Sulawesi, Gorontalo, and West Sulawesi

1. INTRODUCTION

1.1 Background and Notes

Figure 6.1 shows the provinces in Sulawesi Region as defined by the Master Plan for Acceleration and Expansion of Indonesia's Economic Development 2011–2025 (MP3EI).[1] The six provinces with their respective capital cities are South Sulawesi (Makassar), Central Sulawesi (Palu), Southeast Sulawesi (Kendari), North Sulawesi (Manado), Gorontalo (Gorontalo), and West Sulawesi (Mamuju). Gorontalo and West Sulawesi are categorised as young provinces in Indonesia. Gorontalo, formerly part of North Sulawesi, was created in 2000. West Sulawesi became a new province following its separation from South Sulawesi in 2004. Bitung (North Sulawesi) and Palu (Central Sulawesi) have been conferred a Special Economic Zone (SEZ) status in 2014.

In Figure 6.1, inset map (top right) shows the competitiveness ranking by the Asia Competitiveness Institute (ACI) using the traffic light scheme with green representing the Top 10 provinces, followed by the 13 middle-ranking provinces in yellow and the rest of the provinces with lower competitiveness in red. Two Sulawesi provinces emerged in the Top 10, namely South Sulawesi at seventh and North Sulawesi at 10th place. Central Sulawesi is at 21st position while the rest, West Sulawesi (25th), Gorontalo (28th), and Southeast Sulawesi (29th), belong to the Bottom 10.[2]

Sulawesi (formerly known as Celebes) is the 11th biggest island in the world and fourth in Indonesia, after Kalimantan, Sumatra, and Papua, with 188,522.36 km^2 of land area that makes up 9.87% of Indonesia. Sulawesi is bordered by Borneo on the west, the Philippines on the north, Flores Sea on the south, and Maluku on the east.

As of 2011, the population in Sulawesi was approximately 17,624,762 people with diverse backgrounds. The majority of the population in South Sulawesi is Muslim while the dominant religion in North Sulawesi is Christianity. The most well-known and biggest ethnic groups are Buginese, Makassarese, Manadonese, and Torajan. More than 40% of the population resides in South Sulawesi while the most urbanised province is North Sulawesi, with 45% of urban population. Dialects, such as Makassarese or Manadonese, are also commonly spoken alongside the national language, Bahasa Indonesia.

Sulawesi has beautiful natural sceneries such as volcanoes, mountains, canyons, tropical rain forests, lakes, rivers, and white sand beaches. The island is surrounded by coral reefs and is home to beautiful Marine Parks, such as Bunaken, Banggai, Taka Bonerate National Park in Selayar, and Wakatobi National Park, where endangered species are protected in their natural habitats. Tana Toraja is another tourist site where the traditional Torajans live in their ancestral houses, *Tongkonan.*

Sulawesi is endowed with abundant natural resources and fertile grounds suitable for agricultural commodities. Its vast maritime area also has a lot of potential for fisheries and tourism activities. The MP3EI has designated Sulawesi Region with the development theme as "A Centre of Production and Processing of National Agriculture, Plantation, Fishery, Oil, Gas, and Mining". It has identified five main economic activities, namely agriculture (rice, corn, soybean and cassava), cocoa, fishery, nickel, and oil and gas.

---

[1] Coordinating Ministry for Economic Affairs, *Master Plan for Acceleration and Expansion of Indonesia's Economic Development 2011–2025 (MP3EI)* (Jakarta: Coordinating Ministry for Economic Affairs, 2011).

[2] See Tan Khee Giap *et al.*, *Competitiveness Analysis and Development Strategies for 33 Indonesian provinces* (Singapore: World Scientific, 2013) and Tan Khee Giap and Mulya Amri, "Subnational Competitiveness and National Performance: Analysis and Simulation for Indonesia," *Journal of Centrum Cathedra (JCC): The Business and Economics Research Journal* Vol. 6, No. 2 (2013): 173–192 that mark the first attempt to rank provinces based on their competitiveness level.

Figure 6.1. Map of Sulawesi Region

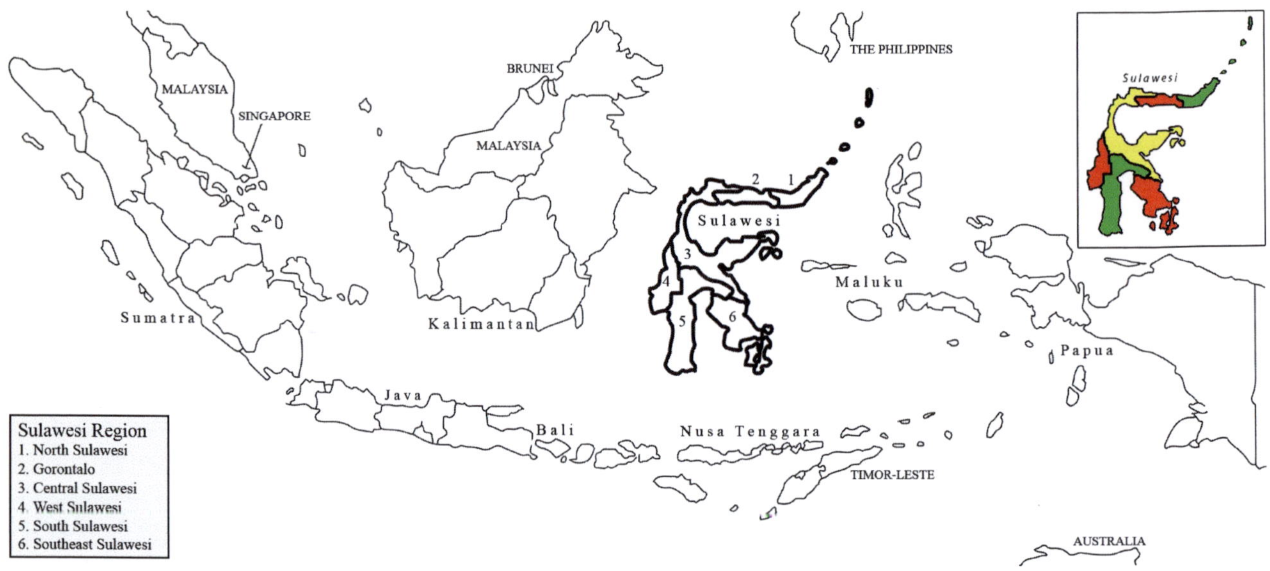

Source: Asia Competitiveness Institute

Table 6.1 shows that its Gross Regional Domestic Product (GRDP) has significantly increased from 79,152,635 million Rupiah in 2006 to 115,132,900 million Rupiah in 2011, which was a 45% increase. From the GRDP breakdown, it is obvious that the region is not heavily reliant on oil, gas and mineral despite the MP3EI's focus to develop oil and gas sector. The tertiary sector contributed the most at 47.93%, followed by the primary sector at 33.47%. Concurrently, the region's poverty rate has decreased from 17.79% in 2006 to 12.17% in 2011 and Human Development Index (HDI) has risen from 69.28 in 2006 to 72.21 in 2011.

1.2 Major Sectors and Activities

Table 6.2 reiterates the diversity of economic activities in Sulawesi. As indicated in Table 6.1, the primary sector contributed to 33.47% of the GRDP in the region. Each province has its own characteristic in terms of economic activity. Central Sulawesi accounts for Indonesia's largest fishery production and has the potential to be an excellent centre of seaweed production. Central Sulawesi and South Sulawesi contribute to 75% of the cocoa bean exports and output from Indonesia. West Sulawesi has been a centre of rice production as it consistently produces a surplus of rice since 2009, and has subsequently targeted 140,000 tons of maize production by 2014. There are three districts in Gorontalo, namely North Gorontalo, Boalemo and Pohuwato, that have been assigned as centre of fishery-based economy, or locally known as "Minapolitan" programme. The pilot programme in Pohuwato district focuses on aquaculture. For mining, Sulawesi has abundant reserves of nickel in Sorowako in East Luwu district of South Sulawesi, Morowali district in Central Sulawesi, Pomalaa in Kolaka district and Konawe district in Southeast Sulawesi.

The secondary sector is still relatively underdeveloped. Nickel smelting in Southeast Sulawesi is expected to produce up to 25,000 unit of nickel pig iron per year. Central Sulawesi is focusing on the downstream industry from its cocoa and rattan resources as well as refinery from its mineral resources. North Sulawesi's industries include canned fish and food and beverages. With the appointment of Palu and Bitung as SEZs, contribution from the secondary sector is expected to grow exponentially.

As the dominant contributor to the GRDP (47.93%), the tertiary sector is mostly driven by trade and tourism. Given Makassar's prominent role as the centre of trade for eastern Indonesia, it is not surprising that the whole-sale and retail trade of South Sulawesi contributed to more than 10 trillion Rupiah in 2012.[3] As a region, Sulawesi

[3] Based on 2000 Constant Price.

Table 6.1. Sulawesi Region: Basic Economic Indicators

A. Population	**2006**	**2011**
Total population	16,051,981	17,624,762
% urban	28.44	33.61
B. Area		**2011**
Km^2		188,522.36
% equivalent to country		9.87
C. Gross Regional Domestic Product (GRDP)	**2006**	**2011**
Rupiah (million)	79,152,635	115,132,900
Rupiah (million) without oil & gas	78,927,700	114,675,000
Rupiah (million) without oil & gas & mineral	74,931,627	110,674,653
D. Economic composition, as % GRDP	**2006**	**2011**
Primary sector	39.05	33.47
Secondary sector	18.41	18.60
Tertiary sector	42.54	47.93
E. GRDP per capita	**2006**	**2011**
Rupiah (million)	4.93	6.53
Rupiah (million) without oil & gas	4.92	6.51
Rupiah (million) without oil & gas & mineral	4.67	6.28
F. Poverty Rate	**2006**	**2011**
% of population	17.79	12.17
G. Human Development Index	**2006**	**2011**
Index	69.28	72.21

GRDP based on 2000 Constant Price
Source: Asia Competitiveness Institute using data from Indonesia Statistical Yearbook

Table 6.2. Major Products and Activities

Primary	Rice, cocoa, corn, soy bean, peanut, clove, coffee, tea, palm oil, rubber, timber, rattan, seaweed, fishery, nickel, coal, copper, oil, and gas
Secondary	Food and beverages, textiles, petrochemical, steel, gas, and water supply
Tertiary	Tourism, MICE (Meetings, Incentives, Conferences, and Exhibitions), transportation, and trade

Source: Asia Competitiveness Institute

is rich in cultural diversity, culinary and natural scenery with a rising hospitality sector. Sulawesi is not only attractive for sightseeing but also for MICE (Meetings, Incentives, Conferences, and Exhibitions) activities, which are engines for growth especially in Manado and Makassar.

1.3. Infrastructure Provision

For land transportation, Trans Sulawesi is the main route connecting provinces in the region. The length of paved roads varied among the provinces, ranging from 16,472 km in South Sulawesi, to 2,055 km in West Sulawesi, which can be attributed to the variation in the area size. However, the region suffers from serious setback in road quality. In general, the quality of road infrastructure is perceived to be poor.[4] Acknowledging the importance of land transportation for inter- and intra-province connectivity, the MP3EI has identified several road improvement projects across the region. This is imperative to boost the efficiency and effectiveness of supply chain within Sulawesi.

In terms of air transportation, although there are several local airports in every province, there are only two international airports in Sulawesi, namely Sultan Hasanuddin International Airport in Makassar (South Sulawesi) and Sam Ratulangi Airport in Manado (North Sulawesi). The main airports in other provinces are Tampa Padang Airport in Mamuju (West Sulawesi), Jalaluddin Airport (Gorontalo), Mutiara Airport in Palu (Central Sulawesi) and Haluoleo Airport in Kendari (Southeast Sulawesi). According to Angkasa Pura, passenger traffic in Hasanuddin Airport has reached 9.6 million, which is beyond its capacity of 7.5 million per year. The airport operator aims to further develop the airport capacity to 30 million passengers per year to anticipate future growth in air traffic.

For sea transportation, Soekarno-Hatta Port in Makassar is the only international seaport in Sulawesi. The volume of containers received by the port has significantly increased from 372,532 twenty-foot equivalent units (TEUs) in 2009 to over 500,000 TEUs in 2012 and is expected to grow further in the coming years. The state-owned port operator PT. Pelindo IV has been planning to construct the much anticipated Makassar New Port with a capacity between 250,000–300,000 TEUs to help support the existing Soekarno-Hatta Port and to further ease the distribution of goods not only in Sulawesi, but also in other eastern regions such as Maluku and Papua. Furthermore, Bitung's status as an SEZ will spur the need for a more developed seaport to support its industrial activities.

Electricity supply varies across the region, which has become one of the hurdles for achieving balanced regional growth in all provinces. According to PT PLN, state-owned electricity company, electrification ratio in 2011 in some provinces were considered high — 77.99% in North Sulawesi, 71.97% in South Sulawesi, 67.38% in Gorontalo, and 62.03% in Central Sulawesi. However, the rates were particularly low for West Sulawesi and Southeast Sulawesi, at 33.56% and 51.08%, respectively.[5] With Sulawesi ramping up its posture to be the centre of development in the eastern part of Indonesia, significant improvement in energy supply is imperative. To fulfil such aspiration, the MP3EI has identified 18 projects related to power and energy that span from geothermal power plant to transmission network and substation development across region.

2. RELATIVE COMPETITIVENESS OF REGIONS

The competitiveness framework for the region follows the same approach with the provincial competitiveness, as explained in Chapter 1 in greater detail. Further explanation on the aggregation of individual province's indicators into regional scores can be found in Chapter 2.

[4] Organisation for Economic Cooperation and Development (OECD), "Structural Policy Country Notes: Indonesia," in *Southeast Asian Economic Outlook 2013: With Perspectives on China and India* (OECD Publishing, 2013).
[5] PT PLN, *Statistik PLN 2012* (Jakarta: PLN, 2012).

2.1 Competitiveness Ranking of Six Regions — Rank and Score by Environment[6]

Table 6.3. 2014 Overall Competitiveness: Ranking and Score

Rank	Region	Score
1	Java Region	1.7233
2	Kalimantan Region	0.6511
3	*Sulawesi Region*	*–0.0392*
4	Sumatra Region	–0.0741
5	Bali–Nusa Tenggara Region	–0.9839
6	Maluku–Papua Region	–1.2772

Source: Asia Competitiveness Institute

Sulawesi Region holds third position in Overall Competitiveness ranking (Table 6.3). Its score (–0.0392) is far below Java (first) and Kalimantan (second).

Sulawesi's competitiveness can be attributed to South Sulawesi and North Sulawesi's high position at seventh and 10th, respectively, in Overall Competitiveness provincial ranking. However, its regional score is pulled down by the mediocre performance of Central Sulawesi (21st), West Sulawesi (25th), Gorontalo (28th), and Southeast Sulawesi (29th). Such competitiveness ranking encourages inter-regional friendly rivalry to eventually improve Indonesia's competitiveness at the global level.

Table 6.4. 2014 Macroeconomic Stability: Ranking and Score

Rank	Region	Score
1	Java Region	2.0461
2	Sumatra Region	0.1112
3	Kalimantan Region	0.0350
4	*Sulawesi Region*	*–0.3896*
5	Maluku–Papua Region	–0.7943
6	Bali–Nusa Tenggara Region	1.0085

Source: Asia Competitiveness Institute

From Table 6.4, Sulawesi Region is at fourth place with a negative score (–0.3896) for Macroeconomic Stability. The result is consistent with the provincial performance as none of its provinces are at the Top 10 in Macroeconomic Stability ranking of the 33 provinces. The highest rank is South Sulawesi at 11th place, while the lowest is Gorontalo at 25th position. The remaining provinces are placed in the middle ranking.

Although Maluku–Papua Region occupies the fifth position with a much lower score of –0.7943, Sulawesi should avoid being complacent and strive to address issues related to Macroeconomic Stability to improve its performance.

Table 6.5. 2014 Government and Institutional Setting: Ranking and Score

Rank	Region	Score
1	Java Region	1.4124
2	*Sulawesi Region*	*0.7733*
3	Kalimantan Region	0.5582
4	Sumatra Region	–0.4219
5	Bali–Nusa Tenggara Region	–0.8284
6	Maluku–Papua Region	–1.4937

Source: Asia Competitiveness Institute

Sulawesi is the runner-up in terms of Government and Institutional Setting, scoring 0.7733 which is almost half of the score of Java (1.4124; Table 6.5). Sulawesi's commendable position reflects the strength of each province in obtaining relatively higher rank in this environment. Three out of the six provinces join the Top 10 group, with South Sulawesi leading the pack at third place, followed by North Sulawesi at eighth and West Sulawesi at 10th.

Opportunities remain abundant for Sulawesi to be on par or even better than Java if it further strives to improve its indicators in Government and Institutional Setting. This is particularly relevant for the other three provinces in the Middle 13 such as Central Sulawesi (12th), Gorontalo (18th), and Southeast Sulawesi (22nd).

[6] Results for the 2014 competitiveness study are based on official data in 2011 and survey data collected in 2013. Conventionally due to collation, compilation, and publication of official data, such a lag of data before reaching end-users is acceptable.

Table 6.6. 2014 Financial, Businesses and Manpower Conditions: Ranking and Score

Rank	Region	Score
1	Java Region	1.6700
2	Kalimantan Region	1.0027
3	Maluku–Papua Region	–0.3552
4	Sumatra Region	–0.3940
5	*Sulawesi Region*	*–0.7693*
6	Bali–Nusa Tenggara Region	–1.1543

Source: Asia Competitiveness Institute

Sulawesi is placed fifth in Financial, Businesses, and Manpower Conditions, with a score of –0.7693 (Table 6.6). Considering the large gap with Sumatra, Sulawesi has to work hard to boost its rank. The region's poor performance is a reflection of the respective provincial ranking for this environment. South Sulawesi is the only province in the Top 10 while North Sulawesi is the only province in the Middle 13. The remaining provinces are in the Bottom 10 with Gorontalo attaining the lowest rank (33rd) for this environment.

Table 6.7. 2014 Quality of Life and Infrastructure Development: Ranking and Score

Rank	Region	Score
1	Java Region	1.0603
2	Kalimantan Region	0.7425
3	Sumatra Region	0.4385
4	*Sulawesi Region*	*0.2448*
5	Bali–Nusa Tenggara Region	–0.5423
6	Maluku–Papua Region	–1.9438

Source: Asia Competitiveness Institute

As seen in Table 6.7, Sulawesi occupies the fourth place with a score of 0.2448. Although its gap with Bali– Nusa Tenggara Region (fifth) is quite significant, Sulawesi should not be too contented in achieving its current standing and should strive to improve its Quality of Life and Infrastructure Development.

South Sulawesi (ninth) consistently performs well in the provincial ranking while North Sulawesi is ranked at 12th. Nevertheless, disparities exist as the other provinces attain lower ranks — Central Sulawesi 20th, Southeast Sulawesi 24th, Gorontalo 27th, and West Sulawesi 29th. Poor infrastructure has been an issue in most provinces located in the eastern part of Indonesia. With the MP3EI driving more balanced growth across Indonesia, more infrastructure projects are in the pipeline and these are expected to improve Sulawesi's score.

2.2 Analysis of Median and Maximum Competitiveness Webs

To better understand Sulawesi's relative strengths and weaknesses, it is useful to compare and contrast its attainment against the median and the maximum scores of Indonesia's six regions for the 12 sub-environments. The median competitiveness web plots Sulawesi's attained scores for each of the 12 sub-environments.

Sulawesi's Overall Competitiveness (Table 6.3) is ranked at third among the six regions, which makes it the median performing region. This is illustrated in Figure 6.2, where the Median Competitiveness scores for the six Indonesian regions are shown in dashed line, while the scores for Sulawesi are in solid line.

Sulawesi far exceeds the median scores in two out of the 12 sub-environments, namely Competition, Regulatory Standards and Rule of Law and Institutions, Governance and Leadership. These two sub-environments are under Government and Institutional Setting environment where Sulawesi holds runner-up position, the best rank that Sulawesi attains at environment level.

Other sub-environments that are above the median include Standard of Living, Education and Social Stability and Attractiveness to Foreign Investors while Technological Infrastructure is almost equal to the median score. The latter is very crucial for dynamic versus static growth and competitiveness.

The remaining sub-environments are relatively lower than the median scores. Two sub-environments, Openness to Trade and Services and Financial Deepening and Business Efficiency, appear to be far lower than the median scores and require serious improvements. Sulawesi's poor achievement in Financial, Businesses and Manpower Conditions, as shown in Table 6.6, is also reflected in its below-median scores for all its respective sub-environments. Progress in boosting these microeconomic indicators is the key for Sulawesi to ramp up its competitiveness posture.

Figure 6.2. 2014 Median Competitiveness Web Analysis for Sulawesi Region

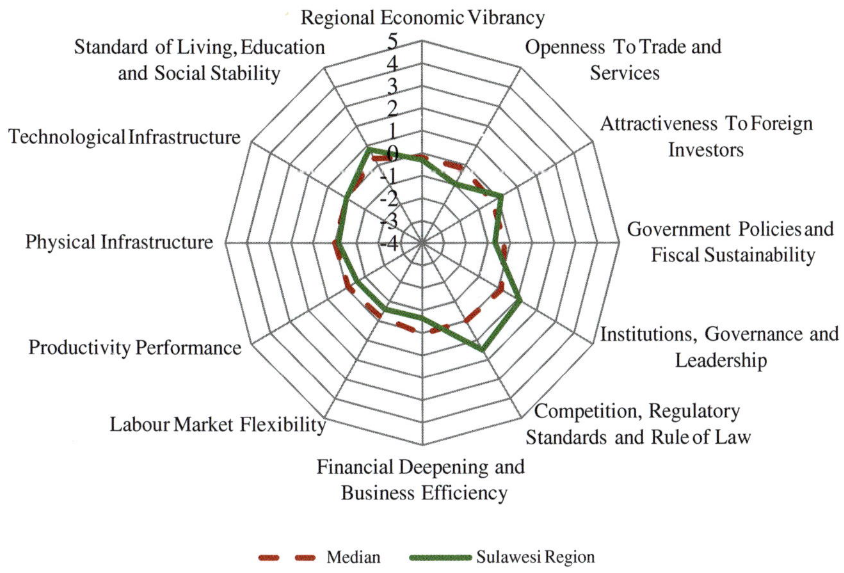

Source: Asia Competitiveness Institute

Figure 6.3. 2014 Maximum Competitiveness Web Analysis for Sulawesi Region

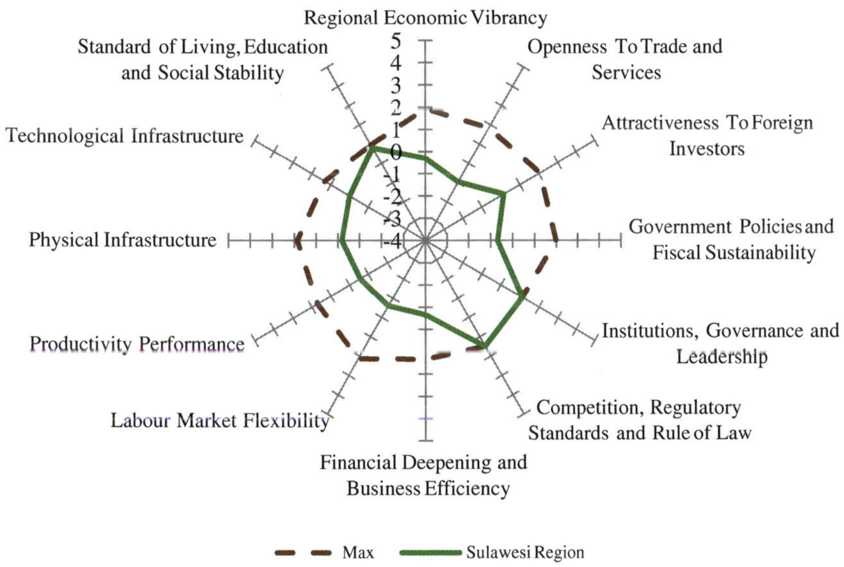

Source: Asia Competitiveness Institute

The maximum competitiveness web in Figure 6.3 shows how far the best score for each sub-environment is, in relation to Sulawesi Region's score. The maximum scores for the six regions are shown in dashed line, while the scores for Sulawesi are shown solid line.

As illustrated in Figure 6.3, Sulawesi achieves maximum score in two out of the 12 sub-environments, namely Institutions, Governance and Leadership and Competition, Regulatory Standards and Rule of Law, both are under Government and Institutional Setting environment. This is consistent with Table 6.5 that highlights remarkable achievement of Sulawesi as the runner-up in this environment. One sub-environment, which is Standard of Living, Education and Social Stability, is very close to the maximum score.

Sulawesi still needs to close the gap with the maximum scores in nine out of the 12 sub-environments. These include Physical Infrastructure; Technological Infrastructure; Labour Market Flexibility; Regional Economic Vibrancy; Openness to Trade and Services; Attractiveness to Foreign Investors; Government Policies and Fiscal Sustainability; Productivity Performance; and Financial Deepening and Business Efficiency.

Based on the median and maximum competitiveness web analysis, it is worth noting that Sulawesi performs extremely well in Government and Institutional Setting. The region should capitalise on this strength to enhance the performance in the other environments.

2.3 Analysis of Strengths and Weaknesses

Tables 6.8 and 6.9 list the strongest and weakest indicators of Sulawesi Region. Table 6.8 shows the region's top 20% or 21 strongest indicators out of a total of 104 indicators, in descending order. Table 6.9 shows the top 20% of weakest indicators in ascending order.[7]

The top three strongest indicators are Urban Population Growth, Government Progress and Expectation, and Quality of Physical Infrastructure. Overall, most of the top 20% strongest indicators are those related to Government and Institutional Setting (nine indicators) and Quality of Life and Infrastructure Development

Table 6.8. 2014 Top 20% Strongest Indicators List for Sulawesi Region

Rank	20% Strongest Indicator	Score	Environment
1	Urban Population Growth	1.7594	QLID
2	Government Progress & Expectation	1.7398	GIS
3	Quality of Physical Infrastructure	1.7054	QLID
4	Rule of Law	1.6458	GIS
5	Provincial Governing Capacity	1.5767	GIS
6	Regulatory Governance	1.5542	GIS
7	Ease of Acquiring Property	1.5023	QLID
8	Government Efficiency	1.4778	GIS
9	Coordination of Local Governments	1.4534	GIS
10	Lack of Corruption	1.4321	GIS
11	Investment Promotion and Management	1.3900	MS
12	GRDP Growth	1.3826	MS
13	Student-Teacher Ratio (Junior High)	1.3677	QLID
14	Government Inclusiveness and Accountability	1.2126	GIS
15	Security	1.1301	GIS
16	Affordability and Accessibility of Goods	1.0177	QLID
17	Student-Teacher Ratio (Primary)	0.8958	QLID
18	Student-Teacher Ratio (Senior High)	0.8940	QLID
19	Firms' Performance	0.8808	FBMC
20	Inflation	0.8558	MS
21	Firms' Human Resource Capacity	0.8270	FBMC

Note: MS = Macroeconomic Stability; GIS = Government and Institutional Setting; FBMC = Financial, Businesses and Manpower Conditions; QLID = Quality of Life and Infrastructure Development
Source: Asia Competitiveness Institute

[7] These 21 strongest and 21 weakest indicators are obtained by sorting all of the 104 indicators' scores that the region received, from the highest to the lowest. Those that appear at the top 21 are identified as the region's strengths, and those that appear at the bottom 21 are identified as the region's weaknesses. The comparison is done relatively among the indicator scores of said region, without comparing to the indicator scores of other regions.

Table 6.9. 2014 Top 20% Weakest Indicators List for Sulawesi Region

Rank	20% Weakest Indicator	Score	Environment
84	Government Expenditure	–0.6272	GIS
85	Government Revenue	–0.6679	GIS
86	School Enrollment Rate (Junior High)	–0.6720	QLID
87	GRDP Per Capita	–0.6741	MS
88	Cargo at International Seaport	–0.6802	QLID
89	Passengers of International Air Traffic	–0.7223	QLID
90	RGDP of Primary Industry	–0.7282	MS
91	Urban Population	–0.7353	QLID
92	Cargo at Inter-island Seaport	–0.8062	QLID
93	Secondary Industry Productivity	–0.8242	FBMC
94	Exports, Non-oil & gas	–0.8433	MS
95	Corruption Perception Index	–0.8491	GIS
96	Exports	–0.9212	MS
97	Gini Ratio	−1.0141	QLID
98	Fiscal Balance	−1.1767	GIS
99	Openness To Trade	−1.2402	MS
100	Life Expectancy at Birth	−1.3598	QLID
101	Firms' Application of IT	−1.5157	FBMC
102	Labor Force Participation Rate	−1.5755	FBMC
103	Crime Rate	−1.6670	GIS
104	Non-Performing Loans per Total Bank Loans	−1.6878	FBMC

Note. MS = Macroeconomic Stability; GIS = Government and Institutional Setting; FBMC = Financial, Businesses and Manpower Conditions; QLID = Quality of Life and Infrastructure Development
Source: Asia Competitiveness Institute

environment (seven indicators). Other indicators from Government and Institutional Setting that should be further leveraged are Rule of Law (#4), Provincial Governing Capacity (#5), and Regulatory Governance (#6). The other top 20% strongest indicators from Quality of Life and Infrastructure Development are Ease of Acquiring Property (#7) and Student-Teacher Ratio (Junior High) (#13).

The other strengths are related to Macroeconomic Stability such as Investment Promotion and Management (#11), GRDP Growth (#12), and relatively low inflation (#20). For Financial, Businesses, and Manpower Conditions environment, Sulawesi is particularly strong in Firms' Performance (#19) and Firms' Human Resources Capacity (#21).

The top 20% of weakest indicators are dominated by Quality of Life and Infrastructure Development environment (seven indicators). This environment also contributes an equal number of indicators in the top 20% of strongest indicators (Table 6.8). The weakest indicators include Non-Performing Loans per Total Bank Loans (#104), Crime Rate (#103), and Labour Force Participation Rate (#102); two of which are from Financial, Businesses and Manpower Conditions. These contribute to Sulawesi's poor performance ranking, as shown in Table 6.6. Even though the Government and Institutional Setting environment appears strong in Sulawesi Region, three out of the five indicators under Government Policies and Fiscal Sustainability sub-environment are listed in the top 20% of weakest indicators.

The three weakest indicators from Quality of Life and Infrastructure Development are Life Expectancy at Birth (#100), Gini Ratio (#97), and Cargo at Inter-island Seaport (#92). As economic development and competitiveness improve, the quality of life indicators will also improve. For Macroeconomic Stability, its three weakest indicators are Openness to Trade (#99), Exports (#96), and Exports of Non-oil and Gas (#94).

3. POLICY THEMES AND DEVELOPMENT STRATEGIES

3.1 Official Policies[8]

Sulawesi is highly endowed with vast natural resources, from food crops, horticulture, estate crops and fisheries, to nickel, oil and gas. These are essentially the main economic activities identified in the MP3EI. The region is a well-known trading hub for economic activities in the eastern part of Indonesia and is also home to many attractive tourist destinations.

Under the MP3EI, several policy recommendations have been outlined in order to accelerate the development in key sectors. In the context of agriculture, some policies in the pipeline include optimisation of land use, improvement in storage quality, and promoting empowerment and institutional capacity building and financing access for farmers. For cocoa, the policies are not only intended to improve productivity, sustainability and quality of cocoa beans, but also to produce processed and refined products that will be attractive for the export market.

Sulawesi has abundant maritime resources and as such, the MP3EI also assigns fishery as the champion sector to further develop fishery-based economy in capitalising on the large potential of aquaculture especially for high-value shrimp culture. Holistic efforts are put in place to ensure conducive environment for growing the fishery sector; from optimising supporting infrastructure, such us fishing ports, processing units and storage activities, to increasing industrial processing standard. With the newly launched Maritime Vision under the leadership of President Joko Widodo, more specific policies targeted at spearheading fishery sector will be in place.

The MP3EI also lists nickel as the main economic commodity as Sulawesi has the largest nickel reserves in Indonesia. The region is looking to simplify rules and bureaucracy while taking into account sustenance of ecosystems. The next step involves creating downstream industry to leap from mining to smelting and refining process.

Apart from those economic activities related to the key sectors, the central and local government have agreed to develop the infrastructure for Sulawesi Region, especially for those supporting Bitung and Palu SEZ. This includes building the capacity of respective ports and ensuring adequate electricity supply. In fact, a number of projects related to the development of power plant, substation and transmission network in all provinces are currently underway.

The National Medium-Term Development Plan (RPJMN 2010–2014) highlighted the need to develop a selection of highly competitive commodities through cross-sector and cross-province cooperation in management and marketing.[9] Sulawesi is designated to be the centre of agriculture and fisheries production, thus its role as the national food storage.

Following the MP3EI and RPJMN, each province has its own Medium-Term Development Plan (RPJMD) that outlines specific strategies over the next few years.[10]

In South Sulawesi, improving competitiveness is one of its key targets outlined in its RPJMD 2013–2018. It aims to increase cooperation among districts and cities, as well as regional cooperation with other provinces in Sulawesi and the eastern part of Indonesia. Additionally, the province is also committed to build conducive business environment and develop local innovation system to position South Sulawesi as the hub for goods and services in eastern Indonesia. Primary commodities listed in the MP3EI, such as cocoa and seaweed, also appear as

---

[8] At national level, Indonesia's development plan is documented in the 2005–2025 National Long-Term Development Plan (RPJPN 2005–2025). It was in the second phase of implementation under the 2010–2014 National Medium-Term Development Plan (RPJMN 2010–2014). Provincial governments must take into account the RPJMN 2010–2014 when formulating or adjusting their respective Provincial Medium-Term Development Plan (RPJMD) to reach national development targets. The MP3EI is not intended to replace RPJMN or the ongoing national and provincial development plans. It is a complementary working document for the abovementioned development plans aimed at accelerating and expanding economic development in Indonesia.

[9] Ministry of National Development and Planning Agency, *National Medium-Term Development Plan (RPJMN) 2010–2014* (Jakarta: Ministry of National Development and Planning Agency, 2010).

[10] Provincial Development and Planning Agency, *Medium-Term Development Plan (RPJMD) of various provinces across various time spans.*

the strategic commodities in RPJMD, illustrating the alignment between the development envisioned by the central and local government.

For North Sulawesi, its RPJMD also similarly encourages the stakeholders in the province to cooperate and collaborate in optimising its entire capacity to achieve prosperous North Sulawesi. The province has developed several clusters such as tourism, especially for MICE activities. This sector is not listed in the MP3EI but has been acknowledged as another economic activity that provides contribution to overall development of the region. North Sulawesi also plans to develop an integrated metropolitan area, covering the cities of Manado, Bitung and Tomohon. Manado is designated as the centre for government, trade and services while Bitung holds a more prominent role as the port centre, especially after it has been conferred an SEZ status.

Central Sulawesi's vision is to be on par with developed provinces in eastern Indonesia and to accelerate economic growth through high quality agribusiness and marine industries supported by competitive human resources. For agriculture, the local government focuses on seaweed as a major commodity by building several clusters and establishing the processing industry for seaweed.

West Sulawesi's main focus is to accelerate the economic growth and welfare of its people with development strategies that are pro-growth, pro-poor, pro-employment, pro-human development, and pro-environment. Its RPJMD 2011–2016 puts emphasis on expanding and improving the quality of infrastructure to support its key sectors such as agro-industry, palm oil, oil and gas, and minerals. West Sulawesi also iterates the importance of sustainable development and is committed to maintain and rehabilitate the protected area.

For Gorontalo, its vision is to accelerate equitable economic development in the province. In its mission, Gorontalo aims to develop potential cluster of fishery and agriculture, which is in alignment with the MP3EI theme for Sulawesi Region.

Southeast Sulawesi government envisages the province to be a prosperous, self-sufficient and competitive province. Kendari is identified as a hub for fishery sector, while other areas in the province are identified as nickel mining activity nodes and food estate hub, capitalising on the agriculture production. An "economic connecting lane" will also connect Kendari with Palu in Central Sulawesi, Makassar in South Sulawesi, and Mamuju in West Sulawesi.

In their RPJMD, all provinces have incorporated strategies to improve access and quality of education and health in order to ensure adequate human resources in supporting its growth trajectory. Local government revitalisation also becomes their strategic focus in promoting good governance.

3.2 Development Strategies

Given its stellar performance as the runner-up in Government and Institutional Setting environment, Sulawesi should leverage on its capable government to drive the acceleration of economic development in the region. South Sulawesi can be a good role model for other provinces as it has earned numerous accolades that affirm its good governance practice. This is vital as Gorontalo and Southeast Sulawesi are falling behind at 18th and 22nd place, respectively, in terms of governance. One way to build on this is to ensure that development plans across all layers of government — central, provincial, district and city — are in sync. With such committed and trusted local government, it will render the region attractive as an investment destination for both domestic and foreign investors. The government should also capitalise on their well-rounded capability to convince private sector to take part in Public-Private-Partnership (PPP) infrastructure projects.

The provinces within Sulawesi would benefit if the region enforces effective collaboration to create integrated framework of value chain for their key products. For example, industry clusters can be coordinated at the regional level based on provincial competitiveness. Other cities may act as processing centres that eventually transport these goods to Makassar or Manado to be shipped elsewhere.

By streamlining rule of law and regulation, the region can even create an integrated one-stop-service that will ease the process of starting and conducting businesses in the region. With this, the region can benefit from economies of scale and scope. Infrastructure plays a vital role to facilitate connectivity in this archipelago. This highlights the importance of seaports that have far been underdeveloped, as shown in the ACI's top 20% weakest indicators list (Table 6.9) that includes the low capacity of Cargo at International Seaport (#88) and Cargo at

Inter-Island Seaport (#92). The Governor of South Sulawesi has persistently urged the realisation of Makassar New Port to ease the congestion in Soekarno-Hatta Seaport. The increased capacity of seaports will facilitate and relieve the pressure from Tanjung Priok and Tanjung Perak Seaports that are located in Java Island. Infrastructure to connect the region by land is also imperative as an alternative means of transport. Repairing of damaged roads allows for better connection between farms and trading centres, which can enhance productivity level in agricultural sector.

To unleash Sulawesi's potential in agriculture, one alternative is to strengthen "Agropolitan". It is a bottom-up rural development strategy that encompasses "integration of agricultural and non-agricultural activities, physical and institutional support system, optimal use of resources, and development of local service centres as the interface between urban and metropolitan centres".[11] This primary sector is not inferior to others. With innovative approach, technology adoption and intensification of Research and Development (R&D), it is possible to increase productivity from this sector.

For the development of processing industry, the opportunities are abundant, especially after the central government granted Palu and Bitung the SEZ status. At the initial stage, the Coordinating Ministry for Economic Affairs had recorded a number of domestic and foreign investors from various sectors, such as nickel processing, automotive, and property, who were keen to set up their production in the SEZs. The region should capture this opportunity to further promote downstream industries for its raw materials. At the same time, knowledge and technology transfer, as well as involvement of small and medium–sized enterprises (SMEs) should take place to ensure that the benefits are shared locally. The capital-intensive sector will further enhance the Secondary Industry Productivity (#93), which is currently listed as one of the weaknesses (Table 6.9).

Simultaneously, the region has to strengthen its human resources to ensure that the rapid growth of secondary sector is supported by a capable and skilled workforce. Enhancing vocational track is one strategy that can be taken up by the private sector. A notable example is from Astra, which established its own vocational institute, *Politeknik Manufaktur Astra*. Additionally, the private sector can collaborate with the existing vocational schools, by contributing curriculum and equipment, to ensure that the students are equipped with the relevant skills required in the industry. Vocational training centre (BLK) also plays a pivotal role in re-training the existing workforce to cope with more advanced technology. This prepares the workforce for any structural change in the industry composition in the region.

Sustainability should not be neglected as the region gears up for rapid industrial growth. The RPJMN, as echoed by the provincial plans, also underlined policies to maintain and rehabilitate conservation areas for, at least, 40% of the total area of Sulawesi Island. All economic activities should abide to environmental laws. This includes upholding moratorium for forest concessions. Currently, there are a number of sites in Sulawesi that have been assigned as Key Biodiversity Area (KBA). This identification is important to address biodiversity conservation at the site scale. The government plays an important role in ensuring that these areas are preserved to protect the livelihood of diverse flora and fauna. In addition, the region has to ensure comprehensive environmental impact assessment to avoid the trade-off between industrial growth and environmental damage.

The provinces in the region also envision equitable growth that is pro-poor. According to the ACI's strength and weakness analysis, the region has a relatively high Gini Ratio (#97) and low Life Expectancy at Birth (#100). These can be addressed by promoting equal access to good quality education and health through provision of scholarship and affordable health coverage for the poor. The region should also ensure that each locality is equipped with sufficient number of schools and health centres, as well as teachers and medical staff.

Overall, Sulawesi Region has what it takes to be the hub for the eastern part of Indonesia and play an active role in the national economic development. Not only is the region endowed with vast natural resources and scenic destinations, it has also grown to be an exemplary model for good governance. As such, the government is capable to drive the economic development and attract private sectors to partake in the development of various industries. A committed and trustworthy government can further pave the way for Sulawesi to continuously increase its competitiveness.

---

[11] A. Buang *et al.*, "The Agropolitan Way of Re-Empowering the Rural Poor", *World Applied Sciences Journal (Special Issue of Human Dimensions of Development)* Vol. 13 (2011): 01–06.

REFERENCES

Buang, A., A. Habibah, J. Hamzah, and Y.S. Ratnawati. "The Agropolitan Way of Re-Empowering the Rural Poor". *World Applied Sciences Journal (Special Issue of Human Dimensions of Development)* Vol. 13 (2011): 01–06.

Coordinating Ministry for Economic Affairs. *Master Plan for Acceleration and Expansion of Indonesia's Economic Development 2011–2025 (MP3EI).* Jakarta: Coordinating Ministry for Economic Affairs, 2011.

Ministry of National Development and Planning Agency. *National Medium-Term Development Plan (RPJMN) 2010–2014.* Jakarta: Ministry of National Development and Planning Agency, 2010.

Organisation for Economic Cooperation and Development (OECD). "Structural Policy Country Notes: Indonesia." In *Southeast Asian Economic Outlook 2013: With Perspectives on China and India.* OECD Publishing, 2013.

Provincial Development and Planning Agency. *Medium-Term Development Plan (RPJMD) of various provinces across various time spans.*

PT PLN. *Statistik PLN 2012.* Jakarta: PLN, 2012.

Tan, Khee Giap, and Mulya Amri. "Subnational Competitiveness and National Performance: Analysis and Simulation for Indonesia." *Journal of Centrum Cathedra (JCC): The Business and Economics Research Journal* Vol. 6, No. 2 (2013): 173–192.

Tan, Khee Giap, Mulya Amri, Linda Low, and Tan Kong Yam. *Competitiveness Analysis and Development Strategies for 33 Indonesian Provinces.* Singapore: World Scientific, 2013.

Chapter 7
Competitiveness Analysis on the Bali–Nusa Tenggara Region

Bali, West Nusa Tenggara, and East Nusa Tenggara

1. INTRODUCTION

1.1 Background and Notes

Figure 7.1 shows the provinces in Bali–Nusa Tenggara Region as defined by the Master Plan for Acceleration and Expansion of Indonesia's Economic Development 2011–2025 (MP3EI).[1] The three provinces with their respective capital cities are Bali (Denpasar), West Nusa Tenggara (Mataram), and East Nusa Tenggara (Kupang). Altogether, the three islands cover an area of 73,070.48 km^2. Geographically, the region is bordered by the island of Java on the west, Java Sea on the north, Indian Ocean on the south, and the Democratic Republic of Timor-Leste on the east.

From Figure 7.1, inset map (top right) shows the competitiveness ranking by the Asia Competitiveness Institute (ACI) using the traffic light scheme with green representing the Top 10 provinces, followed by the 13 middle-ranking provinces in yellow and the remaining provinces with lower competitiveness in red. Bali and West Nusa Tenggara are part of the middle-ranking provinces, ranked 14th and 22nd, respectively. East Nusa Tenggara falls behind at 32nd place.[2]

The three islands have their own unique characteristics. Historically, Bali has been largely influenced by the Hindu culture and tradition. Its unique cultural heritage and its scenic beaches mark Bali as a major international tourism attraction. West Nusa Tenggara, on the other hand, is strongly influenced by Islam; more than 90% of its population are Muslim. Besides the pristine beaches, there are Mount Rinjani National Park and Segara Anak Lake that draw tourists into the province. By contrast, East Nusa Tenggara's population is predominantly Christian. One of its most attractive tourist destinations is Komodo National Park, a home for the endangered giant lizard Komodo.

According to the MP3EI, the development theme for Bali–Nusa Tenggara Economic Corridor is "Gateway for Tourism and National Food Support." The corridor comprises four major economic centres, namely Denpasar, Lombok Island, Mataram, and Kupang. Given that the major strength of this region is its outstanding environmental quality, the emphasis on key sectors of tourism, fishery, and animal husbandry is well aligned.[3]

Despite its relatively close proximity to Java as the most economically advanced region in Indonesia, Bali–Nusa Tenggara Region faces low investment level, either from foreign or domestic investors, when compared to other regions. The region is also associated with high income disparity and sat at the bottom of Human Development Index (HDI) in 2011 as indicated by West Nusa Tenggara's (32nd) and East Nusa Tenggara (31st) ranks. The gap between Bali and Nusa Tenggara was also pertinent in terms of unequal poverty rate, with 4.59% for Bali, 19.67% for West Nusa Tenggara and 20.48% for East Nusa Tenggara in 2011. The uneven ratio must be addressed for the region to achieve its role as designated by the MP3EI.

---

[1] Coordinating Ministry for Economic Affairs, *Master Plan for Acceleration and Expansion of Indonesia's Economic Development 2011–2025 (MP3EI)* (Jakarta: Coordinating Ministry for Economic Affairs, 2011).

[2] See Tan Khee Giap et al., *Competitiveness Analysis and Development Strategies for 33 Indonesian provinces* (Singapore: World Scientific, 2013) and Tan Khee Giap and Mulya Amri, "Subnational Competitiveness and National Performance: Analysis and Simulation for Indonesia," *Journal of Centrum Cathedra (JCC): The Business and Economics Research Journal* Vol.6, No. 2 (2013):173–192 that mark the first attempt to rank provinces based on their competitiveness level.

[3] As seen from the favourable score of Environment Quality Index as part of Quality of Life and Infrastructure Development environment in ACI's Competitiveness Framework, which is an aggregate index of air pollution, water pollution, and forest coverage.

Figure 7.1. Map of Bali–Nusa Tenggara Region

Source: Asia Competitiveness Institute

Table 7.1 shows that Bali–Nusa Tenggara's economic composition is dominated by the tertiary sector (55.14%). The Gross Regional Domestic Product (GRDP) per capita also increased from 4.00 million Rupiah in 2006 to 4.77 million Rupiah in 2011.

1.2 Major Sectors and Activities

Both Table 7.1 and Table 7.2 illustrate the importance of agriculture, fishery, and animal husbandry. In Bali, agriculture and fishery made up the bulk of primary economic activities, contributing to almost 20% of the island's GRDP as of 2011; whereas in East Nusa Tenggara, animal husbandry and agriculture contributed to approximately 38% of the province's GRDP in 2011. Seaweed is another potential commodity that has yet to be fully tapped in East Nusa Tenggara, as the province possesses vast suitable areas for such industry. For West Nusa Tenggara, aside from the quite robust activities in animal husbandry and agriculture, mining is also an important pillar that greatly contributes to its export earnings. When the New Mining Law that bans the export of unprocessed minerals became effective on 12 January 2014, it has adversely affected mining contribution to the province's income. The law aims to boost downstream higher value-added activities that create better jobs and prospects.

The secondary sector in Bali–Nusa Tenggara Region remains underdeveloped. In Bali, manufacturing activities are generally discouraged to maintain the environmental quality of the island, except for small-scale manufacturing activities such as food processing and garment production. Hence, the secondary sector only contributed to approximately 15% of the province's GRDP in 2011. The secondary sector in East Nusa Tenggara was also relatively low and only contributed to approximately 9% of the GRDP. This includes food and beverages industry, textile, furniture, and other small and medium-sized enterprises (SMEs). This also applies to West Nusa Tenggara, which needs economic restructuring in order to increase its competitiveness, particularly for the meat processing industry.

The tertiary sector was the most dominant sector in Bali–Nusa Tenggara Region, especially in Bali and East Nusa Tenggara, which contributed to 66.35% and 52.69% of the GRDP, respectively, in 2011. Hotels and tourism industry in both provinces serve as the main economic catalyst for growth. Apart from the scenic beaches, beautiful oceans and reefs for ecotourism, cultural tourism also serves as this region's specialty.

Table 7.1. Bali–Nusa Tenggara Region: Basic Economic Indicators

A. Population	**2006**	**2011**
Total population	12,027,468	13,293,476
% urban	34.32	39.21
B. Area		**2011**
Km^2		73,070.48
% equivalent to country		3.82
C. Gross Regional Domestic Product (GRDP)	**2006**	**2011**
Rupiah (million)	48,156,959	63,435,700
Rupiah (million) without oil & gas	48,156,959	63,435,700
Rupiah (million) without oil & gas & mineral	44,400,328	58,681,817
D. Economic composition, as % GRDP	**2006**	**2011**
Primary sector	37.37	32.01
Secondary sector	12.01	12.85
Tertiary sector	50.61	55.14
E. GRDP per capita	**2006**	**2011**
Rupiah (million)	4.00	4.77
Rupiah (million) without oil & gas	4.00	4.77
Rupiah (million) without oil & gas & mineral	3.69	4.41
F. Poverty Rate	**2006**	**2011**
% of population	22.21	15.46
G. Human Development Index	**2006**	**2011**
Index	65.69	68.75

GRDP based on 2000 Constant Price
Source: Asia Competitiveness Institute using data from Indonesia Statistical Yearbook

Table 7.2. Major Products and Activities

Primary	Animal husbandry, food crops (corn and rice), fishery, and mining (copper, gold, silver, and iron sand)
Secondary	Handicrafts, food processing, textile, and furniture
Tertiary	Tourism, restaurant, hotel, trade, and services

Source: Asia Competitiveness Institute

1.3 Infrastructure Provision

The provision of sound infrastructure is one key agenda outlined in the MP3EI to enable the acceleration of Bali–Nusa Tenggara's economic growth. As part of the MP3EI landmark projects, the 12.7 km-long toll road construction that connects Nusa Dua–Ngurah Rai–Tanjung Benoa had been completed in only 14 months and was widely regarded as a success. The toll road is called 'Bali Mandara' and is aimed for mitigating the overly congested traffic of Nusa Dua–Ngurah Rai route, thereby improving tourism development in Bali.

There are two international airports in this region, namely Ngurah Rai International Airport in Bali and Lombok International Airport in West Nusa Tenggara. With almost 40% of international air traffic arrivals in Indonesia destined for Bali, a major expansion had been undertaken in Ngurah Rai International Airport to significantly increase the capacity of the airport in accommodating flights and passengers.

As an archipelagic region, sea transportation plays an important role in connecting the islands. In Bali, on top of the three ferry or passenger ports, the province also has two container ports in Benoa in the south and Celukan Bawang in the north. For West Nusa Tenggara, there are three major seaports, namely Lembar, Badas and Bima Ports, with the former having the biggest capacity. Meanwhile, East Nusa Tenggara has one international seaport of Tenau in Kupang and several national ports such as Wini in the district of Central Timor, Larantuka in East Flores, and Labuan Bajo in West Manggarai.

The region has acknowledged the importance of increasing its electricity supply as consumption is expected to rise in line with the number of projects developing in the pipeline. Some efforts to boost electricity supply have been undertaken in Bali. The construction of Java-Bali underwater cable, Celukan Bawang power plant and Bali Crossing project for high voltage electricity transmission will significantly increase the much-needed electricity supply.

2. RELATIVE COMPETITIVENESS OF REGIONS

The competitiveness framework for the region follows the same approach with the provincial competitiveness, as explained in Chapter 1 in greater detail. Further explanation on the aggregation of individual province's indicators into regional scores can be found in Chapter 2.

2.1 Competitiveness Ranking of Six Regions — Rank and Score by Environment[4]

Table 7.3. 2014 Overall Competitiveness: Ranking and Score

Rank	Region	Score
1	Java Region	1.7233
2	Kalimantan Region	0.6511
3	Sulawesi Region	–0.0392
4	Sumatra Region	–0.0741
5	*Bali–Nusa Tenggara Region*	*–0.9839*
6	Maluku–Papua Region	–1.2772

Source: Asia Competitiveness Institute

As seen from Table 7.3, Bali–Nusa Tenggara Region is ranked fifth for Overall Competitiveness, with a score of –0.9839 that is slightly better than Maluku–Papua Region at the bottom (–1.2772). Individually, the three provinces have diverse performance with Bali at 14th, West Nusa Tenggara at 22nd and East Nusa Tenggara close to the bottom rank (32nd). Nevertheless, all of their scores are negative, meaning that their performances remain below the national average.

The gap in score between Bali–Nusa Tenggara Region and Sumatra Region is wider than that of Maluku–Papua Region. It will be harder for Bali–Nusa Tenggara to surpass Sumatra.

A well-planned strategy and carefully concerted implementation are required if the region wants to improve its score and climb up from the presently near-bottom position to a more secured and competitive place in the ACI's ranking.

[4]Results for the 2014 competitiveness study are based on official data in 2011 and survey data collected in 2013. Conventionally due to collation, compilation, and publication of official data, such a lag of data before reaching end-users is acceptable.

Table 7.4. 2014 Macroeconomic Stability: Ranking and Score

Rank	Region	Score
1	Java Region	2.0461
2	Sumatra Region	0.1112
3	Kalimantan Region	0.0350
4	Sulawesi Region	–0.3896
5	Maluku–Papua Region	–0.7943
6	*Bali–Nusa Tenggara Region*	*–1.0085*

Source: Asia Competitiveness Institute

However, Bali–Nusa Tenggara Region scores even lower than Maluku–Papua Region and Sulawesi Region, being the last in rank for Macroeconomic Stability with a score of –1.0085 (Table 7.4).

Bali–Nusa Tenggara's low rank in this particular environment can be attributed to the fact that two of the provinces in this region, West Nusa Tenggara and East Nusa Tenggara, stand at the Bottom 10 in the Macroeconomic Stability Ranking of the 33 provinces (27th and 33rd, respectively), while Bali is only at the 18th position.

As the disparity in score between Bali–Nusa Tenggara with Maluku–Papua is not large, Bali–Nusa Tenggara should be able to be on par or better than Maluku-Papua through greater efforts in comprehensive development strategy and implementation.

Table 7.5. 2014 Government and Institutional Setting: Ranking and Score

Rank	Region	Score
1	Java Region	1.4124
2	Sulawesi Region	0.7733
3	Kalimantan Region	0.5582
4	Sumatra Region	–0.4219
5	*Bali–Nusa Tenggara Region*	*–0.8284*
6	Maluku–Papua Region	–1.4937

Source: Asia Competitiveness Institute

It can be seen from Table 7.5 that Bali–Nusa Tenggara Region is at the fifth place (–0.8284) in Government and Institutional Setting. This is also reflected from the provincial ranking where West Nusa Tenggara ranks 15th, Bali and East Nusa Tenggara rank 24th and 32nd, respectively.

While it may be possible to catch up to Sumatra's position (fourth), Bali–Nusa Tenggara will most likely struggle to climb up to higher ranking. This is because the disparity in score between Bali–Nusa Tenggara Region and Kalimantan Region (third) is considerably wide.

Table 7.6. 2014 Financial, Businesses and Manpower Conditions: Ranking and Score

Rank	Region	Score
1	Java Region	1.6700
2	Kalimantan Region	1.0027
3	Maluku–Papua Region	–0.3552
4	Sumatra Region	–0.3940
5	Sulawesi Region	–0.7693
6	*Bali–Nusa Tenggara Region*	*–1.1543*

Source: Asia Competitiveness Institute

For Financial, Businesses and Manpower Conditions environment, Bali–Nusa Tenggara Region ranks last with a score of –1.1543 (Table 7.6). There is a big difference in score with Sulawesi Region (–0.7693), which makes it difficult to catch up.

To move up the ladder, each individual province has to significantly improve. Bali and West Nusa Tenggara only rank 17th and 20th, respectively, while East Nusa Tenggara is at the lower-end (29th) in the provincial ranking.

Table 7.7. 2014 Quality of Life and Infrastructure Development: Ranking and Score

Rank	Region	Score
1	Java Region	1.0603
2	Kalimantan Region	0.7425
3	Sumatra Region	0.4385
4	Sulawesi Region	0.2448
5	*Bali–Nusa Tenggara Region*	*–0.5423*
6	Maluku–Papua Region	–1.9438

Source: Asia Competitiveness Institute

For Quality of Life and Infrastructure Development, Bali–Nusa Tenggara scores –0.5423 and holds fifth in rank (Table 7.7). Despite Bali's stellar performance at the provincial level (ranked eighth), the region's score is pulled down by West Nusa Tenggara and East Nusa Tenggara, which are at the Bottom 10 (ranked 26th and 32nd, respectively).

At the current place, Bali–Nusa Tenggara is well above Maluku–Papua. However, the region needs to exert significant efforts if it seeks to catch up to Sulawesi. Augmenting information and communications technology (ICT) is a feasible strategy as it will not only upgrade Bali–Nusa Tenggara's standing in this environment, but also give a multiplier effect of enhancing productivity performance.

2.2 Analysis of Median and Maximum Competitiveness Webs

To better understand Bali–Nusa Tenggara's relative strengths and weaknesses, it is useful to compare and contrast its attainment against the median and the maximum scores of Indonesia's six regions for the 12 sub-environments. The median competitiveness web plots Bali–Nusa Tenggara's attained scores for each of the 12 sub-environments.

In Figure 7.2, the median scores for all the regions are shown in dashed line, while the scores for Bali–Nusa Tenggara are in solid line.

Bali–Nusa Tenggara's scores in all sub-environments are below the median. This reflects Bali–Nusa Tenggara's fifth position in Overall Competitiveness ranking. The sub-environments in which Bali–Nusa Tenggara score slightly below the median are Standard of Living, Education and Social Stability; Labour Market Flexibility; Institutions, Governance and Leadership; Government Policies and Fiscal Sustainability; and Attractiveness to Foreign Investors. On the other hand, Bali–Nusa Tenggara scores are considerably lower than

Figure 7.2. 2014 Median Competitiveness Web Analysis for Bali–Nusa Tenggara Region

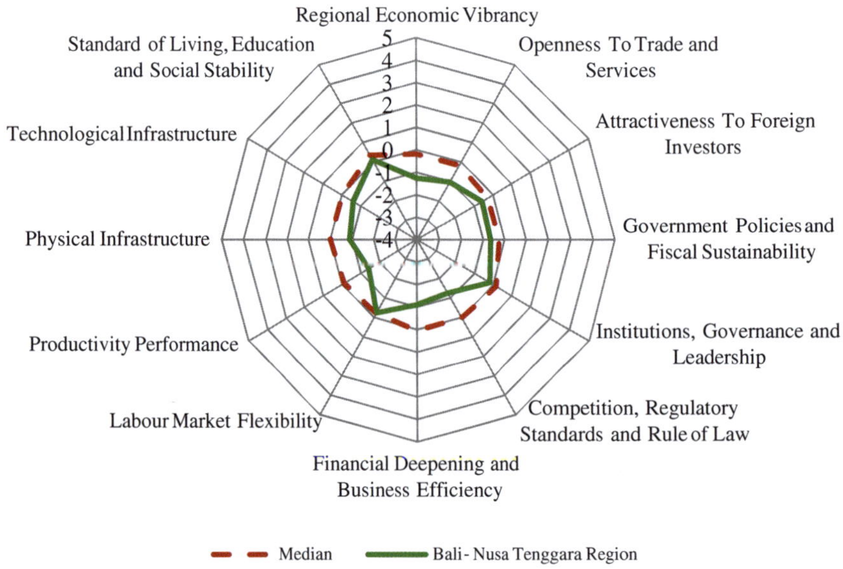

Source: Asia Competitiveness Institute

Figure 7.3. 2014 Maximum Competitiveness Web Analysis for Bali–Nusa Tenggara Region

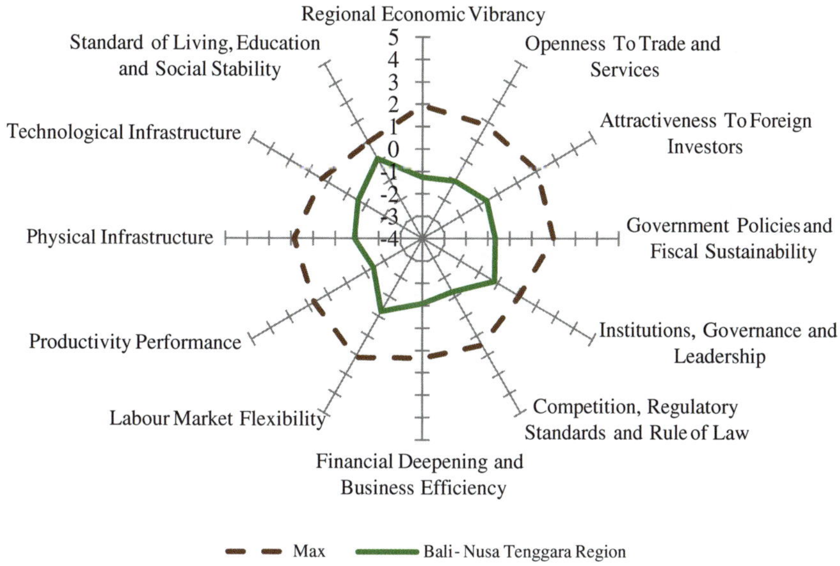

Source: Asia Competitiveness Institute

other regions, especially in two sub-environments: Competition, Regulatory Standards and Rule of Law, and Productivity Performance.

The maximum competitiveness web (Figure 7.3) shows how far the best score for each sub-environment is, in relation to Bali–Nusa Tenggara Region's scores. The maximum scores for the six regions are shown in dashed line, while the scores for Bali–Nusa Tenggara are shown in solid line.

All of Bali–Nusa Tenggara's 12 sub-environments are still lower than the national maximum score. The main sub-environments where Bali's score are relatively close to the maximum score are Standard of Living, Education and Social Stability, and Institutions, Governance and Leadership. Two notable sub-environments where the region is further behind are Regional Economic Vibrancy and Productivity Performance, implying that the region has to address the bottlenecks in these two sub-environments to improve its competitiveness.

2.3 Analysis of Strength and Weakness

Tables 7.8 and 7.9 respectively show the strongest and weakest indicators of Bali–Nusa Tenggara Region. Table 7.8 shows the region's top 20% or 21 strongest indicators out of a total of 104 indicators, in descending order. Table 7.9 shows the top 20% of weakest indicators in ascending order.[5]

Based on Table 7.8, most of Bali–Nusa Tenggara Region's top 20% strengths come from indicators related to the Quality of Life and Infrastructure Development environment (total of 12 indicators). They include Population per Health Facility (#3), Senior High School Enrollment Rate (#4), Households with pipe water services (#5), Junior High School Enrollment Rate (#6), and Environmental Quality Index (#8).

Three other environments also contribute to Bali–Nusa Tenggara's strengths. At the top of the strengths list is the Corruption Perception Index (#1), followed by Crime Rate (#13) and Tax Revenue/Government Revenue

[5]These 21 strongest and 21 weakest indicators are obtained by sorting all of the 104 indicators' scores that the region received, from the highest to the lowest. Those that appear on the top 21 are identified as the region's strengths, and those that appear at the bottom 21 are identified as the region's weaknesses. The comparison is done relatively among the indicator scores of said region, without comparing to the indicator scores of other regions.

Table 7.8. 2014 Top 20% Strongest Indicators List for Bali–Nusa Tenggara Region

Rank	20% Strongest Indicator	Score	Environment
1	Corruption Perception Index	2.0077	GIS
2	Unemployment Rate	1.8546	FBMC
3	Population Per Health Facility	1.5689	QLID
4	School Enrollment Rate (Senior High)	1.2822	QLID
5	Households with pipe water services	1.2358	QLID
6	School Enrollment Rate (Junior High)	1.1486	QLID
7	Non-Performing Loans per Total Bank Loans	1.0103	FBMC
8	Environmental Quality Index	1.0028	QLID
9	Firms' Application of IT	0.7408	FBMC
10	Minimum Wage Per Month	0.7011	FBMC
11	Non-Performing Loans	0.5513	FBMC
12	Passengers of International Air Traffic	0.5446	QLID
13	Crime Rate	0.4754	GIS
14	Population Per Medical Worker	0.4125	QLID
15	Gini Ratio	0.4111	QLID
16	School Enrollment Rate (Primary)	0.3693	QLID
17	Student-Teacher Ratio (Senior High)	0.3658	QLID
18	Labour Force Participation Rate	0.3245	FBMC
19	Student-Teacher Ratio (Junior High)	0.2828	QLID
20	Fatalities due to Natural Disaster	0.2770	QLID
21	Tax Revenue/Government Revenue	0.2302	GIS

Note: MS = Macroeconomic Stability; GIS = Government and Institutional Setting; FBMC = Financial, Businesses and Manpower Conditions; QLID = Quality of Life and Infrastructure Development
Source: Asia Competitiveness Institute

(#21), which are part of the Government and Institutional Settings environment. Unemployment Rate (#2), Rate of Non-Performing Loans per Total Bank Loans (#7) and Firms' Application of IT (#9) are from the Financial, Businesses and Manpower Conditions environment.

In Table 7.9, Bali–Nusa Tenggara Region's weaknesses come from all four environments. The primary weakness is the problem in Ease of Dealing with Banks (#104), which is under Financial, Businesses and Manpower Conditions environment. Labour Relations (#100), Secondary Industry Productivity (#101), Overall Labour Productivity (#97), and Overall Labour Productivity, Non-oil & gas (#98) are also some of the notable weaknesses in this environment.

Indicators related to governance also feature in the top 20% of weakest indicators, including Vibrancy of Competition and Collaboration (#103) and Government Efficiency (#90). Similarly, many indicators from the Quality of Life and Infrastructure Development are part of the weaknesses. These include Life Expectancy at Birth (#95), Human Development Index (#93), Mean Years of Schooling (#91), and Ease of Acquiring Property (#88). Indicators from Macroeconomic Stability environment as weaknesses include relatively low GRDP Growth (#102), higher Inflation (#99), and a lower degree of Openness to Trade (#96).

Table 7.9. Top 20% Weakest Indicators List for Bali–Nusa Tenggara Region

Rank	20% Weakest Indicator	Score	Environment
84	GRDP of Primary Industry	−1.0071	MS
85	Exports	−1.0112	MS
86	Tertiary Industry Productivity	−1.0319	FBMC
87	Internet Access in Handphone	−1.0420	QLID
88	Ease of Acquiring Property	−1.1749	QLID
89	Firms' Human Resource Capacity	−1.1815	FBMC
90	Government Efficiency	−1.1947	GIS
91	Mean Years of Schooling	−1.2211	QLID
92	GRDP Per Capita	−1.2302	MS
93	Human Development Index	−1.2310	QLID
94	GRDP Per Capita, Non-oil & gas	−1.2442	MS
95	Life Expectancy at Birth	−1.2653	QLID
96	Openness To Trade	−1.3149	MS
97	Overall Labour Productivity	−1.3390	FBMC
98	Overall Labour Productivity, Non-oil & gas	−1.3629	FBMC
99	Inflation	−1.4324	MS
100	Labour Relations	−1.4486	FBMC
101	Secondary Industry Productivity	−1.5052	FBMC
102	GRDP Growth	−1.8188	MS
103	Vibrancy of Competition and Collaboration	−1.8858	GIS
104	Ease of Dealing With Banks	−2.0767	FBMC

Note: MS = Macroeconomic Stability; GIS = Government and Institutional Setting; FBMC = Financial, Businesses and Manpower Conditions; QLID = Quality of Life and Infrastructure Development
Source: Asia Competitiveness Institute

3. POLICY THEMES AND DEVELOPMENT STRATEGIES

3.1 Official Policies[6]

Bali–Nusa Tenggara Region, as envisioned by the MP3EI as the "Gateway for Tourism and National Food Support", focuses at three main economic activities with strong competitive edge — tourism, fisheries, and animal husbandry. Bali is still Indonesia's centrepiece for tourism as 36% of 8.04 million foreign tourists in 2012 arrived through Bali, in contrast to the negligible percentage of arrival in Lombok International Airport (West Nusa Tenggara). Ngurah Rai airport has seen a 12.9% increase in cumulative passengers, from 3.76 million to 4.24 million in 2013.

The MP3EI has identified projects specifically catered to boost the region's tourism sector. The development of Bali International Park has been swift with more than 80% of the project has been completed. This project is expected to elevate the island through an integrated tourism area that supports arts, culture, industry, and sustainable community. The Mandalika Integrated Resort, which is another major investment project in West Nusa

[6]At national level, Indonesia's development plan is documented in the 2005–2025 National Long-Term Development Plan (RPJPN 2005–2025). It was in the second phase of implementation under the 2010–2014 National Medium-Term Development Plan (RPJMN 2010–2014). Provincial governments must take into account the RPJMN 2010–2014 when formulating or adjusting their respective Provincial Medium-Term Development Plan (RPJMD) to reach national development targets. The MP3EI is not intended to replace RPJMN or the ongoing national and provincial development plans. It is a complementary working document for the above-mentioned development plans aimed at accelerating and expanding economic development in Indonesia.

Tenggara, faces several strategic issues such as land clearing and the issuance of environmental impact assessment documents (AMDAL) that need to be resolved before further development can take place.[7]

The MP3EI is a comprehensive plan that also encompasses the areas of security, promotion and marketing, governance, and connectivity. A safe and secure environment for tourists is paramount, considering previous incidents in Bali and West Nusa Tenggara.

Promotion and marketing strategies and activities tailored to suit different target markets will help brand Bali–Nusa Tenggara as a leading world-class destination as it goes head-to-head against other tourist attractions in Southeast Asia. Strategies to empower the tourism board in marketing and promotion and increase the awareness of locals to strengthen environmental standards, expanding public services in transportation, electricity, and communication facilities will help with the objective to increase length of stay and hence tourists' spending. Finally, connectivity between Bali–Nusa Tenggara and neighbouring provinces is as important to create a holistic "Bali and Beyond" tourism experience. This supports the MP3EI's objective for this region as a gateway for tourism in Indonesia.

Fishery, as another main economic activity of Bali–Nusa Tenggara Region, is a great potential yet underexploited, especially in Nusa Tenggara area. Of the approximately 25,000 ha of area with potential for pearls, only 7% were effectively utilised in 2008. Similarly for seaweed, only 30% out of approximately 20,000 ha of potential area were exploited. Likewise, marine fishery has a potential of around 2,000 ha area but only 30% of which has been effectively exploited. Policymakers need to develop further actions to improve such an important sector for Nusa Tenggara as it contributes to 73% of its export.

Strategic initiatives to boost fishery sector in the region have been proposed under the MP3EI. Among those, the most important is the establishment of fisheries-related infrastructure, such as seed centres, ponds, and training centres, aimed to upgrade the capacity and capability of the fishery sector. The infusion of technology and industrial know-how will also support the production of high value-added processed fishery such as frozen fish, canned fish, fish meal processing, and seaweed flour processing.

The MP3EI outlines and supports high value-added fishery industry within industrial clusters and this can establish further foreign cooperation and marketing of these products. Another interesting initiative is the plan to establish salt-producing Minapolitan region in East Nusa Tenggara given the province's extensive land suitable for salt production. The plan is aimed at increasing national salt production, which currently faces shortages and is partly eased by importing salt. As of 2011, the provincial government has prepared 9000 ha of land to support this project with the involvement of both foreign and domestic investors.[8]

Another main economic activity for Bali–Nusa Tenggara Region is animal husbandry, particularly beef cattle that also provides derivative products such as milk, leather, natural fertilisers, and biogas. The general acceleration strategies in this particular field include creating conducive farm business climate, increasing productivity of cattle to achieve self-sufficiency in meat, increasing downstream as well as regulatory and institutional farms, and strengthening infrastructure. Focus will be given on the development of beef processing industries such as bone meal, leather, organic fertiliser, and biogas industries. These products are consumed locally with high export potential.

In the provincial context, each province's Medium Term Development Plan (RPJMD) generally complements each other and is broadly aligned with the MP3EI.[9] Bali's RPJMD 2008–2013, for example, proposed a mission to increase prosperity through, among others, intensifying tourism while at the same time preserving the environment and culture. Improving inter-religious and inter-community tolerance was identified as one of the strategies to create a safe and secure environment needed for growth. Much like the MP3EI, the development

[7] Committee for the Acceleration and Expansion of Indonesia's Economic Development (KP3EI), *Laporan Perkembangan Pelaksanaan MP3EI s.d. Maret 2013* (Jakarta: Coordinating Ministry for Economic Affairs, 2013), pp. 39–41.

[8] Ade Marboen, "NTT siapkan 9000 hektar padang garam", *Antara News*, September 26, 2011, retrieved on June 24, 2014, <http://www.antaranews.com/berita/277166/ntt-siapkan-9000-hektare-padang-garam>.

[9] Provincial Development and Planning Agency, *Medium-Term Development Plan (RPJMD) of various provinces across various time spans.*

plan also stressed the importance of sound infrastructure and facilities in accelerating this growth, particularly in tourism sector.

On the other hand, in conjunction with the MP3EI's identification of animal husbandry and fishery as the lead sectors of growth in this region, West Nusa Tenggara champions three prime commodities — cow, corn and seaweed — in its development plan. In fact, the province has targeted a population of one million cows through the 'Land of One Million Cows' programme. Tourism development is also given a high priority with Mandalika Resort mega-project being fully supported by the provincial government. Lastly, the development plan also stresses the importance of nurturing human capital as a source of competitive advantage and support growth in all of these sectors.

East Nusa Tenggara in its RPJMD 2013–2018 also follows the spirit of the MP3EI in stressing the importance of tourism, animal husbandry, and fishery as the lead engines of growth. To support its aspiration in developing fishery, the province has boldly designated itself as the 'Marine and Fishery Province' and set a number of strategies to attain this goal. These include, among others, marketing programmes for fisheries products and technical guidance for fishermen. Tourism development is placed in the broader context of economic growth and includes strategies such as scaling-up promotion, investment cooperation and developing tourists' destination.

As infrastructure upgrading is a core mission of the MP3EI, it lists down several major projects for Bali–Nusa Tenggara Region. These include development of railways in Bali, water transmission network and water intake in Guyangan Klungkung spring in Bali, improvement of fiber optic coverage in the metro region and the deployment of base stations in Bali–Nusa Tenggara, and Bangau-Dompu-Ramba-Labuan Bajo road improvement (159.25 km) in East Nusa Tenggara.

The Bali railway project has captured much attention as it was initially intended to support tourism and economic development, and also mitigate the increasing traffic congestion on the island. The railway was planned to be 560 km long, encircling Bali and connecting the capital city of the province, Denpasar, in the south with the other districts. However, the result of the feasibility studies conducted by the Indonesian Railway Corporation (PT KAI) in 2012 demonstrated that the project was still not economically feasible and therefore had to be postponed.

3.2 Development Strategies

It is clearly stipulated that the MP3EI is not meant to substitute the existing development strategy plans at the national level, which include the National Medium-Term Development Plan (RPJMN) and National Long-Term Development Plan (RPJPN). The MP3EI remains an integral part of the national development planning system. As such, greater streamlining efforts between these development plans need to be conducted if the objectives and vision of the MP3EI are to be achieved.

Under RPJMN 2010–2014, the conventional 'Java-Bali' mindset still prevailed.[10] The strategy to develop Bali–Nusa Tenggara as one single region was still sidelined as East Nusa Tenggara and West Nusa Tenggara were often treated as separate entities from Bali in terms of developmental strategy. Moreover, while the development plan endorsed tourism, fisheries and animal husbandry for Nusa Tenggara region, it put heavier emphasis on manufacturing and services industry for Java-Bali area. Nevertheless, it also conveyed the sustainability philosophy and preservation of cultural heritage in Bali, which is also advocated by the MP3EI. These inform us that greater streamlining efforts to align all national development planning strategies are necessary if the objectives of the MP3EI are to be met, especially as events and conditions are ever changing. All relevant players at the national and local levels should also be resilient in ensuring the implementation of all projects while being sensitive to the dynamics of the plan.

The ACI's analysis, particularly the strength and weakness analysis, has direct policy implications for Bali–Nusa Tenggara. Among the most crucial weaknesses are those related to Financial, Businesses and Manpower

---

[10] Ministry of National Development and Planning Agency. *National Medium-Term Development Plan (RPJMN) 2010–2014* (Jakarta: Ministry of National Development and Planning Agency, 2010).

Conditions as they may hamper accelerated economic growth in the region. They can also negatively affect other environments such as Macroeconomic Stability, particularly in relation to GRDP per capita and GRDP growth. Issues in financing and productivity at the secondary and tertiary sectors, as well as the capacity of human resources must be dealt with accordingly. Preserving the region's strengths as identified is crucial.

With regard to financing, for example, dealing with banks is still not easily accomplished within the region and is especially prevalent in Bali. The extremely low standardised score in this indicator may in turn affect business owners to resort to other channels that offer non-competitive rates, which may even increase the likelihood of default.

To facilitate development in the tertiary sector, especially as a hub for tourism, ease in access to financing is an integral part of efforts to create conducive business environment. To mitigate the problem, intensive communication and coordination between business owners and banking industries, including state, private, and regional banks, is necessary to ensure a win-win situation between the parties. Administrative requirement should be made practical while business owners should strengthen their business plan and avoid moral hazard that can disrupt the trust with the banks. Additional initiative includes empowerment and mentoring programme for SMEs as a joint-programme that involves all key partners, including government, banks, business communities and civil societies. Maximising the role of BPD (*Bank Pembangunan Daerah* — Regional Development Bank) is also an alternative to reach out to more prospective entrepreneurs as means to foster the vibrancy of business activities in the region.

Low productivity of secondary industry in Bali may be a trade-off due to the preservation of environmental quality at the expense of manufacturing. Yet, this should not fully discourage secondary economic activities from expanding as long as careful planning and rigorous environmental requirements are in place. West Nusa Tenggara and East Nusa Tenggara, which consist of several major islands, can actually take advantage of their geography and designate one specific island as the centre for processing raw resources so as not to harm the environment of other islands where tourism forms the main economic activity.

Low overall labour productivity and tertiary industry productivity are also issues to be solved swiftly. This can be done by intensifying vocational education and training in tourism and hospitality to enhance the capability of human resources in the respective industry and thereby increase productivity. This strategy is not solely the responsibility of the government. Through the Public-Private Partnerships (PPP), the private sector as the end-user of workforce should take part by establishing training centres or supporting government's vocational training programmes. Quintessentially, the government should continuously play a proactive role in promoting the importance and benefit of further education and changing the mindset of people to internalise a lifelong learning culture.

Complementing the above strategy, the full use of ICT in tourism and hotel industries is needed to increase productivity. Likewise, ICT should be integrated in public sector to enhance public service provision and thereby increase the government's efficiency, which is sub-optimum currently. Based on the survey conducted by the Indonesian Association of Internet Service Provider in 2012, internet penetration in major cities throughout Bali–Nusa Tenggara region is still relatively low. For example, in Denpasar, internet penetration is only at 33.7% of total population whereas in Mataram and Kupang, the figure is around 36.4% and 20.2%, respectively.[11] This provides a sense of urgency for the government to expand the accessibility of internet throughout the region in order to support both productivity enhancement and government efficiency, as in e-government. The improvement of fibre optic coverage as a strategic commitment under the MP3EI is a step in the right direction and needs to be upheld.

When discussing development strategies pertaining to Bali–Nusa Tenggara Region, an important fact that should not be overlooked is the disparity between Bali, West Nusa Tenggara, and East Nusa Tenggara. In terms of Overall Competitiveness for example, based on the ACI's ranking, Bali ranks 14th while West Nusa Tenggara and East Nusa Tenggara only hold 22nd and 32nd position, respectively. Disparity was also seen in the GRDP and income per capita in which Bali outstood the other two provinces with 30.75 trillion Rupiah of GRDP and 7,744,100 Rupiah income per capita whereas the figures for West Nusa Tenggara were only 19.43 trillion

[11] Asosiasi Penyelenggara Jasa Internet Indonesia (APJII), *Profil Pengguna Internet Indonesia 2012* (Jakarta: APJII, 2012), 29.

Rupiah and 4,274,900 Rupiah in 2011, respectively. Likewise, East Nusa Tenggara's GRDP in 2011 was 13.25 trillion Rupiah and its income per capita was 2,773,900 Rupiah; all far behind Bali's.

Thus, the MP3EI may be the right answer to close the inter-provinces' disparity 'gap' throughout Indonesia, not just between Bali and Nusa Tenggara.[12] This is because the MP3EI firstly emphasises enhancement based on the unique and distinctive economic potential of each region and then improving the interconnectivity of regions nationally and internationally to create an integrated system of economic activities. Through this plan, economic development will not be concentrated on a particular region, but more diversified as each region will have its own distinctive economic potential to focus on and a greater access to international and domestic market. Moreover, the MP3EI gives special attention to the upgrading of human resources capability across the regions, which is necessary to close the economic disparities across provinces and regions.

REFERENCES

Asosiasi Penyelenggara Jasa Internet Indonesia (APJII). *Profil Pengguna Internet Indonesia 2012*. Jakarta: APJII, 2012.

Committee for the Acceleration and Expansion of Indonesia's Economic Development (KP3EI). *Laporan Perkembangan Pelaksanaan MP3EI s.d. Maret 2013*. Jakarta: Coordinating Ministry for Economic Affairs, 2013.

Coordinating Ministry for Economic Affairs. *Master Plan for Acceleration and Expansion of Indonesia's Economic Development 2011–2025 (MP3EI)*. Jakarta: Coordinating Ministry for Economic Affairs, 2011.

Kuncoro, Mudrajad. "Economic Geography of Indonesia: Can MP3EI Reduce Inter-Regional Inequality?" Working paper presented at the Kuala Lumpur International Business, Economics, and Law Conference (KLIBEL) 2013, Hotel Putra, Kuala Lumpur, Malaysia, 8–9 April, 2013.

Marboen, Ade. "NTT siapkan 9000 hektar padang garam". *Antara News*, September 26, 2011. Retrieved on June 24, 2014. <http://www.antaranews.com/berita/277166/ntt-siapkan-9000-hektare-padang-garam>.

Ministry of National Development and Planning Agency. *National Medium-Term Development Plan (RPJMN) 2010–2014*. Jakarta: Ministry of National Development and Planning Agency, 2010.

Provincial Development and Planning Agency. *Medium-Term Development Plan (RPJMD) of various provinces across various time spans.*

Tan, Khee Giap, and Mulya Amri. "Subnational Competitiveness and National Performance: Analysis and Simulation for Indonesia." *Journal of Centrum Cathedra (JCC): The Business and Economics Research Journal* Vol. 6, No. 2 (2013): 173–192.

Tan, Khee Giap, Mulya Amri, Linda Low, and Tan Kong Yam. *Competitiveness Analysis and Development Strategies for 33 Indonesian Provinces*. Singapore: World Scientific, 2013.

[12] Mudrajad Kuncoro, "Economic Geography of Indonesia: Can MP3EI Reduce Inter-Regional Inequality?" (working paper presented at the Kuala Lumpur International Business, Economics, and Law Conference (KLIBEL) 2013, Hotel Putra, Kuala Lumpur, Malaysia, 8–9 April, 2013).

Chapter 8
Competitiveness Analysis on the Maluku–Papua Region

Maluku, North Maluku, Papua, and West Papua

1. INTRODUCTION

1.1 Background and Notes

Figure 8.1 shows the provinces in Maluku–Papua Region as defined by the Master Plan for Acceleration and Expansion of Indonesia's Economic Development 2011–2025 (MP3EI). [1] The four provinces with their capital cities are Maluku (Ambon), North Maluku (Sofifi), Papua (Jayapura), and West Papua (Manokwari). Among the six regions, it is the second largest in land area after Kalimantan. Measuring about 494,956 km^2, Maluku–Papua Region covers 25.9% of Indonesia's land area. Despite its vast size, the region is home to only 2.7% of Indonesia's population. The archipelagic provinces of Maluku and North Maluku have sea covering 90.5% of the area. The provinces of Papua and West Papua, however, are both part of a large land mass that makes up half of New Guinea Island, to also share with Papua New Guinea in administration.

As seen from Figure 8.1, inset map (top right) shows the competitiveness ranking by the Asia Competitiveness Institute (ACI) using the traffic light scheme with green representing the Top 10 provinces, followed by the 13 middle-ranking provinces in yellow and the remaining provinces with lower competitiveness in red. Only Maluku (23rd) is part of the Middle 13 provinces while the others are in the Bottom 10.[2]

As of 2011, the population of the Maluku–Papua Region was approximately 6,419,425 people, with 63% of the population in their productive age (15–64 years old). Papua and West Papua had two of the highest population growth rates in Indonesia, 5.57% and 3.76%, respectively. However, their population densities were the lowest in the country with nine and eight people per km^2, respectively. On the other hand, Maluku and North Maluku had a density of 33 and 32 people per km^2, with a moderately high population growth rate of 2.77% and 2.41% respectively. The region has a good mix of ethnicity and indigenous groups residing with a significant number of migrants, mainly from Java and Sulawesi.

Maluku–Papua Region is rich with energy and mineral, where nearly 40% of its total Gross Regional Domestic Product (GRDP) comes from oil, gas and minerals. Most of these resources are found in Papua and West Papua. In addition, the region has a vast coastal area due to the archipelagic nature of Maluku. Coupled with the presence of deep waters, this provides the region with tremendous fishery potential.

In the MP3EI, Maluku–Papua Region is designated to be the "Centre for Development of Food, Fisheries, Energy and National Mining." Supported by seven economic centres (Sofifi, Ambon, Sorong, Manokwari, Timika, Jayapura, and Merauke), the main economic activities are focused on food agriculture, copper, nickel, oil and gas mining, as well as fishery. Connectivity by land and sea transport is imperative to realise the potential of the region.

Despite numerous plans, development in the Maluku–Papua Region remains challenging. Even with an average GRDP growth of 7% per year between 2006 and 2009, its GRDP is still not on par with other adjacent regions. Other than the district of Mimika, most districts in Papua and West Papua have far lower GRDP per capita than

[1] Coordinating Ministry for Economic Affairs, *Master Plan for Acceleration and Expansion of Indonesia's Economic Development 2011–2025 (MP3EI)* (Jakarta: Coordinating Ministry for Economic Affairs, 2011).

[2] See Tan Khee Giap *et al.*, *Competitiveness Analysis and Development Strategies for 33 Indonesian provinces* (Singapore: World Scientific, 2013) and Tan Khee Giap and Mulya Amri, "Subnational Competitiveness and National Performance: Analysis and Simulation for Indonesia," *Journal of Centrum Cathedra (JCC): The Business and Economics Research Journal* Vol. 6, No. 2 (2013): 173–192 that mark the first attempt to rank provinces based on their competitiveness level.

Figure 8.1. Map of Maluku–Papua Region

Source: Asia Competitiveness Institute

the national average. The relatively high GRDP growth has not been transformed into opportunities to develop the secondary and tertiary sectors along with their employment opportunities. Although poverty rate had decreased by 8% during 2006–2011, it was still staggeringly high at above 20%.

Some of the most pressing issues in the region are high investment risk, low business certainty, limited irrigation facilities to support agricultural productivity, and lack of physical infrastructure. Economies of scale are also difficult to achieve with only a small number of population spread thinly over steep mountainous terrain throughout most of the island, except for the vast flat land in the south. Security issues in Papua and West Papua also remain apparent. In the remote mountainous areas of Papua, the daily situation could turn unstable when members of secessionist movements encounter members of the Indonesian army or international mining companies operating in the area. These companies have difficulty in hiring lowly educated locals, hence fuelling negative sentiments towards extractive mining companies. Instead, migrant workers viewed as foreigners seem to be taking the land, livelihood, and job opportunities away from the locals. These issues make policy implementation in Maluku–Papua even more challenging.

Maluku–Papua Region's heavy reliance on extraction activities can be seen from the significant difference between its total GRDP with and without mining (Table 8.1). Primary sector's contribution to the GRDP stood as high as 65.20% in 2006 and 46.15% in 2011. On the other hand, revenue from this sector equipped this region with the ability to improve the welfare of its people as seen through the decrease in poverty rate from 33.79% in 2006 to 25.23% in 2011.

1.2 Major Sectors and Activities

Table 8.2 shows that Maluku–Papua Region is highly dependent on the economic activities of its primary sector, which consists of energy and raw material extraction such as oil, gas, coal, and mineral wealth like copper, nickel and gold. Based on mining activities, the disparity of GRDP among districts is prominent.

Substantial oil and gas reserves have been identified in Sorong, West Coast Block Sarmi, Sermai, and Teluk Bintuni. Nickel is abundantly found in Weda of Central Halmahera district while copper has been mined in Timika. Copper reserves are abundant in Papua, with the largest mining activities currently operated by PT Freeport Indonesia.

Fishing is the main activity in the highly potential Maluku waters, designated as the National Fish Reserves. Fishery activities in North Maluku are concentrated in processing and distribution. The Morotai Mega Minapolitan zone in North Maluku is thus initiated based on this characteristic.

Table 8.1. Maluku–Papua Region: Basic Economic Indicators

A. Population	**2006**	**2011**
Total population	4,889,527	6,419,425
% urban	26.65	29.38
B. Area		**2013**
Km^2		494,956.85
% equivalent to country		25.90
C. Gross Regional Domestic Product (GRDP)	**2006**	**2011**
Rupiah (million)	29,750,695	40,791,100
Rupiah (million) without oil & gas	28,390,700	35,394,800
Rupiah (million) without oil & gas & mineral	18,533,609	24,216,979
D. Economic composition, as % GRDP	**2006**	**2011**
Primary sector	65.20	46.15
Secondary sector	11.04	25.83
Tertiary sector	23.76	28.02
E. GRDP per capita	**2006**	**2011**
Rupiah (million)	6.08	6.35
Rupiah (million) without oil & gas	5.81	5.51
Rupiah (million) without oil & gas & mineral	3.79	3.77
F. Poverty Rate	**2006**	**2011**
% of population	33.79	25.23
G. Human Development Index	**2006**	**2011**
Index	65.98	68.17

GRDP based on 2000 Constant Price
Source: Asia Competitiveness Institute using data from Indonesia Statistical Yearbook

Table 8.2. Major Products and Activities

Primary	Mining (copper, nickel, gold, silver, crude oil, natural gas, and steel), plantation (cocoa, coconut, and coffee), fisheries (brackish cultivation, cage cultivation, fishery catch, floating cage cultivation, fresh water pond culture, rice field cultivation, and aquaculture), agriculture (sugar cane, sago, rice, corn, and banana), stockbreeding (pig, cow, buffalo, goat, horse, and sheep), and spices (nutmeg and cloves)
Secondary	Oil and gas processing, construction, furniture, and handicraft
Tertiary	Tourism, restaurant, hotel, real estate, and business services

Source: Asia Competitiveness Institute

The secondary sector has increased by twofold since 2006. Manufacturing activities in the two Papua provinces are primarily driven by liquefied natural gas (LNG) processing activities in Bintuni, West Papua. Aside from the LNG processing activities, other types of manufacturing remain relatively small with activities in food and beverages sector, including fish processing in Sorong, and furniture making. The sector is also largely dominated by construction services, which have contributed to over 22% of the total GRDP of Papua in 2011.

In the Maluku archipelago, manufacturing is growing but still underdeveloped. The main manufacturing industries in Maluku are metal and chemical, agricultural products, forestry products, and small industry and handicrafts. In addition to that, most of the industries in North Maluku are in sectors related to food and beverages, apparel, printing, metal products, and furnitures.

The tertiary sector is driven by the growth of primary and secondary sector as well as a budding tourism industry. Trade and services are dominating in Papua due to the abundant natural resources and spillover from its mining activity. West Papua is home to world-renowned diving site, Raja Ampat, and is rich in biodiversity of flora and fauna, though, much less known. The tourism industry in these regions, however, is still hampered by the lack of infrastructure, which renders accessing these regions challenging. Furthermore, there is also difficulty in recruiting and training staff locally.

1.3 Infrastructure Provision

Air transport is the main method of connecting the relatively vast and mountainous land of Maluku–Papua Region. There are four airports in Papua, namely Frans Kaisiepo in Biak, Sentani Airport in Jayapura, Mopah Airport in Merauke, and Wamena Airport. A number of plans have been designed to improve the quality of current airports and to build new ones. Sentani airport's runway is going to be extended to 3,000 metres. Mopah Airport's runway is going to be overlaid to anticipate for higher loading. Mountaineous area, such as Deiyai, will soon see the construction of Waghete, a small airport. In addition to that, Mozes Kilangin Airport in Timika, which was mostly used as a helicopter landing area, is now being developed by central, provincial, and Mimika district government. This is to accelerate the process towards providing supporting infrastructure for National Sport Week (*Pekan Olahraga National* — PON), planned to be held in Papua in 2020.

West Papua also improves the quality of existing airports while constructing new ones. The two existing airports are Rendani in Manokwari and Domine Eduard Osok in Sorong. The newly constructed airports are Fakfak Airport in Fakfak district and Kaimana Airport in Kaimana. The Ministry of Transportation has signed a Memorandum of Understanding (MoU) with the local government to develop fences along the runway of Domine Eduard Osok Airport.

Maluku has 11 airports, comprising Amahai, Bandanaira, Bula, Dobo, Dumatubun, Kisar, Larat, Namlea, Nomrole and Orolit, with only Pattimura Airport in the capital city of Ambon serving international flights. In North Maluku, there are a total of 11 airports across seven districts and one city. However, only Sultan Baabullah Airport is considered as a "class 2" airport which serves inter-provinces routes. An international airport, Leo Wattimena, is planned in Daruba, Morotai Island, benefiting from an ex-world war airport with seven runways. In addition to that, three more airports have been planned, more specifically in West Halmahera (Domato Airport), South Halmahera (Obi Island), and Central Halmahera.

Water or maritime transportation is the main method of transporting goods in the major urban areas. In terms of water connectivity, currently there are only two international seaports, which are located in the city of Jayapura in Papua and Sorong in West Papua. Apart from these, there are also two national seaports, each located in Manokwari and Kaimana. With an understanding that connectivity is the backbone of the region, the central government, through its coordinating ministry, has undertaken many works in progress to promote the spirit of inter-regional cooperation.

Integrated connectivity for all economic centres is also crucial. Trans-Maluku as a combination of road and sea transportation improvement project is in the pipeline. In 2012, Maluku already has 19 from the required 40 quays. North Maluku has only one main seaport, Ahmad Yani Port in Ternate Island. Additionally, the province also has 40 concrete ports, 15 semi-permanent ports, 53 wooden ports, and one beach port. For ferry crossing, there are eight existing crossing ports with another eight under construction.

In Papua, there is one international port, which is located in the city of Jayapura, as well as 25 national ports, one regional port, and 78 local ports. On the other hand, there are container ports in Manokwari and Sorong in West Papua. The province also plans to develop new ports in Bintuni, where BP natural gas operations are located, and South Kaimana.

With regard to roads, a number of long distance intercity roads have cut through the Papua province, which demonstrate that progress is taking place. These include the Manokwari-Sorong and the Sorong-Mega Sausapor road. In addition to that, road networks are also improving. Some of the planned strategic road networks in the province are Jayapura-Hamadi-Holtekamp, Jayapura-Sarmi, Jayapura-Wamena-Mulia, Merauke-Tanah Merah-Waropko, and Timika-Mapuru Jaya-Pomako. Despite ongoing efforts, rapid growth is not yet matched with the current pace of road construction and maintenance.

Electrification ratio has increased in the region but remains below the national average at 72%. Maluku's electrification rate in 2011 was 61.80% while North Maluku, Papua and West Papua's were 53.48%, 30.79%, and 54.29%, respectively.[3]

Telecommunication infrastructure has also improved, to some extent, with a growing reliance on cellular phones. However, the distribution of such infrastructure has not been fairly distributed across provinces. Cellular network has been expanding in the region, but not as fast as in other regions of Indonesia. Internet access via broadband remains challenging and internet connection via cell phone networks is also relatively slow. Phone landline penetration by the government could only reach less than 15% of total villages. This inadequacy has hindered any improvement towards the implementation of e-system, both for the government and businesses. In addition to that, the uptake of information and communications technology (ICT) is mostly found in the provincial capital and main districts. Low education level and high illiteracy rate in this region render it more difficult to increase ICT uptake.

Infrastructure for clean water is still very limited. Clean water provided by state-service could only be enjoyed by very few villages, less than 10% of total villages. The majority of the population must rely on manual pumps, spring sources, rivers and lakes, as well as rainwater.

2. RELATIVE COMPETITIVENESS OF REGIONS

The competitiveness framework for the region follows the same approach with the provincial competitiveness, as explained in Chapter 1 in greater detail. Further explanation on the aggregation of individual province's indicators into regional scores can be found in Chapter 2.

2.1 Competitiveness Ranking of Six Regions — Rank and Score by Environment[4]

Table 8.3. 2014 Overall Competitiveness: Ranking and Score

Rank	Region	Score
1	Java Region	1.7233
2	Kalimantan Region	0.6511
3	Sulawesi Region	–0.0392
4	Sumatra Region	–0.0741
5	Bali–Nusa Tenggara Region	–0.9839
6	*Maluku–Papua Region*	*–1.2772*

Source: Asia Competitiveness Institute

This section describes the performance of each region and its provincial ranking. It begins from the overall ranking and subsequently elaborates further on the ranking for each environment.

Based on Table 8.3, Maluku–Papua Region places last in Overall Competitiveness. The difference in score between Maluku–Papua Region (–1.2772) and Bali–Nusa Tenggara Region (–0.9839) is relatively narrow. However, the gap between the two regions and Sumatra Region (fourth) is substantial. Given Maluku–Papua's abundance in natural resource, this region must start to manage its potential and improve its human resources.

Maluku–Papua Region's low Overall Competitiveness can be attributed primarily to the performance of North Maluku (33rd) and Papua (31st) in provincial ranking. Maluku and West Papua perform better at 23rd and 26th place, respectively.

[3] PT PLN, *Statistik PLN 2012* (Jakarta: PLN, 2012), 20.

[4] Results for the 2014 competitiveness study are based on official data in 2011 and survey data collected in 2013. Conventionally due to collation, compilation, and publication of official data, such a lag of data before reaching end-users is acceptable.

Table 8.4. 2014 Macroeconomic Stability: Ranking and Score

Rank	Region	Score
1	Java Region	2.0461
2	Sumatra Region	0.1112
3	Kalimantan Region	0.0350
4	Sulawesi Region	–0.3896
5	*Maluku–Papua Region*	*–0.7943*
6	Bali–Nusa Tenggara Region	–1.0085

Source: Asia Competitiveness Institute

As seen from Table 8.4, Maluku–Papua Region ranks fifth for Macroeconomic Stability. Focusing on the score difference between Maluku–Papua Region (–0.7943) and Bali–Nusa Tenggara Region (–1.0085), it is clear that Bali–Nusa Tenggara can easily catch up to Maluku–Papua. It is also possible for Maluku–Papua to be on par with Sulawesi Region as the score difference is relatively narrow. This means that there is intense competition among regions in the bottom half of the ranking.

Based on the ACI's provincial ranking, West Papua is the only province from Maluku–Papua Region in the Middle 13 group, at 14th place while others are in the Bottom 10 group with North Maluku as 32nd.

Table 8.5. 2014 Government and Institutional Setting: Ranking and Score

Rank	Region	Score
1	Java Region	1.4124
2	Sulawesi Region	0.7733
3	Kalimantan Region	0.5582
4	Sumatra Region	–0.4219
5	Bali–Nusa Tenggara Region	–0.8284
6	*Maluku–Papua Region*	*–1.4937*

Source: Asia Competitiveness Institute

Maluku–Papua Region is in the last place for Government and Institutional Setting environment (Table 8.5). Maluku–Papua Region has a substantially wide gap with Bali–Nusa Tenggara Region. It could be a daunting task to be on par with Bali–Nusa Tenggara in the future. Despite so, the scores for both regions are negative, underlining that they have similar issues with regard to Government and Institutional Setting in their respective provinces.

Maluku (20th) exceeds its peers in this environment and is the only province in the Middle 13. North Maluku is last (33rd). The region cannot malinger and should focus on improving its weaknesses to unleash its potential.

Table 8.6. 2014 Financial, Businesses and Manpower Conditions: Ranking and Score

Rank	Region	Score
1	Java Region	1.6700
2	Kalimantan Region	1.0027
3	*Maluku–Papua Region*	*–0.3552*
4	Sumatra Region	–0.3940
5	Sulawesi Region	–0.7693
6	Bali–Nusa Tenggara Region	–1.1543

Source: Asia Competitiveness Institute

Based on Table 8.6, Maluku–Papua Region performs better in Financial, Businesses and Manpower Conditions environment than in other environments. It ranks third with a score that is by far, the best score for the region. Clearly, this is an environment where Maluku–Papua can strengthen and develop further to reach higher position in the ranking.

As seen from Table 8.6, Maluku–Papua Region scores –0.3552, right below Kalimantan Region in second place, (1.0027). With such a wide score difference, Maluku–Papua has to put in significant efforts to catch up with Kalimantan Region.

Based on the provincial ranking, Papua and West Papua rank 11th and 12th, respectively. However, both Maluku (23rd) and North Maluku (31st) perform poorly. The relatively good performance of Papua and West Papua contributes to the higher competitiveness of Maluku–Papua Region in this environment, overtaking its closest rival, Sumatra Region.

Table 8.7. 2014 Quality of Life and Infrastructure Development: Ranking and Score

Rank	Region	Score
1	Java Region	1.0603
2	Kalimantan Region	0.7425
3	Sumatra Region	0.4385
4	Sulawesi Region	0.2448
5	Bali–Nusa Tenggara Region	–0.5423
6	*Maluku–Papua Region*	*–1.9438*

Source: Asia Competitiveness Institute

Table 8.7 illustrates the extremity of the Quality of Life and Infrastructure Development in the Maluku–Papua Region, at the bottom in rank (–1.9438) with quite a far distance behind the other regions.

Maluku–Papua Region has a significant gap with Bali–Nusa Tenggara Region (fifth; –0.5423), which needs serious intervention by incentives with specific targets for improvement.

This regional position is attributed to the individual performance of Maluku (23rd), West Papua (28th), North Maluku (31st), and Papua (33rd) in the provincial ranking. The scores are heavily skewed towards the bottom.

To boost the region's productivity, a particular aspect that needs concerted effort by the central, provincial, and local governments, is education. Primary school enrolment rate is much lower compared to the national average, especially in Papua.

2.2 Analysis of Median and Maximum Competitiveness Webs

To better understand Maluku–Papua Region's relative strengths and weaknesses, it is useful to compare and contrast its attainment against the median and the maximum scores of Indonesia's six regions for the 12 sub-environments. The median competitiveness web plots Maluku–Papua Region's attained scores for each of the 12 sub-environments.

In Figure 8.2, the median scores for six Indonesian regions are shown in dashed line while the scores for Maluku–Papua are in solid line.

Based on the Overall Competitiveness ranking, Maluku–Papua ranks sixth, making it the worst performing region in the 12 sub-environments. Financial Deepening and Business Efficiency is the only sub-environment where Maluku–Papua performs above the national average. The remaining sub-environments are lower than the median scores; some with narrow margins and some with wide margins. The sub-environments with narrow margins are Regional Economic Vibrancy; Openness to Trade and Services; and Productivity Performance. The

Figure 8.2. 2014 Median Competitiveness Web Analysis for Maluku–Papua Region

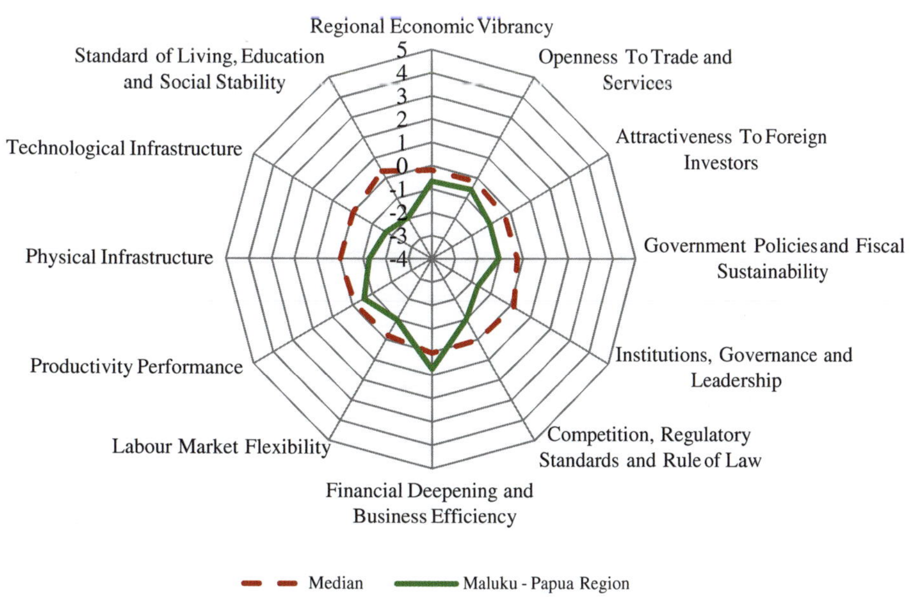

Source: Asia Competitiveness Institute

Figure 8.3. 2014 Maximum Competitiveness Web Analysis for Maluku–Papua Region

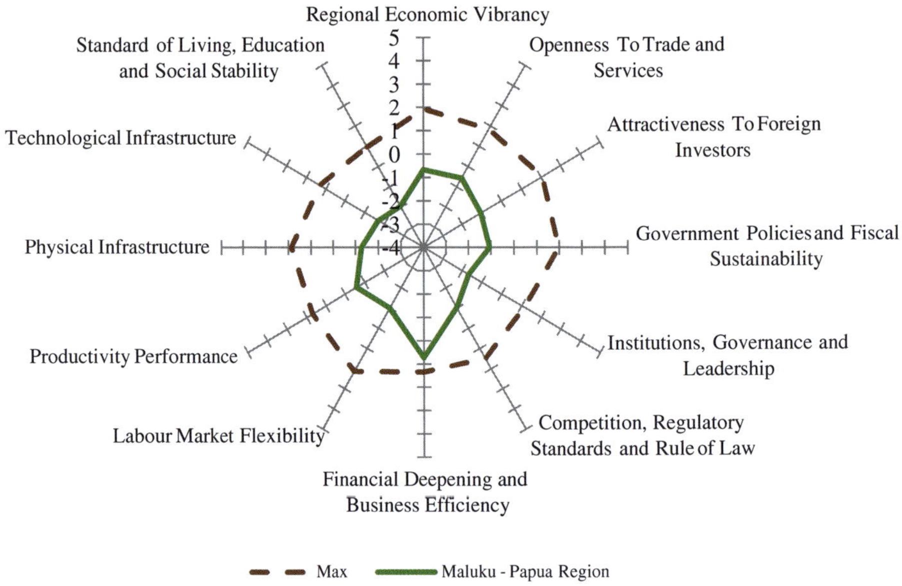

Source: Asia Competitiveness Institute

analysis once again shows that Maluku–Papua lags far behind the median scores in Standard of Living, Education and Social Stability; Technological Infrastructure; and Physical Infrastructure sub-environments under Quality of Life and Infrastructure Development environment, which raise red flags for attention.

The maximum competitiveness web (Figure 8.3) shows how far the best score for each sub-environment is, in relation to Maluku–Papua Region's score. The maximum scores for the six regions are shown in dashed line while the scores for Maluku–Papua are shown in solid line.

Maluku–Papua Region has the narrowest gap to the maximum score in Financial Deepening and Business Efficiency. Nonetheless, the region cannot afford to be complacent. The overall high scores of the top-performing region, Java Region, has set the benchmark high, which are evident from Table 8.3 to Table 8.7. However, this gap shows that Maluku–Papua does have the potential to compete, even with Java Region.

Unfortunately, the scores for the remaining sub-environments are far below the maximum. Two particular sub-environments that need full attention are Standard of Living, Education and Social Stability and Institutions, Governance and Leadership. It is time for the central, provincial, and local governments to pull all efforts and join all the dots to improve these two sub-environments as they play a crucial role in uplifting other sub-environments.

2.3 Analysis of Strengths and Weaknesses

Tables 8.8 and 8.9 list the strongest and weakest indicators of Maluku–Papua Region. Table 8.8 shows the region's top 20% or 21 strongest indicators out of a total of 104 indicators, in descending order. Table 8.9 shows the top 20% of weakest indicators in ascending order.[5]

Based on Table 8.8, some indicators from Financial, Businesses and Manpower Conditions (10 indicators) and Quality of Life and Infrastructure Development (eight indicators) environments dominate Maluku–Papua Region's strength. The top three strongest indicators are Population Growth (#1), Firms' Equipment Capacity (#2), and Firms' Strategy (#3).

[5] These 21 strongest and 21 weakest indicators are obtained by sorting all of the 104 indicators' scores that the region received, from the highest to the lowest. Those that appear at the top 21 are identified as the region's strengths, and those that appear at the bottom 21 are identified as the region's weaknesses. The comparison is done relatively among the indicator scores of said region, without comparing to the indicator scores of other regions.

Table 8.8. 2014 Top 20% Strongest Indicators List for Maluku–Papua Region

Rank	20% Strongest Indicator	Score	Environment
1	Population Growth	2.1357	QLID
2	Firms' Equipment Capacity	2.0734	FBMC
3	Firms' Strategy	1.9182	FBMC
4	Firms' Application of IT	1.5292	FBMC
5	Registered Motor Vehicles per Km of Paved Road	1.4375	QLID
6	Population per Number of Bank Branches/Offices	1.0438	FBMC
7	Secondary Industry Productivity	0.8913	FBMC
8	Inflation	0.8864	MS
9	Non-Performing Loans per Total Bank Loans	0.7457	FBMC
10	Urban Population Growth	0.7080	QLID
11	Non-Performing Loans	0.5877	FBMC
12	Ease of Dealing With Banks	0.5493	FBMC
13	Labour Force Participation Rate	0.4939	FBMC
14	Environmental Quality Index	0.4345	QLID
15	Population Per Health Facility	0.4234	QLID
16	Fatalities due to Natural Disaster	0.3908	QLID
17	Openness To Trade	0.3771	MS
18	Vibrancy of Competition and Collaboration	0.1119	GIS
19	Life Expectancy at Birth	0.1096	QLID
20	Unemployment Rate	–0.0132	FBMC
21	Student-Teacher Ratio (Senior High)	–0.0254	QLID

Note: MS = Macroeconomic Stability; GIS = Government and Institutional Setting; FBMC = Financial, Businesses and Manpower Conditions; QLID = Quality of Life and Infrastructure Development
Source: Asia Competitiveness Institute

Other promising strengths are Firm's Application of IT (#4), Secondary Industry Productivity (#7), Non-Performing Loans (#11), Ease of Dealing with Banks (#12), and Labour Force Participation Rate (#13). These reflect a strong Financial, Businesses and Manpower Conditions environment. Alongside these strengths, Urban Population Growth (#10), Openness to Trade (#17), and Vibrancy of Competition and Collaboration (#18) show promising leads for Maluku–Papua to grow even further.

Interestingly, along with Government and Institution Setting, some indicators from Quality of Life and Infrastructure Development also dominate the top 20% weakest indicators list. Poor performance of government adversely affects the quality of basic education and health provision.

The detailed scores in Table 8.9 indicate that the government must take serious measures to balance the gains from natural resources with the capability of human resources. Primary School Enrolment Rate (#104), Primary School Student-Teacher Ratio (#102), Adult Illiteracy Rate (#97), and Junior High School Enrolment Rate (#96) are among the indicators with the lowest scores. Infrastructure-wise, Quality of Technological Infrastructure (#101) and Households with State Electricity Services (#98) indicate that collaboration between the central, provincial, and local governments are needed to bring about investments to support their development.

Nonetheless, improvement in those indicators requires strong leadership and management from the local government. Security (#103) is also among the lowest indicators. This is essential to keep the businesses running and ensure the safety of school children. Tax Revenue per Government Revenue (#99) is also among the weakest indicators, along with corruption (#89). These two indicators could be related by the low perceived performance of Government Inclusiveness and Accountability (#92) and Coordination of Local Governments (#91).

Table 8.9 2014 Top 20% Weakest Indicators List for Maluku–Papua Region

Rank	20% Weakest Indicator	Score	Environment
84	Regulatory Governance	−1.4673	GIS
85	Provincial Governing Capacity	−1.4742	GIS
86	Internet Access at School	−1.4992	QLID
87	Human Development Index	−1.5022	QLID
88	Student-Teacher Ratio (Junior High)	−1.5047	QLID
89	Lack of Corruption	−1.6001	GIS
90	Minimum Wage Per Month	−1.6055	FBMC
91	Coordination of Local Governments	−1.6060	GIS
92	Government Inclusiveness and Accountability	−1.6445	GIS
93	Quality of Healthcare	−1.6654	QLID
94	Telephone Ownership	−1.6681	QLID
95	Affordability and Acessibility of Goods	−1.6695	QLID
96	School Enrolment Rate (Junior High)	−1.7856	QLID
97	Adult Illiteracy Rate	−1.8238	QLID
98	Households with state electricity services	−1.8998	QLID
99	Tax Revenue/Government Revenue	−1.9089	GIS
100	Handphone Ownership	−1.9240	QLID
101	Quality of Technological Infrastructure	−1.9360	QLID
102	Student-Teacher Ratio (Primary)	−1.9713	QLID
103	Security	−2.0462	GIS
104	School Enrolment Rate (Primary)	−2.2259	QLID

Note: MS = Macroeconomic Stability; GIS = Government and Institutional Setting; FBMC = Financial, Businesses and Manpower Conditions; QLID = Quality of Life and Infrastructure Development
Source: Asia Competitiveness Institute

3. POLICY THEMES AND DEVELOPMENT STRATEGIES

3.1 Official Policies[6]

Known for its natural resources potential, the Maluku–Papua Region is envisioned by the MP3EI to be the centre of food, agriculture, and fisheries, as well as mining development. Merauke region in Papua has been specifically designated as the centre of food reserves to cultivate food and non-food crops through the development of Merauke Integrated Food and Energy Estate (MIFEE). Maluku Islands have a huge potential in fishery and have been designated as the National Fish Reserves. Morotai Mega Minapolitan in North Maluku has been set as the pioneer of such idea. Policies and regulations in each strategy are in alignment to support the implementation. Supporting infrastructures to enhance connectivity between these strategic centres have also been identified and crafted into an investment plan.

The MIFEE is clustered into 10 Agricultural Production Centres (KSPP). During the short-term development period in 2011–2014, agricultural production centres within MIFEE have been developed in Merauke, Kali Kumb, Yeinan, and Bian. These agri-business activities are supported by the idea of an industrial system that is

[6]At national level, Indonesia's development plan is documented in the 2005–2025 National Long-Term Development Plan (RPJPN 2005–2025). It was in the second phase of implementation under the 2010–2014 National Medium-Term Development Plan (RPJMN 2010–2014). Provincial governments must take into account the RPJMN 2010–2014 when formulating or adjusting their respective Provincial Medium-Term Development Plan (RPJMD) to reach national development targets. The MP3EI is not intended to replace RPJMN or the ongoing national and provincial development plans. It is a complementary working document for the abovementioned development plans aimed at accelerating and expanding economic development in Indonesia.

based on science and technology, capital, organisation, and management. This further emphasises that agricultural sector is not inferior to other sectors. One of the priorities of MIFEE is to meet the national sugar demand, especially with Papua's vast land that is suitable for sugar cane.

The Ministry of Marine Affairs and Fisheries has set plans for fishery processing industry in Tual and Seram in Maluku. Despite tremendous opportunities, these plans are still in the pipeline and the quality of processed fish is not yet on par to compete in the more lucrative export markets.

Mining development of nickel and copper has been set as most promising commodities for this region. However, nickel is only produced in its crude form as nickel ore. To support a higher value of export, it is necessary to develop infrastructure for refinery and smelting activities, as well as to facilitate the development of smelting industries.

So far, the technical draft of the National Medium-Term Development Plan (RPJMN 2015–2019) is closely aligned with the MP3EI.[7] Plans to develop six industrial areas in Maluku–Papua region are clearly spelled out. There are two other national level initiatives that have an impact on the development in the Maluku–Papua Region. The first is the Draft Law on Acceleration of Development in Archipelagic Areas (RUU PPDK). Maluku and North Maluku provinces are among the seven provinces defined as archipelagic, and therefore will fall under the draft law once it is formally adopted. The draft law envisions development in archipelagic areas to be conducted with a maritime-based regional approach, in addition to the standard sectoral approach commonly used throughout the country. It aims to put a halt on illegal fishing activities by foreign vessels in the seas of these provinces. However, the long delay in the process of ratifying the draft law means further delay in implementing any plans to build National Fish Reserves in Maluku and North Maluku.

The other initiative at the national level related to Papua and West Papua is the central government Unit for the Acceleration of Development in Papua and West Papua (UP4B). This unit works specifically in assisting both provinces to achieve their targets in governance, physical infrastructure, local economy, and education.[8] Since 2001, a special autonomy law was applied to the provinces in Papua region. The law stipulates that natural resource revenues coming from Papua region are mostly to be returned to the provinces of Papua and West Papua, to be utilised under greater provincial autonomy. However, since the application of the law, the development has been less than expected; corruption cases have proliferated, politics have been dominated by conflicts over money, and quality of life has not improved significantly. The UP4B is thus expected to help the provinces make internal reforms and achieve tangible development results.

Each province has its own medium term development plan (RPJMD) that is, to some extent, aligned with the MP3EI and other national level initiatives. [9] For Maluku, its RPJMD for 2014–2019 will most likely continue on those that were stipulated in the RPJMD 2008–2013, which outlined three priorities, namely improvement of basic services and rural development, acceleration of sustainable economic growth supported by development in agriculture, infrastructure, and energy, and strengthening good local governance by scaling up anti-corruption measures, bureaucracy reform, and peace-keeping efforts. In a more practical term, the provincial government envisages the province to excel as the national fish reserves (Golden Fishing Ground), in maritime and sea tourism, plantation and spices (mainly nutmeg and clove), oil, gas, and mineral.

For North Maluku, according to its RPJMD 2009–2014, the goals were to increase living standards, productivity and usage of marine and plantation resources, the availability, quality, and accessibility of transportation mode, and to create a balanced development between the northern and southern part of Maluku and between the land, sea, and air. Based on its RPJMD, the development pattern for Papua will be based on three essential aspects, namely, people-centred development, inclusive and sustainable growth, and a balanced development within the province. These aspects are chosen with the awareness of development disparity between areas, for example between high mountainous and coastal areas.

---

[7] Ministry of National Development and Planning Agency, *National Medium-Term Development Plan (RPJMN) Technocratic Draft* (Jakarta: Ministry of National Development and Planning Agency, 2014).

[8] "Strategi Percepatan Pembangunan Provinsi Papua dan Papua Barat," *National Development and Planning Agency*, April 24, 2014, retrieved on July 24, 2014, <http://www.bappenas.go.id/berita-dan-siaran-pers/strategi-percepatan-pembangunan-provinsi-papua-dan-papua-barat/>.

[9] Provincial Development and Planning Agency, *Medium-Term Development Plan (RPJMD) of various provinces across various time spans.*

To facilitate business, Papua has also established a one-stop service for business licence application and Papua investment promotion houses in China and Germany. The focus on special autonomy remains critical due to the widespread anxiety of the survival of indigenous Papuans. They are at risk as a result of direct competition with migrants living in the province or as a result of outsiders' presence that could lead to a negative impact in their livelihood. No explicit policies or initiatives are being carried out to address this issue. A particular example in this regard is PT Freeport in Mimika district, which is a company known to recruit locals as workers. Nonetheless, the number of local recruits are consistently low as they are not equipped with the necessary qualifications or skills. It is evident, from this example, that the government must step in to improve the current formal education system in order to produce more competent workers.

West Papua's RPJMD for 2012–2016 identifies eight main missions that include: (1) to implement the special autonomy law, with a focus on building a sense of fairness and justice to the indigenous Papuans, (2) to accelerate the local economy, with a focus on human resource development, natural resource management, and creation of better business climate, (3) to alleviate poverty, (4) to improve governance, with a focus on providing good and services and eradicating corruption and inefficiencies, (5) to ensure distribution of benefits, with a focus on addressing the urban-rural divide, (6) to develop human resources that can contribute meaningfully to the economy, (7) to use natural resources for people's welfare, with a focus on better natural resource management, and (8) to ensure environmental sustainability. Similar to Papua, the status of special autonomy and the need to accommodate indigenous Papuans in the pursuit of more modern economic activities are also part of its development plan.

3.2 Development Strategies

Based on the ACI's competitiveness analysis, Maluku–Papua Region is the least competitive in terms of Overall Competitiveness (Table 8.3). However, looking into the issue in greater detail, it can be seen that the region enjoys better prospects in Macroeconomic Stability and Financial, Businesses and Manpower Conditions environment (see Table 8.4 and Table 8.6) compared to its performance in Government and Institutional Setting and Quality of Life and Infrastructure Development environment (see Table 8.5 and Table 8.7). This implies that the region is business-friendly, although it could just be spillover effects from the fact that the region has abundant natural resources potential and large public finances resulting from the extraction industry. Monetising this wealth is key to do better.

Improving government capacity and accountability at the provincial level has to be pursued more rigorously. The need to strengthen its governance, starting from having a system that ensures accountability, should be supported by leadership that can be trusted by stakeholders and promote changes for collective improvement. Capacity and capability development of civil servants are important, but an incentive system that allows them to work with integrity and build a personal commitment to reform is as crucial. This may seem common sensical in any strategy, but it has proven to be complicated with North Maluku and West Papua, being young provinces. It is also important for both Papua and West Papua to manage large public funding, which is the result of special autonomy law where provincial revenues are mostly channelled back to the province by the central government. It is key that the funding goes to the less developed areas for improvement in infrastructure and public goods provision. It requires a tremendous and concerted effort across all layers of government.

Currently, a number of regulations, be it at the central, provincial, and local levels, need to be better coordinated to further stimulate economic growth in Maluku–Papua Region. Inconsistencies in regulations between the central and local government or between ministries have caused slow issuance of mining permits for exploration activity. For example, the risk of regulatory uncertainty has hindered the development of copper industry in Papua. Therefore, resolving this issue is pertinent to the success of each strategy in the long run.

The government has already conducted several debottlenecking measures, including revising regulations pertaining to ease of doing business, such as land acquisition and fiscal incentives. What needs to be done is to monitor its implementation closely and make sure that all relevant parties (investors and local population) are benefiting from the regulations.

Implementing comprehensive incentives for businesses will help spur more rapid investment. At the same time, it helps to ensure that all players are respectful to each other. Nonetheless, an equal contribution for this effort must come from both government and business players. A consultative process must also involve local community, with the rationale that any future investment on extractive activities must be cognisant of the potential conflict between priorities of business, human rights, and climate change.

To promote business operations practically, Maluku–Papua needs infrastructure and connectivity among its regions. It is time to call for efficient infrastructure than can reach people living in the outermost and forefront regions, and in least developed islands. It means not only big boats connecting the large islands, but transportation to connect small islands as also necessary. This may also be one of the answers to reduce price gaps between the western and eastern part of Indonesia. This is also in line with the ACI's findings that highlight the dire conditions of both physical and technological infrastructure in the region.

Apart from governance and infrastructure aspects, the economic engines of the region, especially in Papua and West Papua, need to be expanded beyond the primary, natural resource-based sector. Currently, Papua and West Papua's key sectors are resource-intensive and capital-intensive sectors. This places limitations on creating employment for the locals and the area's sustainability. In other words, while the MP3EI strategy shows its superiority in terms of generating output in Java, Sumatra, and Sulawesi, it may not yield similar output in Maluku–Papua.

It is time to move into a broader-based investment that maintains the growth potential and reduces poverty incidence in Papua and West Papua. Expansion of value-added activities to process primary products is essential to engender more inclusive industrialisation in the region. Maluku and North Maluku also need to take the challenge of industrialisation and expand its simple agriculture and fishery production into processing industry, especially for Maluku, which ranks the highest in the region in terms of Overall Competitiveness (23rd). For industrialisation to succeed, economies of scale need to be considered carefully. Therefore, Maluku–Papua Region needs to strengthen its centres of production and consumption and mobilise the presence of a critical mass of producers and consumers.

Employment creation for the prosperity of future generation must be put as high priority. Nationally born and bred, the locals possess knowledge of the local setting, but need concerted and relentless support from the central and local governments to be truly qualified workers. Business operators are expected to contribute in the form of non-formal and vocational training for people in their productive age. This should be in line with the MP3EI. Nonetheless, political will and leadership by the government are required in each province.

In developing the agriculture sector in Maluku–Papua Region, there needs to be cooperation across various sectors, including forestry and fisheries. Food security is needed and Papua has the potential to provide food through MIFEE and other programmes. Papua is also one of the world's sources of oxygen and its lush rainforests are home to a rich biodiversity. Managing this precious resource responsibly is the most important part of the general strategy in developing the region.

Finally, in order to upgrade the region's productivity and hence its competitiveness, investment in infrastructure, human development, good governance, and resource management must be targeted. Education, in formal and non-formal settings, should be prioritised to achieve better quality of life among the local population. On the other hand, good governance needs to be strengthened by building the capacity of public officials at provincial and district level. This is intended to streamline bureaucracy process and boost its effectiveness in providing public services.

An in-depth analysis on challenges and obstacles as identified in this chapter is beneficial to help the government and investors to collaborate and devise development strategies. The second phase of the MP3EI should build a solid foundation for the final phase, which is due to be completed in 2025. By that time, Maluku–Papua Region must become a sustainable economic entity with access to rich natural resources and capable workforce and be recognised as one of the most competitive regions in Southeast Asia.

REFERENCES

Coordinating Ministry for Economic Affairs. *Master Plan for Acceleration and Expansion of Indonesia's Economic Development 2011–2025 (MP3EI)*. Jakarta: Coordinating Ministry for Economic Affairs, 2011.

Ministry of National Development and Planning Agency. *National Medium-Term Development Plan (RPJMN Technocratic Draft)*. Jakarta: Ministry of National Development and Planning Agency, 2014.

Ministry of National Development and Planning Agency. "Strategi Percepatan Pembangunan Provinsi Papua dan Papua Barat, April 24, 2014. Retrieved on July 24, 2014. <http://www.bappenas.go.id/berita-dan-siaran-pers/strategi-percepatan-pembangunan-provinsi-papua-dan-papua-barat/>.

Provincial Development and Planning Agency. *Medium-Term-Development Plan (RPJMD) of various provinces across various time spans.*

PT PLN. *Statistik PLN 2012*. Jakarta: PLN, 2012.

Tan, Khee Giap, and Mulya Amri. "Subnational Competitiveness and National Performance: Analysis and Simulation for Indonesia." *Journal of Centrum Cathedra (JCC): The Business and Economics Research Journal* Vol. 6, No. 2 (2013): 173–192.

Tan, Khee Giap, Mulya Amri, Linda Low, and Tan Kong Yam. *Competitiveness Analysis and Development Strategies for 33 Indonesian Provinces*. Singapore: World Scientific, 2013a.

Chapter 9

Geweke Analysis on Causal Linkages for East Java, East Kalimantan, North Maluku, and East Nusa Tenggara

1. RESEARCH MOTIVATION AND EXPECTED CONTRIBUTIONS

The Asia Competitiveness Institute (ACI) has been tracking the competitiveness of Indonesian provinces since 2013 through the annual provincial competitiveness index. A well-constructed index is able to paint a clear composite picture of a situation by aggregating multiple aspects. As competitiveness is a multi-dimensional issue, the ACI has carefully identified 104 relevant indicators, grouped them into four environments and 12 sub-environments. The resulting index is a measure that many Indonesian policy makers have found to be intuitive (conforming to their inherent understanding of the situation), while at the same time, also provides new insights and challenges some conventional wisdom.[1]

Although an index can do a good job in measuring and painting a condition, it does not explain why certain condition came into being. For example, the ACI's provincial competitiveness index can generate up to 104 different dimensions that make DKI Jakarta, East Java, and East Kalimantan the first, second, and third most competitive provinces, respectively, in the country. However, it cannot provide a statistical or detailed explanation as to why the three provinces came to be very competitive. Thus an inquiry into the causes of competitiveness (or lack thereof) has to be answered through different means or methodology other than an index. This chapter reports the results of causality analysis done by the ACI on selected Indonesian provinces, using a methodology developed by Geweke in 1982.[2]

2. RESEARCH METHODOLOGY

Like Granger and Sims[3], Geweke causality analysis focuses on a wide-sense stationary,[4] purely nondeterministic[5] multiple time series Z = {z_t, t real}. Therefore, the vector z_t can be expressed under the following autoregressive representation:

$$Z_t = \sum_{s=1}^{\infty} B_s Z_{t-s} + e_t$$

where e_t is white noise and z_t can be partitioned into $k \times 1$ and $l \times 1$ sub-vectors x_t and y_t. Geweke also showed that a canonical form for the wide-sense stationary time series $z_t = (x_t, y_t)$ is of the following form:

$$x_t = \sum_{s=1}^{\infty} E_{1s} x_{t-s} + u_{1t} \qquad var(u_{1t}) = \Sigma_1 \qquad (1)$$

[1] Tan Khee Giap and Mulya Amri, "Subnational Competitiveness and National Performance: Analysis and Simulation for Indonesia," *Journal of Centrum Cathedra (JCC): The Business and Economics Research Journal* Vol. 6, No. 2 (2013): 173–192. The results are also published in a book and translated into Bahasa; Tan Khee Giap *et al.*, *Competitiveness Analysis and Development Strategies for 33 Indonesian Provinces* (Singapore: World Scientific, 2013a) and Tan Khee Giap *et al.*, *Analisis Daya Saing dan Strategi Pembangunan untuk 33 Provinsi Indonesia* (Singapore: World Scientific, 2013b).

[2] John Geweke, "Measurement of linear dependence and feedback between multiple time series," *Journal of the American Statistical Association* Vol. 77, No. 378 (1982): 304–313.

[3] C.W.J. Granger, "Investigating Causal Relations by Econometric Models and Cross-Spectral Methods," *Econometrica* Vol. 37 (1969): 424–438; Christopher A. Sims, "Money, Income, and Causality," *The American Economic Review* Vol. 62, No. 4 (September 1972): 540-552.

[4] Wide-sense stationary implies that the mean of z_t exists and does not depend on *t*, and for all *t* and *s*, cov (z_t, z_{t+s}) exists and depends on *s* but not on *t*.

[5] Purely nondeterministic implies that the correlation of z_t and z_{t+p} vanishes as p increases.

$$x_t = \sum_{s=1}^{\infty} E_{2s} x_{t-s} + \sum_{s=1}^{\infty} F_{2s} y_{t-s} + u_{2t} \qquad var(u_{2t}) = \Sigma_2 \qquad (2)$$

$$x_t = \sum_{s=1}^{\infty} E_{3s} x_{t-s} + \sum_{s=1}^{\infty} F_{3s} y_{t-s} + u_{3t} \qquad var(u_{3t}) = \Sigma_3 \qquad (3)$$

$$x_t = \sum_{s=1}^{\infty} E_{4s} x_{t-s} + \sum_{s=1}^{\infty} F_{4s} y_{t-s} + u_{4t} \qquad var(u_{4t}) = \Sigma_4 \qquad (4)$$

$$y_t = \sum_{s=1}^{\infty} G_{1s} y_{t-s} + v_{1t} \qquad var(v_{1t}) = \mathrm{T}_1 \qquad (5)$$

$$y_t = \sum_{s=1}^{\infty} G_{2s} y_{t-s} + \sum_{s=1}^{\infty} H_{2s} x_{t-s} + v_{2t} \qquad var(v_{2t}) = \mathrm{T}_2 \qquad (6)$$

$$y_t = \sum_{s=1}^{\infty} G_{3s} y_{t-s} + \sum_{s=0}^{\infty} H_{3s} x_{t-s} + v_{3t} \qquad var(v_{3t}) = \mathrm{T}_3 \qquad (7)$$

$$y_t = \sum_{s=1}^{\infty} G_{4s} y_{t-s} + \sum_{s=-\infty}^{\infty} H_{4s} x_{t-s} + v_{4t} \qquad var(v_{4t}) = \mathrm{T}_4 \qquad (8)$$

2.1 Definition: Measure of Linear Feedback

The measure of linear feedback from Y to X is defined as:

$$F_{Y\to X} = \ln(|\Sigma_1| / |\Sigma_2|) \qquad (9)$$

The measure $F_{Y\to X}$ is always non-negative and takes value of zero only if the linear feedback running from Y to X is absent.

Symmetrically, the measure of linear feedback from X to Y is defined as:

$$F_{X\to Y} = \ln(|\mathrm{T}_1| / |\mathrm{T}_2|) \qquad (10)$$

The instantaneous feedback is defined as:

$$F_{X\cdot Y} = \ln(|\mathrm{T}_2| \times |\Sigma_2| / |\Upsilon|) \qquad (11)$$

where $\Upsilon = \mathrm{var}\begin{pmatrix} u_2 t \\ v_2 t \end{pmatrix} = \begin{bmatrix} \Sigma_2 & C \\ C' & \mathrm{T}_2 \end{bmatrix}$.

Thus, the measure of linear feedback between two vectors X and Y can be decomposed into the sum of measure of linear feedback from X to Y, the measure of linear feedback from Y to X, and the instantaneous linear feedback between the two vectors. That is,

$$F_{X,Y} = F_{X\to Y} + F_{Y\to X} + F_{X\cdot Y} \qquad (12)$$

Geweke also proved that the following set of equations are equivalent:

$$F_{X,Y} = \ln(|\Sigma_1| \times |\mathrm{T}_1| / |\Upsilon|) = \ln(|\Sigma_1| / |\Sigma_4|) = \ln(|\mathrm{T}_1| / |\mathrm{T}_4|) \qquad (13)$$

$$F_{X\to Y} = \ln(|\mathrm{T}_1| / |\mathrm{T}_2|) = \ln(|\Sigma_3| / |\Sigma_4|) \qquad (14)$$

$$F_{Y\to X} = \ln(|\Sigma_1| / |\Sigma_2|) = \ln(|\mathrm{T}_3| / |\mathrm{T}_4|) \qquad (15)$$

$$F_{X\cdot Y} = \ln(|\mathrm{T}_2| \times |\Sigma_2| / |\Upsilon|) = \ln(|\Sigma_2| / |\Sigma_3|) = \ln(|\mathrm{T}_2| / |\mathrm{T}_3|) \qquad (16)$$

2.2 Distribution of Statistics

Under the null hypothesis that there is no unidirectional causality running from Y to X,
e.g. if $F_{Y\to X} = 0$, then

$$n\widehat{F}_{Y\to X} \sim X^2(klp) \tag{17}$$

if $F_{X\to Y} = 0$, then

$$n\widehat{F}_{X\to Y} \sim X^2(klp) \tag{18}$$

if $F_{X\cdot Y} = 0$, then

$$n\widehat{F}_{X\cdot Y} \sim X^2(kl) \tag{19}$$

Since these tests are of nested hypotheses, $\widehat{F}_{Y\to X}, \widehat{F}_{X\to Y}$, and $\widehat{F}_{X\cdot Y}$ are asymptotically independent. The measure of linear feedback between X and Y, $F_{X,Y}$, can be tested at once,
if $F_{X,Y} = 0$.

$$n\widehat{F}_{X,Y} \sim X^2(kl(2p+1)) \tag{20}$$

2.3 Confidence Interval

The 95% confidence interval (CI) can be calculated approximately as following:
For $\hat{F}_{Y\to X,}$

$$\left\{\left[\left(\widehat{F}_{Y\to X} - \frac{klp-1}{3n}\right)^{1/2} - \frac{1.96}{\sqrt{n}}\right]^2 - \frac{2klp+1}{3n}, \left[\left(\widehat{F}_{Y\to X} - \frac{klp-1}{3n}\right)^{1/2} + \frac{1.96}{\sqrt{n}}\right]^2 - \frac{2klp+1}{3n}\right\} \tag{21}$$

For $\hat{F}_{X\to Y,}$

$$\left\{\left[\left(\widehat{F}_{X\to Y} - \frac{klp-1}{3n}\right)^{1/2} - \frac{1.96}{\sqrt{n}}\right]^2 - \frac{2klp+1}{3n}, \left[\left(\widehat{F}_{X\to Y} - \frac{klp-1}{3n}\right)^{1/2} + \frac{1.96}{\sqrt{n}}\right]^2 - \frac{2klp+1}{3n}\right\} \tag{22}$$

For $\hat{F}_{X\cdot Y,}$

$$\left\{\left[\left(\widehat{F}_{X\cdot Y} - \frac{kl-1}{3n}\right)^{1/2} - \frac{1.96}{\sqrt{n}}\right]^2 - \frac{2kl+1}{3n}, \left[\left(\widehat{F}_{X\cdot Y} - \frac{kl-1}{3n}\right)^{1/2} + \frac{1.96}{\sqrt{n}}\right]^2 - \frac{2kl+1}{3n}\right\} \tag{23}$$

For $\hat{F}_{X,Y,}$

$$\left\{\left[\left(\widehat{F}_{X,Y} - \frac{kl(2p+1)-1}{3n}\right)^{\frac{1}{2}} - \frac{1.96}{\sqrt{n}}\right]^2 - \frac{2kl(2p+1)+1}{3n}, \left[\left(\widehat{F}_{X,Y} - \frac{kl(2p+1)-1}{3n}\right)^{\frac{1}{2}} + \frac{1.96}{\sqrt{n}}\right]^2 - \frac{2kl(2p+1)+1}{3n}\right\} \tag{24}$$

3. CASE SELECTION

This chapter explores the possible explanations for the high and low level of competitiveness among Indonesian provinces. To do this, we shall look deeper into four provinces. The criteria for selection include:

a. Provinces that have been ranked consistently high and consistently low in the ACI's provincial competitiveness index in 2013 and 2014,
b. Provinces that are part of different regions within Indonesia to analyse regional variation, and
c. Provinces that have diversity in their population and economic structure.

For the first criterion, as revealed in Chapter 1, the top ranked province is DKI Jakarta. However, considering Jakarta's unique role as the nation's capital and its standardised scores, which are significantly higher than those of other provinces, Jakarta is practically an outlier. Consequently, the choices for East Java and East Kalimantan, as the second and third most competitive province, respectively, are rationalised. These two provinces have consistently held their ranks since 2013. Their Overall Competitiveness standardised scores are also not too far off from each other, 1.82 for East Java and 1.56 for East Kalimantan.[6]

As for the provinces with relatively low competitiveness, the choices go to the 32nd and 33rd province in the ranking, namely East Nusa Tenggara and North Maluku. Their standardised scores are also relatively close, −1.56 for East Nusa Tenggara and −1.71 for North Maluku.

The highly competitive cases, East Java and East Kalimantan, have also scored consistently high (among the top five provinces) on all four environments of competitiveness. Meanwhile, the less competitive provinces, North Maluku and East Nusa Tenggara, have also positioned themselves among the bottom five provinces on three out of the four competitiveness environments in 2013 and 2014.[7]

The second criterion is to select provinces that are part of different regions. Those four provinces come from different regions. East Java is part of the Java Region; East Kalimantan is part of the Kalimantan Region; East Nusa Tenggara is part of the Bali–Nusa Tenggara Region; and North Maluku is part of the Maluku–Papua Region. The diversity of geographic setting is hoped to provide more variation into the provinces that are to be observed in greater detail.[8] Figure 9.1 illustrates the geographical map of the four selected provinces.

The third and final criterion is to select provinces that have diversity in their population and economic structure. The four chosen provinces also have various social and economic backgrounds. East Java is a dense province with a largely urban characteristic and bases its economy on manufacturing and trade. East Kalimantan is a large province in terms of area, with relatively small population and rich natural resources (e.g. oil, gas, and coal). Both East Nusa Tenggara and North Maluku are archipelagic provinces with small population and an economy that is reliant on agriculture and fishery. North Maluku, however, has been more exposed to trade due to the long history of spices production for the international market.

3.1 East Java

3.1.1 *Key Characteristics*

East Java is the second most populous province in Indonesia after West Java. In 2011, its population reached 37.7 million (about 15% of the country's population), while West Java had 43.8 million people. East Java's capital, Surabaya, is Indonesia's second largest city after Jakarta, with 2.8 million residents in 2011. The Surabaya metropolitan area (also called as *Gerbangkertosusila*) was home to 9.1 million people in 2010, or almost a quarter of the province's population. Almost half (47.5%) of the province's population live in urban areas.

---

[6] See Table 1.1 in Chapter 1 for Overall Competitiveness Ranking and Score.

[7] See Tables 1.2 to 1.5 in Chapter 1 for Ranking and Score for all four environments.

[8] See Chapter 2 for more information about regional grouping.

Figure 9.1. Provincial Distribution of Overall Competitiveness

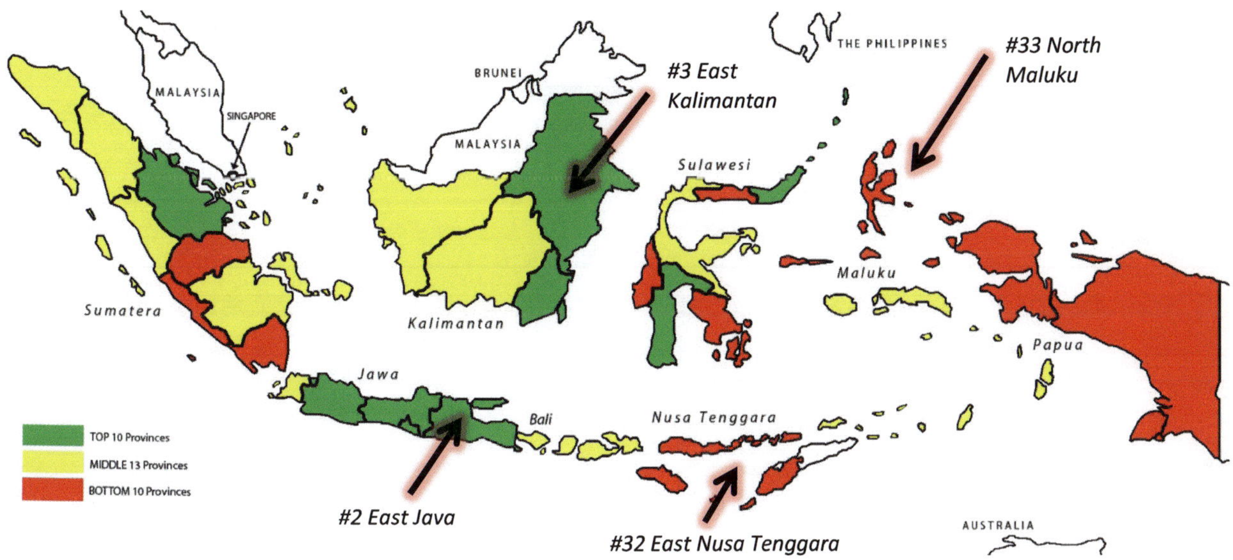

Source: Asia Competitiveness Institute

In terms of economy, East Java has the second highest Gross Regional Domestic Product (GRDP) in the country after DKI Jakarta. In 2011, East Java's GRDP was 366,984 billion Rupiah in 2000 constant price. DKI Jakarta had 422,162 billion Rupiah. In fact, East Java is the runner up in all three sectors of the GRDP. For the GRDP of the primary sector, East Java is second after East Kalimantan. For GRDP of the secondary sector, East Java is second after West Java. Similarly for the GRDP of the tertiary sector, East Java is second after DKI Jakarta. This shows that East Java is well-rounded in competitiveness with good performance in multiple aspects of the economy.

East Java is also Indonesia's second largest source of non-oil and gas exports after DKI Jakarta. The Surabaya metropolitan area is home to one of the country's largest clusters of industrial zones, after the Jakarta metropolitan area (covering DKI Jakarta, West Java, and Banten). Other notable clusters of industrial zones are found in Riau Islands, West Java, and Central Java.

East Java obtained the highest score nationwide for Labour Market Flexibility sub-environment, according to the ACI's provincial competitiveness study. East Java's score for this sub-environment is 3.47 while the second-ranked province is Central Java with a score of 2.96. The difference in score is quite substantial. Among East Java's highlights for this aspect is that it has the highest number of labour force and employment, the lowest unemployment rate, and the second lowest minimum wage across the country.

According to the ACI's Indonesia provincial competitiveness analysis, East Java also boasts of having the highest score for Physical Infrastructure sub-environment. As documented in 2011, East Java had the longest paved roads in the country, as long as 35,539 km, followed by Central Java, with 22,897 km of paved roads. The Surabaya seaport is also the second busiest port in the country after DKI Jakarta's and its airport is the second busiest for domestic travels after Soekarno–Hatta Airport in Banten. The ACI's survey confirms that there is a favourable perception towards the quality of physical infrastructure in East Java.

The ACI's Median Competitiveness Web for East Java (Figure 9.2) underscores the province's good performance in all sub-environments, with particular emphasis on its strength in Labour Market Flexibility, Physical Infrastructure, Regional Economic Vibrancy, and Attractiveness to Foreign Investors.

Despite East Java's good economic performance, it still has room for improvement in reducing poverty rate (13.85% in 2011) and improving human development. In 2011, East Java's Human Development Index (HDI) was 72.18, which placed it at the 17th position (median) among 33 the Indonesian provinces.

Figure 9.2. 2014 Median Competitiveness Web for East Java

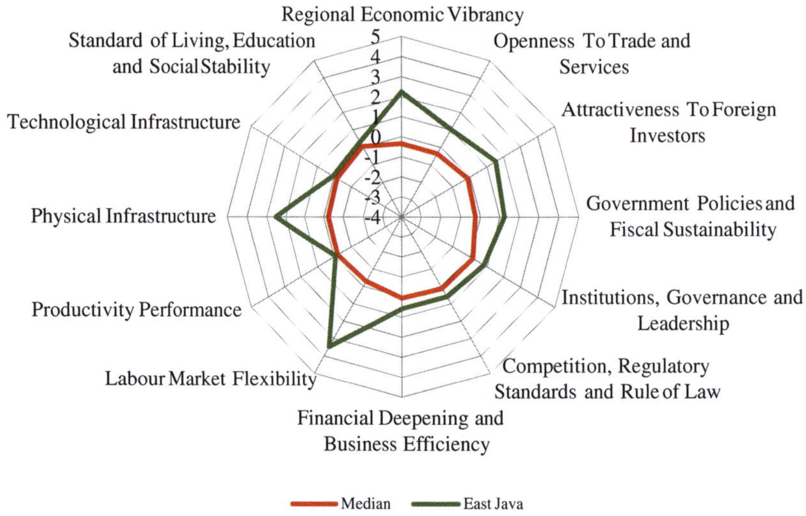

Source: Asia Competitiveness Institute

3.1.2 *Economic Development Trends*

East Java's economic development has been characterised by a strong and steady growth of the tertiary sector that has experienced substantially higher growth than the primary and secondary sectors. This phenomenon can be considered as restructuring of the economy from one that relies primarily on the primary and secondary sector to the tertiary. As seen from Figure 9.3, it is noticeable how the tertiary sector has been rising with a relative decrease in the primary and secondary sectors.

Through closer observation of the top four sub-sectors for East Java between 2000 and 2011, we observed that the trade, hotel and restaurant sub-sector had been growing the fastest and it became the sub-sector with the most economic output, overtaking manufacturing since 2005, as illustrated in Figure 9.4.

The following Geweke causality analysis explores the factors that may drive East Java's restructuring process.

3.1.3 *Hypothesis Testing*

Upon review of East Java's main economic development trends, trade, hotel, and restaurant sub-sector had grown the most between 2000–2011 (in terms of GRDP value) compared to the other sub-sectors. It overtook manufacturing in 2005 to claim the first place as the largest component within East Java's GRDP.

Trade, hotel and restaurant sub-sector as the representative of the services sector is highly dependent on the availability and quality of manpower and infrastructure. The availability of workforces that are well-trained in the service industry and able to engage with employers in harmonious industrial relations provides the hospitality sector with the needed human resources. At the same time, good physical infrastructure enables trade to take place seamlessly.

East Java has the highest scores for Labour Market Flexibility and Physical Infrastructure nationwide in the ACI's competitiveness study. We therefore proposed to test the following hypothesis that **good labour market and good infrastructure contribute to East Java's high service sector growth.**

3.1.4 *Data Description*

The selected dependent variable in the Geweke causality analysis is the change in GRDP in trade, hotel and restaurant sub-sector. It is chosen to represent the growth of East Java's services sector. Here, the change (Δ) is derived from first order difference.

Figure 9.3. East Java's Economic Structure

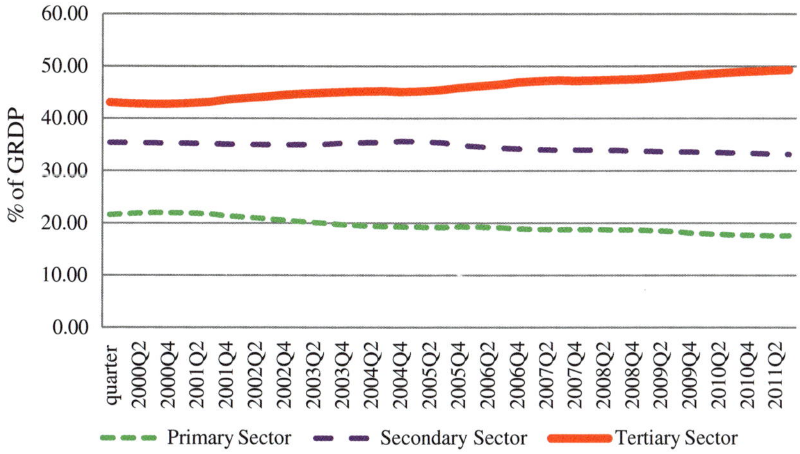

Source: Asia Competitiveness Institute using data from World Bank INDO-DAPOER

Figure 9.4. East Java's GRDP by Sector (2000–2011)

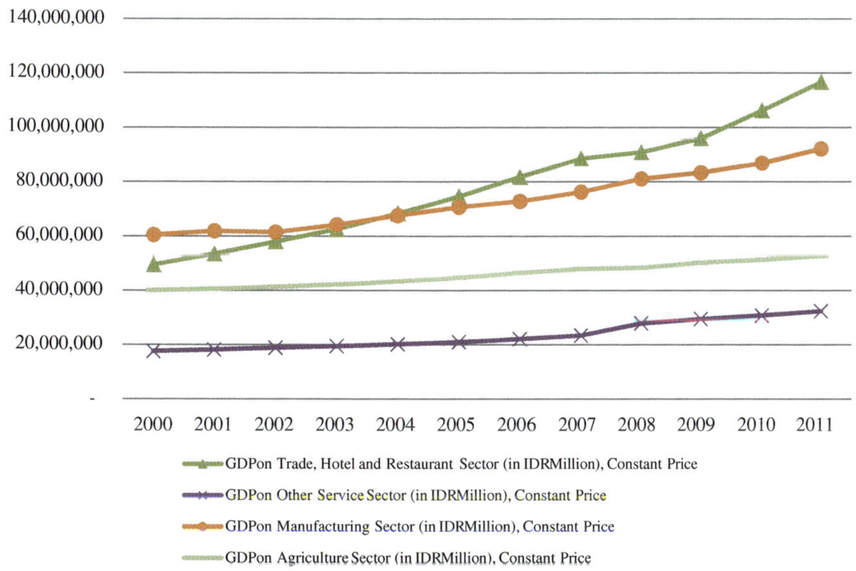

Source: Asia Competitiveness Institute using data from World Bank INDO-DAPOER

The independent variables are employment rate (measured in percentage), which represents the condition of East Java's labour market, and access to electricity (measured in percentage), which represents the province's physical infrastructure (Table 9.1). The data for all three variables were sourced from World Bank's Indonesia Database for Policy and Economic Research (INDO-DAPOER).

To conduct the Geweke causality analysis, we need time series data with at least 30 data points for each indicator. Considering the following issues: (i) limited availability of data at the province level for the previous 30 years and (ii) the presence of several structural breaks in Indonesia's political economic history, we have opted to use quarterly (instead of yearly) data for a period of 12 years (from 2000 until 2011). By converting the yearly data into quarterly data, 48 data points could be obtained.

The conversion from yearly to quarterly data was conducted using Eviews software. The method of conversion used was "Quadratic Match Sum" for the change in GRDP in trade, hotel and restaurant and "Quadratic Match Average" for both employment rate and access to electricity. All variables used in empirical estimations were subjected to statistical checks and stationarity tests.

Table 9.1. Variables used in East Java Geweke Causality Analysis

Variable	Notation	Definition
X	GDPTHR	Δ GRDP in Trade, Hotel, and Restaurant (%)
Y1	EMPRAT	Employment Rate (%)
Y2	ACCELEC	Access to Electricity (%)

Source: Asia Competitiveness Institute

Figure 9.5. East Java's Employment Rate (2000–2011)

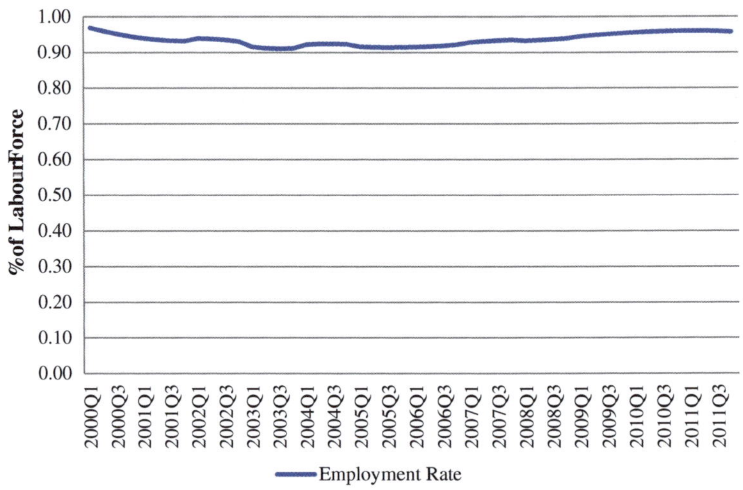

Source: Asia Competitiveness Institute using data from World Bank INDO-DAPOER

Figure 9.6. East Java's Access to Electricity (2000–2011)

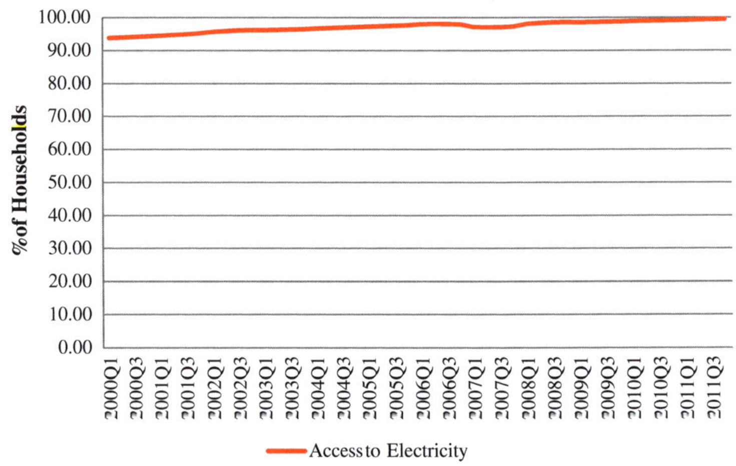

Source: Asia Competitiveness Institute using data from World Bank INDO-DAPOER

Figure 9.5 shows that East Java has a consistently good employment rate (EMPRAT), which was maintained over 90% from the first quarter of 2000 until the fourth quarter of 2011. Some fluctuations happened between 2001 and 2005, but overall, it can be safely concluded that from 2006 onwards, East Java's employment rate has been growing steadily.

Figure 9.6 also shows a very high and increasing level of access to electricity (ACCELEC) throughout the province. Since 2000, East Java already has over 93% of its households connected to the state electricity. The coverage has kept on increasing since then and almost all of the households (over 99%) were covered by 2011.

3.1.5 *Empirical Results*

The Geweke causality analysis was conducted in both bi-variate and multi-variate models. In the bi-variate analysis, association of the dependent variable (X) and independent variables (Y1 and Y2) were tested separately. This means that Geweke tests were conducted between X and Y1 and between X and Y2. In terms of feedback direction, the tests were also conducted separately, from X towards Y1 and vice versa and from X towards Y2 and vice versa. The bi-variate results are presented in Table 9.2.

Table 9.2 shows a significant total association between GDPTHR and EMPRAT in either direction ($F_{X,Y}$ is significant at 1% level for both directions). Most of the association takes place instantaneously between GDPTHR and EMPRAT ($F_{X \cdot Y}$ is significant at 1% level for both directions). However, as seen from each direction, there was no significant feedback for both $F_{X \to Y}$ and $F_{Y \to X}$ when GDPTHR was considered as X and EMPRAT was considered as Y. A significant feedback (up to 10% level of significance) was only seen for $F_{X \to Y}$ when EMPRAT was considered as X and GDPTHR as Y.

Similarly, there is a significant total association between GDPTHR and ACCELEC in either direction ($F_{X,Y}$ is significant at 1% level when GDPTHR was considered as X and ACCELEC as Y and at 5% level when ACCELEC was considered as X and GDPTHR as Y). Most of the association takes place instantaneously between GDPTHR and ACCELEC ($F_{X \cdot Y}$ is significant at 1% level for both directions). However, as seen from each direction, there was no significant feedback for both $F_{X \to Y}$ and $F_{Y \to X}$ when ACCELEC was considered as X and GDPTHR was considered as Y. There is a significant feedback (up to 5% level of significance) for $F_{Y \to X}$ when GDPTHR was considered as X and ACCELEC as Y.

In multi-variate analysis, both the independent variables (Y1 and Y2) were incorporated as Y and its association with the dependent variable (X) was then tested. The multi-variate results are presented in Table 9.3.

Table 9.2. Estimated measures of bi-directional feedback between Change of GRDP in Trade, Hotel and Restaurant (GDPTHR), Employment Rate (EMPRAT), and Access to Electricity (ACCELEC) for East Java, Indonesia, 2000-2011[ab]

Economic aggregates		$H_0(F_{X,Y} = F_{X \to Y} + F_{Y \to X} + F_{X \cdot Y})$			
X	Y	$F_{X,Y}$	$F_{X \to Y}$	$F_{Y \to X}$	$F_{X \cdot Y}$
GDPTHR	EMPRAT	0.4202*** (0.0029)	0.0168 (0.6974)	0.1049 (0.1049)	0.2985*** (0.0003)
EMPRAT	GDPTHR	0.4450*** (0.0018)	0.1234* (0.0704)	0.0230 (0.6097)	0.2985*** (0.0003)
GDPTHR	ACCELEC	0. 4184*** (0.0030)	0.0013 (0.9726)	0.1541** (0.0364)	0.2630*** (0.0008)
ACCELEC	GDPTHR	0.3502** (0.0101)	0.0860 (0.1573)	0.0012 (0.9746)	0.2630*** (0.0008)

[a] *, ** and *** denote 10%, 5% and 1% level of significance, respectively.
[b] Confidence interval will be provided upon request.
Source: Asia Competitiveness Institute

Table 9.3. Estimated measures of multi-directional feedback between Change of GRDP in Trade, Hotel and Restaurant (GDPTHR), Employment Rate (EMPRAT), and Access to Electricity (ACCELEC) for East Java, Indonesia, 2000–2011[ab]

Economic aggregates		$H_0(F_{X,Y} = F_{X \to Y} + F_{Y \to X} + F_{X \cdot Y})$			
X	Y	$F_{X,Y}$	$F_{X \to Y}$	$F_{Y \to X}$	$F_{X \cdot Y}$
GDPTHR	EMPRAT ACCELEC	0.8329*** (0.0001)	0.0341 (0. 8326)	0.3640*** (0.0035)	0.4348*** (0.0001)

[a] *, ** and *** denote 10%, 5% and 1% level of significance, respectively.
[b] Confidence interval will be provided upon request.
Source: Asia Competitiveness Institute

Table 9.3 shows that when EMPRAT and ACCELEC were incorporated as Y, there is a significant total association between X (GDPTHR) and Y (EMPRAT and ACCELEC) at the 1% level of significance. Slightly more than half of that association (0.4348 out of 0.8329 or 52.2%) takes place between X and Y instantaneously while 43.7% of the association (0.3640 out of 0.8329) takes place from Y going towards X. Both of these associations are significant at 1% level of significance. The feedback going from X towards Y, however, is not significant.

Thus, it can be concluded that, in the case of East Java, both employment rate and access to electricity contribute towards a growing GRDP in the trade, hotel and restaurant sub-sector, but not the other way around. The causal direction is not mutual, as we *cannot* say with enough confidence that a growing trade, hotel and restaurant sub-sector in East Java's GRDP contributes to higher employment rate and access to electricity.

3.1.6 *Policy Implications*

The Geweke causality analysis for East Java shows that both high access to electricity and high employment rate contribute positively to a growing GRDP in the trade, hotel, and restaurant sub-sector. This highlights the importance of both infrastructure and human resources for economic development.

As shown from the case of East Java, access to infrastructure, especially in the form of access to electricity, contributes to a growing economy. Roads, water, and information technology are similarly beneficial. In another Geweke causality analysis for East Java (data not shown here), we also found a significant feedback going from the government expenditure in infrastructure towards the growth of exports.

The East Java Geweke tests also show that having a good labour market is just as important to trigger economic development. East Java's high employment rate (the highest among Indonesia's 33 provinces) also contributes to a growing GRDP in the tertiary sector. East Java's favourable labour market is not solely due to high employment rate. The latter may well be associated with the low minimum wage in the province. In 2011, East Java's provincial minimum wage was the second lowest in the country. Furthermore, based on the ACI's surveys with business owners, government, and academics in 2013, all parties confirmed that labour relations in East Java are harmonious.

3.2 East Kalimantan

3.2.1 *Key Characteristics*

East Kalimantan is known as one of Indonesia's well-endowed provinces due to the substantial presence of natural resources. The province's GRDP derived from oil and gas was the second largest in the country, just after Riau in Sumatra. In 2011, East Kalimantan's oil and gas-related GRDP was 40,324 billion Rupiah in 2000 constant price while Riau's was 50,250 billion Rupiah. However, if minerals and coal are included, then East Kalimantan becomes the richest province in terms of oil, gas, minerals, and coal combined. In 2011, the province's GRDP from these combined resources amounted to 75,766 billion Rupiah in 2000 constant price while Riau's was 51,294,855 billion Rupiah. Close to two-thirds (65.74%) of East Kalimantan's GRDP is oil, gas, minerals, and coal-related while the figure is closer to half (49.99%) for Riau.

Natural resources are among the important factors that enable East Kalimantan to have a sizeable public budget. The province has the second highest fiscal balance, after DKI Jakarta. In 2011, East Kalimantan's fiscal balance (the difference between public revenue and public expenditure) was 507,373 million Rupiah while DKI Jakarta's was 806,216 million Rupiah.

Due to the presence of high GRDP with a relatively small population (3.69 million people in 2011), East Kalimantan's GRDP per capita was the second highest in the country after DKI Jakarta. In 2011, East Kalimantan's GRDP per capita was 31,227,100 Rupiah while DKI Jakarta's was 43,389,800 Rupiah in 2000 constant price. The province with the third highest GRDP per capita was Riau Islands with 24,828,600 Rupiah.

The rise of the primary sector has generated many positive spillover effects on the tertiary sector. Trade, hotel, restaurant, and financial services were among the sub-sectors that have experienced positive growth (in absolute and relative terms as percentage of East Kalimantan's GRDP).

The spillover effect of this resource-led growth on the services sector can be seen, among others, in the financial service sub-sector. The ACI surveys confirm that East Kalimantan is ranked among the top three nationwide in terms of Ease of Dealing with Banks.

Another notable aspect of East Kalimantan is the good quality of its infrastructure, be it Physical Infrastructure (ranked seventh nationwide) or Technological Infrastructure (ranked fifth). The province also scores very well in terms of Standard of Living, Education, and Social Stability (ranked fifth). When aggregated at the Quality of Life and Infrastructure Development environment, East Kalimantan is ranked very favourably at the second position (score: 1.59), slightly below DI Yogyakarta at first place (score: 1.65) and above DKI Jakarta at third place (score: 1.55).

The ACI's Median Competitiveness Web for East Kalimantan (Figure 9.7) underscores the province's good performance in almost all sub-environments, except for the Labour Market Flexibility. Among the province's particular strengths are Productivity Performance; Technological Infrastructure; and Competition, Regulatory Standards, and Rule of Law. As for Labour Market Flexibility, one of the challenges faced by East Kalimantan is the spreading of employment opportunities to the wider public, given its high GRDP.

East Kalimantan's good economic performance is coupled with similar good achievements in human development. The province has the fifth highest HDI in the country, with a score of 76.22. Political condition is stable, public services are widely available, and education statistics such as Literacy Rate, School Enrolment Rate and Mean Years of Schooling are favourable.

3.2.2 *Economic Development Trends*

East Kalimantan has substantial oil and gas processing activities, which form a part of the secondary sector. However, coal contributed largely to the primary sector especially during the past decade. The rise of minerals and coal production in East Kalimantan during the 2000 to 2011 period has created a change in the province's economic structure, resulting in a relative decline in the secondary sector (oil and gas processing) contribution to the GRDP.

Figure 9.8 illustrates East Kalimantan's economic structure. With the rise of the primary sector, the secondary sector has been declining while the tertiary sector has been rising (in relative terms as percentage of the GRDP). The secondary sector, albeit declining in trend, still forms a larger share of the GRDP than the tertiary sector, which is rising in trend.

Figure 9.7. 2014 Median Competitiveness Web for East Kalimantan

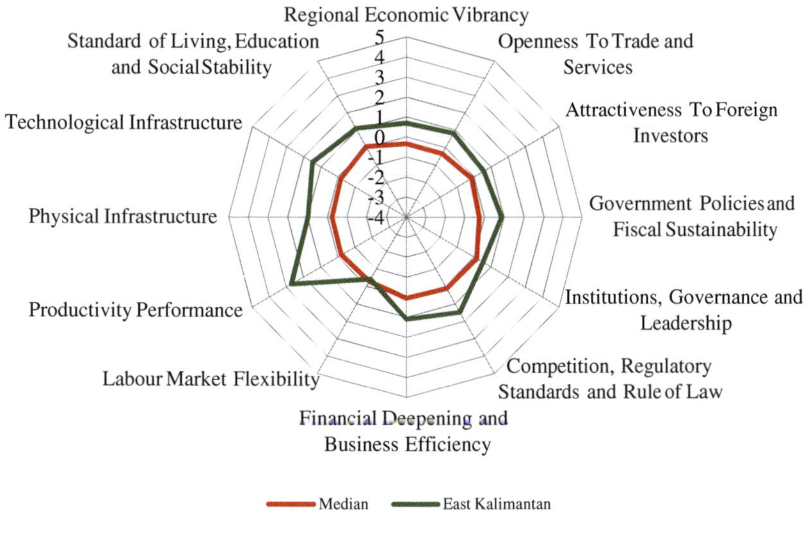

Source: Asia Competitiveness Institute

Figure 9.8. East Kalimantan's Economic Structure

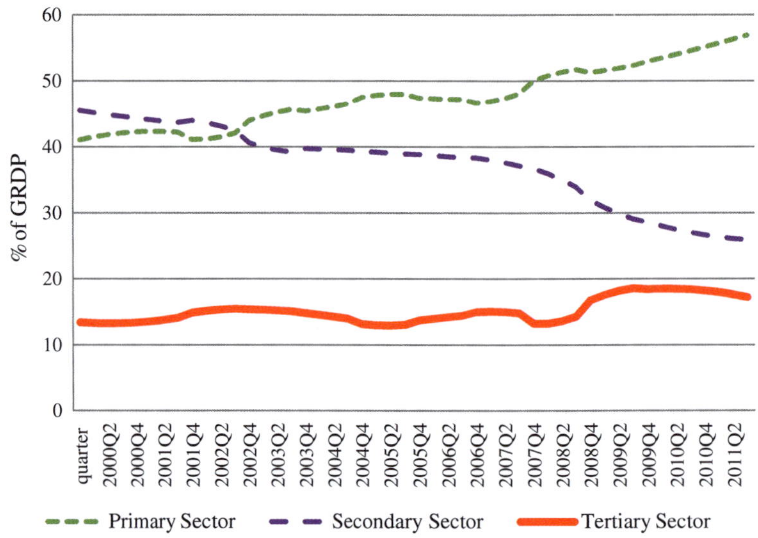

Source: Asia Competitiveness Institute using data from World Bank INDO-DAPOER

Figure 9.9. East Kalimantan's GRDP by Sector (2000–2011)

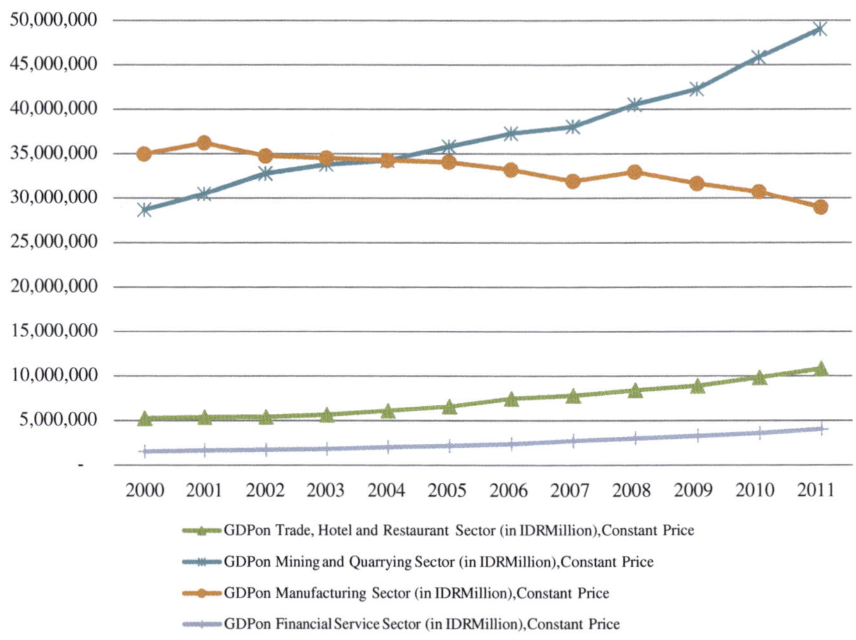

Source: Asia Competitiveness Institute using data from World Bank INDO-DAPOER

With a closer observation, it can be seen that the trade, hotel and restaurant sub-sector is the largest sub-sector among East Kalimantan's tertiary sectors. This pattern was also seen in East Java. Among East Kalimantan's tertiary sub-sectors (Figure 9.9), financial service has been growing, although it is smaller in size than trade, hotel and restaurant. Between 2000 and 2011, the trade, hotel and restaurant sub-sector grew by about 100%, from 5,253 billion to 10,803 billion Rupiah while the financial service sub-sector grew by about 163%, from 1,527 billion Rupiah to 4,023 billion Rupiah in 2000 constant price.

The following Geweke causality analysis explores the factors that may drive East Kalimantan's growth of the trade, hotel and restaurant sub-sector.

3.2.3 *Hypothesis Testing*

Upon review of East Kalimantan's main economic development trends, it can be observed that among the province's tertiary sub-sectors, trade, hotel, and restaurant is the largest sub-sector (51.5%) and has grown by 100% steadily between the period of 2000-2011 (in terms of GRDP value). However, financial service sub-sector has been growing faster at 163%, although it only forms 19.2% of East Kalimantan's tertiary sector.

For the trade, hotel and restaurant sub-sector to flourish, the presence of reliable financial services is important. According to the ACI data and survey results, East Kalimantan is ranked third in Ease of Dealing with Banks, and fourth in Population per Number of Bank Branches. The expansion of financial services depends also on the availability of financial service workers who are well trained. At the same time, good physical infrastructure enables seamless movement of people and goods.

East Kalimantan is ranked fourth in the ACI's Financial Deepening and Business Efficiency sub-environment. At the same time, the province is ranked sixth in the ACI's Physical Infrastructure sub-environment. We therefore proposed to test the following hypothesis that **employment in financial services and good infrastructure contribute to East Kalimantan's high service sector growth.**

3.2.4 *Data Description*

The selected dependent variable in the Geweke causality analysis is the change in GRDP in trade, hotel and restaurant sub-sector. It is chosen to represent the growth of East Kalimantan's services sector. Here, the change (Δ) is derived from first order difference.

The independent variables are employment in financial service sub-sector (measured in number of workers), which represents East Kalimantan's growing financial service sub-sector, and length of paved roads (measured in km), which represents the province's physical infrastructure (Table 9.4). The data for all three variables were sourced from World Bank INDO-DAPOER.

To conduct the Geweke causality analysis, we need time series data with at least 30 data points for each indicator. Considering the following issues: (i) limited availability of data at the province level for the previous 30 years, and (ii) the presence of several structural breaks in Indonesia's political economic history, we have opted to use quarterly (instead of yearly) data for a period of 12 years (from 2000 to 2011). By converting the yearly data into quarterly data, 48 data points could be obtained.

The conversion from yearly to quarterly data was conducted using Eviews software. The method of conversion used was "Quadratic Match Sum" for the change in GRDP in trade, hotel and restaurant and "Quadratic Match Average" for both employment in financial services and length of paved roads. All the variables used in empirical estimations were subjected to statistical checks and stationarity tests.

Figure 9.10 shows that East Kalimantan has experienced an increase in employment in financial services (EMPFIN) from 10,921 people in the first quarter of 2000 to 46,646 in the fourth quarter of 2011. This is an increase of 327% over a period of 12 years. Major fluctuations happened primarily between 2004 and 2010 but generally, the trend is upwards.

Figure 9.11 shows an increasing length of paved roads (ROADS) in the province from 2,171 km in the first quarter of 2000 to 6,166 km in the fourth quarter of 2011. This is an increase of 184% over a period of 12 years. Similar to the data on financial sector workers, there were also fluctuations, which primarily took place between 2005 and 2009.

Table 9.4. Variables used in East Kalimantan Geweke Causality Analysis

Variable	Notation	Definition
X	GDPTHR	Δ GRDP in Trade, Hotel, and Restaurant (%)
Y1	EMPFIN	Employment in Financial Services (number)
Y2	ROADS	Length of Paved Roads (km)

Source: Asia Competitiveness Institute

Figure 9.10. East Kalimantan's Employment in the Financial Services Industry

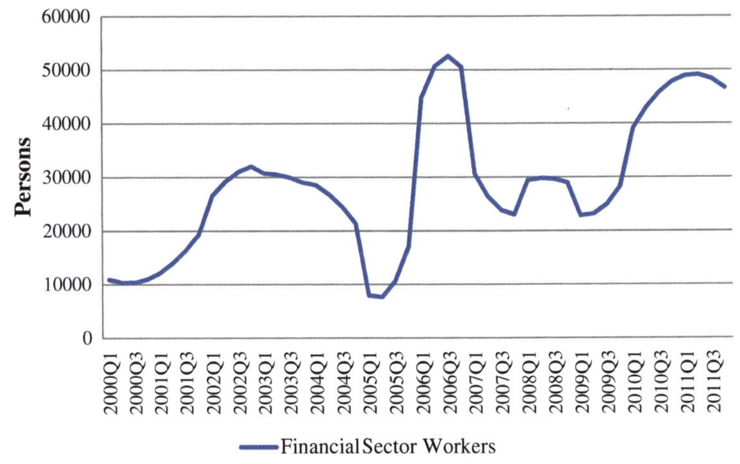

Source: Asia Competitiveness Institute using data from World Bank INDO-DAPOER

Figure 9.11. East Kalimantan's Length of Paved Roads

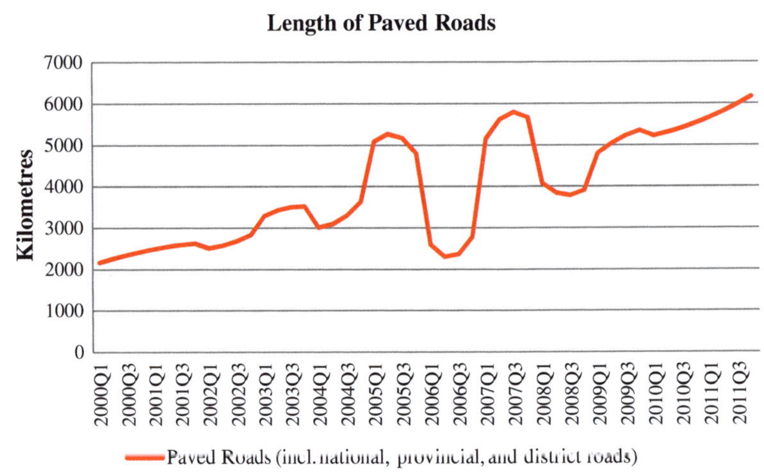

Source: Asia Competitiveness Institute using data from World Bank INDO-DAPOER

3.2.5 *Empirical Results*

The Geweke causality analysis was conducted in both bi-variate and multi-variate models. In the bi-variate analysis, both directions of association between the dependent variable (X) and independent variables (Y1 and Y2) were tested separately. This means that Geweke tests were conducted between X and Y1 and between X and Y2. In terms of feedback direction, the tests were also conducted separately, from X towards Y1 and vice versa and from X towards Y2 and vice versa. The bi-variate results are presented in Table 9.5.

Table 9.5 shows a significant total association between GDPTHR and EMPFIN in either direction ($F_{X,Y}$ is significant at 1% level for both directions). Most of the association takes place instantaneously between GDPTHR and EMPFIN ($F_{X \cdot Y}$ is significant at 1% level for both directions). As seen from each direction, there is a highly significant feedback (at 1% level of significance) for $F_{Y \to X}$ when GDPTHR was considered as X and EMPFIN was considered as Y. This feedback contributed to 0.2524 out of 1.6915 of the total association between GDPTHR and EMPFIN. There is also a significant feedback (at 10% level of significance) for $F_{X \to Y}$ when EMPFIN was considered as X and GDPTHR as Y. This feedback contributed to 0.1215 out of 1.6255 of the total association between EMPFIN and GDPTHR.

Table 9.5. Estimated measures of bi-directional feedback between Change of GRDP in Trade, Hotel and Restaurant (GDPTHR), Employment in Financial Service Sub-Sector (EMPFIN), and Length of Paved Roads (ROAD) for East Kalimantan, Indonesia, 2000–2011[ab]

Economic aggregates		$H_0(F_{X,Y} = F_{X\to Y} + F_{Y\to X} + F_{X\cdot Y})$			
X	Y	$F_{X,Y}$	$F_{X\to Y}$	$F_{Y\to X}$	$F_{X\cdot Y}$
GDPTHR	EMPFIN	1.6915*** (0.000)	0.0333 (0.4892)	0.2524*** (0.0044)	1.4058*** (0.0000)
EMPFIN	GDPTHR	1.6255*** (0.0000)	0.1215* (0.0734)	0.0981 (0.1213)	1.4058*** (0.0000)
GDPTHR	ROAD	1.8243*** (0.0000)	0.0616 (0.2662)	0.6492*** (0.0000)	1.1135*** (0.0000)
ROAD	GDPTHR	1.6901*** (0.0000)	0.3583*** (0.0005)	0.2183*** (0.0091)	1.1135*** (0.0000)

[a]*, ** and *** denote 10%, 5% and 1% level of significance, respectively.
[b]Confidence interval will be provided upon request.
Source: Asia Competitiveness Institute

Table 9.6. Estimated measures of multi-directional feedback between Change of GRDP in Trade, Hotel and Restaurant (GDPTHR), Employment in Financial Service Sub-Sector (EMPFIN), and Length of Paved Roads (ROAD) for East Kalimantan, Indonesia, 2000–2011[ab]

Economic aggregates		$H_0(F_{X,Y} = F_{X\to Y} + F_{Y\to X} + F_{X\cdot Y})$			
X	Y	$F_{X,Y}$	$F_{X\to Y}$	$F_{Y\to X}$	$F_{X\cdot Y}$
GDPTHR	EMPFIN ROAD	2.0054*** (0.000)	0.0509 (0.7014)	0.7440*** (0.0000)	1.2105*** (0.0000)

[a]*, ** and *** denote 10%, 5% and 1% level of significance, respectively.
[b]Confidence interval will be provided upon request.
Source: Asia Competitiveness Institute

Similarly, we found a significant total association between GDPTHR and ROAD in either direction ($F_{X,Y}$ is significant at 1% level for both directions). Most of the association takes place instantaneously between GDPTHR and ROAD ($F_{X\cdot Y}$ is significant at 1% level for both directions). As seen from each direction, there is a highly significant feedback (at 1% level of significance) for $F_{Y\to X}$ when GDPTHR was considered as X and ROAD was considered as Y. This feedback contributed to 0.6492 out of 1.8243 of the total association between GDPTHR and ROAD. A significant feedback (at 1% level of significance) for $F_{X\to Y}$ could also be observed when ROAD was considered as X and GDPTHR as Y. This feedback contributed to 0.3583 out of 1.6901 of the total association between ROAD and GDPTHR.

In the multi-variate analysis, both the independent variables (Y1 and Y2) were incorporated as Y and its association with the dependent variable (X) was then tested. The multi-variate results are presented in Table 9.6.

Table 9.6 shows that when EMPFIN and ROAD were incorporated as Y, there is a significant total association between X (GDPTHR) and Y (EMPFIN and ROAD) at the 1% level of significance. Slightly more than half of that association (1.2105 out of 2.0054 or 60.3%) takes place between X and Y instantaneously while 37.1% of the feedback (0. 7440 out of 2.0054) takes place from Y going towards X. Both of these directions of association are significant at the 1% level of significance. The feedback going from X towards Y, however, is not significant.

Thus, it can be concluded that in the case of East Kalimantan, both employment in the financial service sub-sector and length of paved roads contribute towards a growing GRDP in the trade, hotel and restaurant sub-sector, but not the other way around. The causal direction is not mutual, as we *cannot* say with enough confidence that a growing trade, hotel and restaurant sub-sector in East Kalimantan's GRDP contributes to higher employment in the financial service sub-sector and length of paved roads.

3.2.6 *Policy Implications*

The Geweke causality analysis for East Kalimantan shows that both increase in employment in financial services and paved roads contribute positively to a growing GRDP in the trade, hotel, and restaurant sub-sector. Similar to the conclusion for East Java, this highlights the importance of both infrastructure and human resources for economic development.

The case of East Kalimantan shows that access to infrastructure contributes to a growing economy especially in the form of trade, hotels, and restaurants. The example used in this analysis is roads, but the conclusions and policy implications should similarly be applied to other forms of connecting infrastructure. In another Geweke causality analysis (data not shown here), access to electricity also contributes significantly to tertiary sector growth, as hotels and offices need reliable power sources.

The East Kalimantan Geweke tests also show that the presence of financial sector is needed to support the growth of other services such as trade, hotels, and restaurants. Growing employment in the financial service sub-sector shows that banks are responding positively to the economic potentials in East Kalimantan. This is also seen through the presence of vibrant and responsive banking sector as shown by the ACI's survey.

The presence of labour with appropriate skills that support a growing industry (in this case, the financial industry) is helpful to further trigger economic growth. The challenge is to transform the growth to become more inclusive and more labour-intensive to spread employment opportunities to more people in the province and to reduce unemployment and underemployment rate.

3.3 North Maluku

3.3.1 *Key Characteristics*

North Maluku is an archipelagic province located in eastern Indonesia, between Papua Island and Sulawesi Island. It used to be a part of a larger Maluku province, but North Maluku became a separate province in 1999. The Maluku Islands were once the sole source of nutmeg and mace spices in the world and the islands were treated as a prized possession among European colonisers between the 16th and 19th century. The islands of Ternate and Tidore, now part of the North Maluku province, were once the centres of influential archipelagic sultanates funded by spice trades during pre-colonial times. To this day, Indonesia remains as the world's largest exporter of nutmeg, the bulk of which originates from the Maluku Islands.

As a province, North Maluku's population was the third smallest in Indonesia, with 1.06 million people in 2011. The province with the smallest number of population was West Papua (789,010 people). North Maluku's GRDP at 2011 (3,230 billion Rupiah in 2000 constant price) was the second lowest after Gorontalo's (3,141 billion Rupiah). North Maluku also had the fourth smallest GRDP per capita in 2011, at 3,038,400 Rupiah.

North Maluku was primarily based on agricultural economy, with the primary sector contributing to 41% of the GRDP in 2011. Its most notable primary sector products include nutmeg, mace, clove, and fish. The secondary sector (manufacturing) contributes to about 16% of the GRDP and includes industries such as food and beverages, metal products, and furniture. The bulk of manufacturing activities in North Maluku are in the form of cottage industries that operate at small scale with small productivity. The tertiary sector makes up about 42.5% of North Maluku's GRDP and is dominated by activities related to trade and tourism. Fisheries and tourism are among the province's major potential that still need to be further developed. North Maluku has numerous cultural and historical sites, as well as nature and marine resorts with its white beaches, blue seas, and prime diving sites.

At the moment, North Maluku faces major challenges in terms of productivity. It has the lowest tertiary sector productivity in the country (8.63 million Rupiah per worker per year) and the third lowest primary sector

Figure 9.12. 2014 Median Competitiveness Web for North Maluku

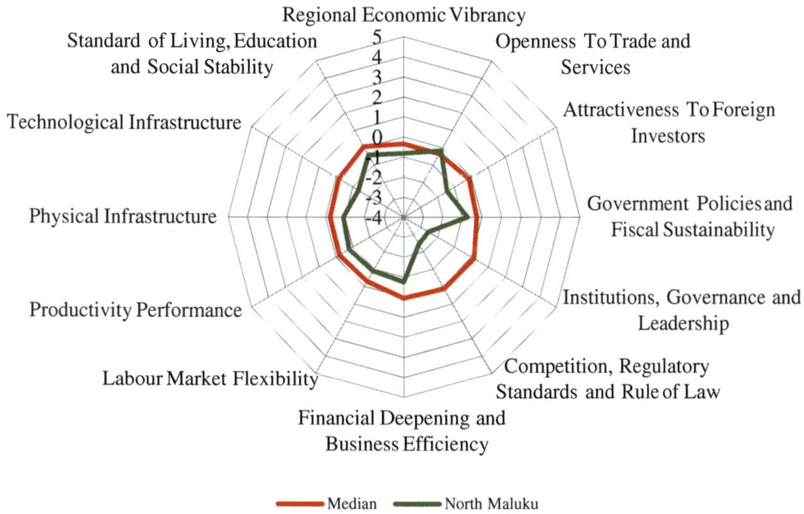

Source: Asia Competitiveness Institute

productivity (5.32 million Rupiah per worker per year). In terms of the secondary sector productivity, North Maluku is doing slightly better at 24th place out of the 33 provinces (17.82 million Rupiah per worker per year).

The ACI's provincial competitiveness analysis found that North Maluku's Government and Institutional Setting deserves further attention as the province is in the last place for this particular environment. Its standardised score was –2.49, which is substantially lower than the score obtained by East Nusa Tenggara at 32nd place (–1.59).

North Maluku's challenges in the social and public services are also reflected through its HDI. As of 2011, its HDI was 69.47. Although this is an improvement compared to 67.50 in 2006, the province was still ranked 30th out of the 33 provinces in 2011.

The ACI's Median Competitiveness Web for North Maluku (Figure 9.12) shows that the province mainly scores below the median for almost all sub-environments, except for Openness to Trade and Services. For some sub-environments, such as Standard of Living, Education and Social Stability, and Government Policies and Fiscal Sustainability, North Maluku's scores are not too far below the median. However, for Institutions, Governance and Leadership; Competition, Regulatory Standards and Rule of Law; and Attractiveness to Foreign Investors, much work needs to be done.

3.3.2 *Economic Development Trends*

As shown in Figure 9.13, North Maluku's economic development from 2000 until 2010 has been characterised by small size economy that has grown from 1,879 billion to 3,230 billion Rupiah in 2000 constant price. In comparison, the economy for an average province grew from 41,378 billion to 67,321 billion Rupiah. The median province in 2011 was Bali with a GRDP of 30,753 billion Rupiah. Therefore, North Maluku's economy has grown by 71.8% over the 10-year period while the average province's has grown by 62.7%.

Although North Maluku's economic growth has been slightly higher than that of the average province, North Maluku needs more economic mass to enable it to compete meaningfully with other Indonesian provinces. North Maluku's GRDP of 3,230 billion Rupiah in 2011 was only 4.79% of the average province's GRDP.

As seen from Figure 9.14, the agriculture sector (including fisheries) is still the largest contributor to North Maluku's GRDP. The province's main products are nutmeg, clove, cocoa, and various types of fish, but most notably, tuna. Trade, hotel and restaurant sector is the second largest contributor, which is growing faster than the primary sector. The trend seems to indicate that the tertiary sector may surpass the primary sector in a few

Figure 9.13. North Maluku's GRDP at 2000 constant prices

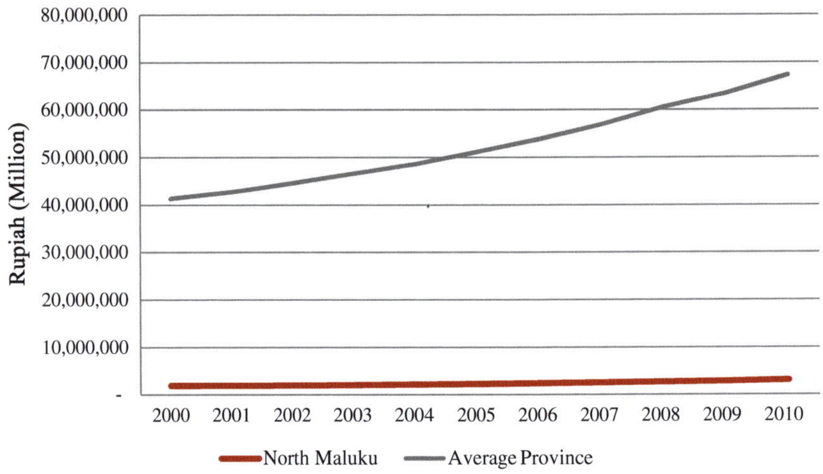

Source: Asia Competitiveness Institute using data from World Bank INDO-DAPOER

Figure 9.14. North Maluku's GRDP by Sector (2000–2011)

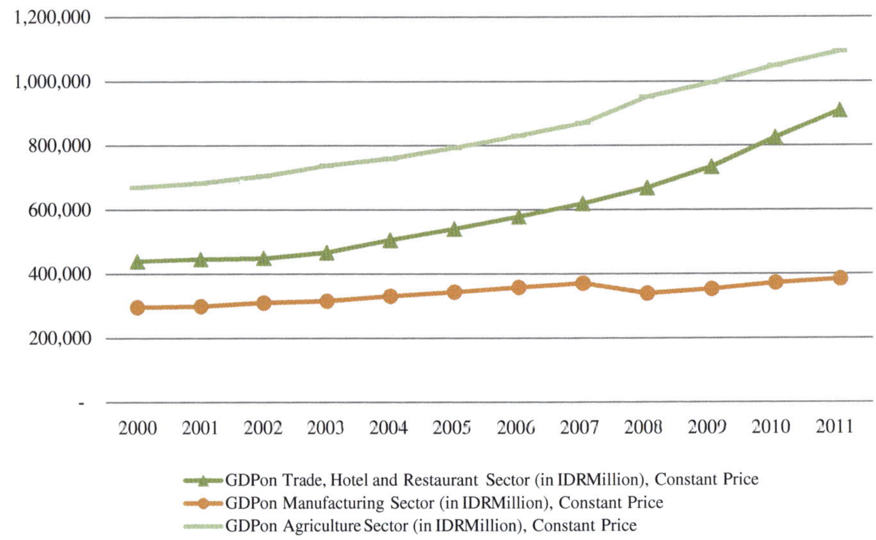

Source: Asia Competitiveness Institute using data from World Bank INDO-DAPOER

years in terms of percentage contribution to GRDP. Meanwhile, the growth of manufacturing sector has been relatively low. For example, the number of businesses dealing with fish processing is small despite the relatively sizeable catch. With limited availability of cold storage, most of the catch is directly sold for exports.

The following Geweke causality analysis explores the factors that may prevent North Maluku from achieving a larger economic mass.

3.3.3 *Hypothesis Testing*

Upon review of North Maluku's economic development trends, it is obvious that the province's GRDP remains small, with a growth rate that is lower than that of the average province. Among the avenues through which an agricultural economy can grow faster, one of them is through transitioning itself to become more manufacturing-oriented. North Maluku has largely been an agricultural (including fisheries) province for a long time and to boost the economic development, it is time to engage in more manufacturing activities. The manufacturing sector could absorb labour from the agriculture sector and create higher value-added products, which are more labour-intensive and thus, more likely to attract people from neighbouring places to migrate into the province.

Currently, North Maluku produces good quality spices (especially nutmeg, mace, and cloves) and fish, but there have been minimal value-adding activities. For many years, the province's economic structure has not changed much, with manufacturing consistently contributing to only about 16%-17% of the GRDP for over more than 10 years. To boost economic development, a larger portion of the province's activities has to involve manufacturing or processing activities.

Furthermore, even with the existing manufacturing activities, higher productivity is needed. In terms of overall productivity, North Maluku is ranked 30th out of the 33 provinces. The province's secondary sector productivity fares better (24th out of the 33 provinces), but there is plenty of room for improvement. We therefore proposed to test the following hypothesis that **North Maluku could have generated higher GRDP growth, but is hampered by low value-adding activities (as represented by small manufacturing sector) and low productivity of the existing manufacturing sector.**

3.3.4 *Data Description*

The selected dependent variable in the Geweke causality analysis is the change in GRDP (overall) of North Maluku. It is chosen to represent the growth of North Maluku's economy. Here, the change (Δ) is derived from first order difference.

The independent variables are change in contribution of secondary sector to GRDP (measured in percentage), which represents the structure of North Maluku's economy, and manufacturing sector productivity (measured in million Rupiah, 2000 constant prices), which represents the productivity of the secondary sector (Table 9.7). The data for all three variables were sourced from World Bank INDO-DAPOER.

Considering the following issues: (i) limited availability of data at the province level for the previous 30 years, and (ii) the presence of several structural breaks in Indonesia's political economic history, we have opted to use quarterly (instead of yearly) data for a period of 12 years (from 2000 to 2011).

To conduct the Geweke causality analysis, we need time series data with at least 30 data points for each indicator. The yearly data therefore had to be converted into quarterly data to obtain 48 data points. The conversion was conducted using Eviews software. The method of conversion from yearly to quarterly data was "Quadratic Match Sum" for the change in GRDP and manufacturing sector productivity and "Quadratic Match Average" for change in contribution of secondary sector to GRDP. All variables used in empirical estimations were subjected to statistical checks and stationarity tests.

As shown in Figure 9.15, North Maluku's economic structure, between 2000 and 2011, has remained unchanged. Each primary and tertiary sector still formed around 40%–42% of the province's GRDP in 2011, comparable to the contributions in 2000. Meanwhile, manufacturing activities or the secondary sector (SECSEC) was still maintained around 16%–17% of North Maluku's GRDP in 2011.

As seen from Figure 9.16, it can be noted that there was an increase in manufacturing sector productivity (PROMAN) from first quarter of 2000 to fourth quarter of 2011. The productivity had fluctuated, but in general, there had been an increase from 4.02 million to 8.74 million Rupiah in 2000 constant price. This is an increase

Table 9.7. Variables used in North Maluku Geweke Causality Analysis

Variable	Notation	Definition
X	GRDP	Δ GRDP
Y1	SECSEC	Δ Percentage of Secondary Sector in GRDP
Y2	PROMAN	Manufacturing Sector Productivity

Source: Asia Competitiveness Institute

Figure 9.15. North Maluku's Economic Structure

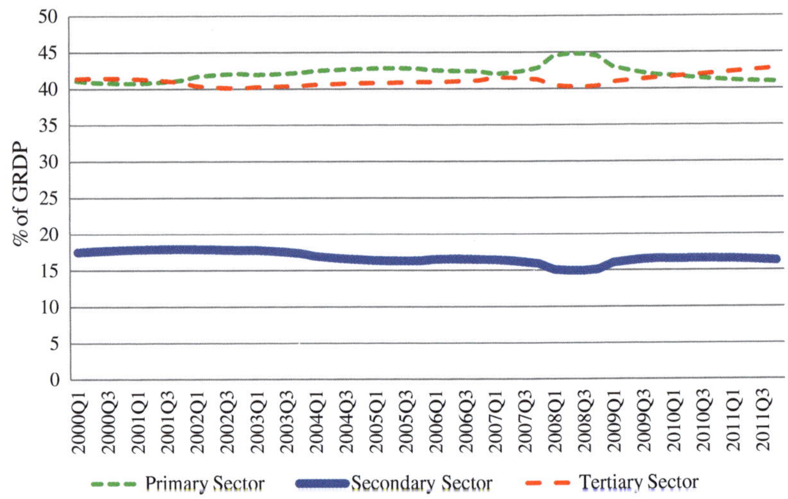

Source: Asia Competitiveness Institute using data from World Bank INDO-DAPOER

Figure 9.16. North Maluku's Productivity of Manufacturing Sector

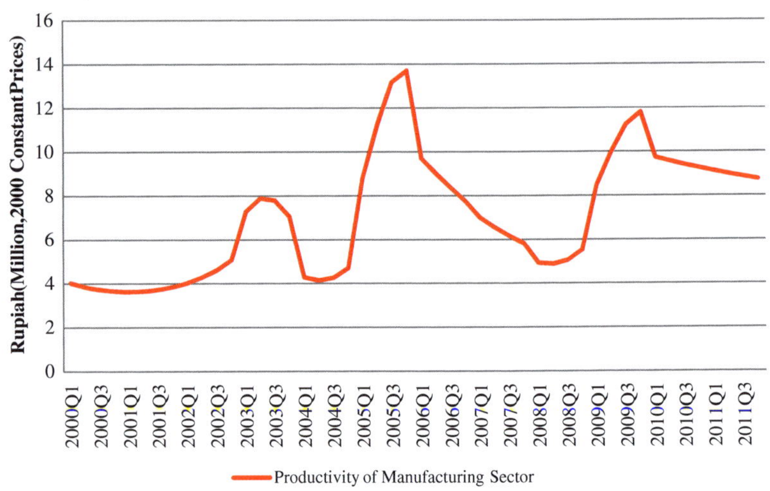

Source: Asia Competitiveness Institute using data from World Bank INDO-DAPOER

in productivity of about 117% in over 11 years, which was quite substantial, but clearly, more could be achieved as North Maluku was ranked 24th out of the 33 provinces in manufacturing sector productivity in 2011.

3.3.5 *Empirical Results*

The Geweke causality analysis was conducted in both bi-variate and multi-variate models. In the bi-variate analysis, both directions of association between the dependent variable (X) and independent variables (Y1 and Y2) were tested separately. This means that Geweke tests were conducted between X and Y1, as well as between X and Y2. In terms of feedback direction, the tests were also conducted separately from X towards Y1 and vice versa and from X towards Y2 and vice versa.

Table 9.8 shows that there is a significant total association between GRDP and SECSEC in either feedback direction ($F_{X,Y}$ is significant at 5% level when X = GRDP and Y = SECSEC and at 10% level when X = SECSEC and Y=GRDP). Most of the association takes place instantaneously between GRDP and SECSEC

Table 9.8. Estimated measures of bi-directional feedback between Change of Economic Output (GRDP), Percentage of Secondary Sector in GRDP (SECSEC), and Productivity of Manufacturing Sector (PROMAN) for North Maluku, Indonesia, 2000–2011[ab]

Economic aggregates		$H_0(F_{X,Y} = F_{X\to Y} + F_{Y\to X} + F_{X\cdot Y})$			
X	**Y**	$F_{X,Y}$	$F_{X\to Y}$	$F_{Y\to X}$	$F_{X\cdot Y}$
GRDP	SECSEC	0.2258** (0.0173)	0.0079 (0.5522)	0.1076** (0.0278)	0.1103** (0.0259)
SECSEC	GRDP	0.1491* (0.0817)	0.0356 (0.2053)	0.0032 (0.7045)	0.1103** (0.0259)
GRDP	PROMAN	0.2175* (0.0959)	0.0209 (0.6378)	0.1387* (0.0507)	0.0579 (0.1147)
PROMAN	GRDP	0.2727** (0.0388)	0.1040 (0.1069)	0.1108* (0.0923)	0.0579 (0.1147)

[a] *, ** and *** denote 10%, 5% and 1% level of significance, respectively.
[b] Confidence interval will be provided upon request.
Source: Asia Competitiveness Institute

Table 9.9. Estimated measures of multi-directional feedback between Change of Economic Output (GRDP), Percentage of Secondary Sector in GRDP (SECSEC), and Productivity of Manufacturing Sector (PROMAN) for North Maluku, Indonesia, 2000–2011[ab]

Economic aggregates		$H_0(F_{X,Y} = F_{X\to Y} + F_{Y\to X} + F_{X\cdot Y})$			
X	**Y**	$F_{X,Y}$	$F_{X\to Y}$	$F_{Y\to X}$	$F_{X\cdot Y}$
GRDP	SECSEC PROMAN	0.4474** (0.0373)	0.1074 (0.3287)	0.1882* (0.0882)	0.1518** (0.0382)

[a] *, ** and *** denote 10%, 5% and 1% level of significance, respectively.
[b] Confidence interval will be provided upon request.
Source: Asia Competitiveness Institute

($F_{X\cdot Y}$ is significant at 5% level for both directions). As seen from each feedback direction, there is a significant feedback (at 5% level of significance) for $F_{Y\to X}$ when GRDP was considered as X and SECSEC was considered as Y. However, there is not any significant feedback (either for $F_{X\to Y}$ or $F_{Y\to X}$) when SECSEC was considered as X and GRDP as Y.

Similarly, there is a significant total association between GRDP and PROMAN in either feedback direction ($F_{X,Y}$ is significant at 10% level for when X = GRDP and Y = PROMAN, and at 5% level for when X = PROMAN and Y = GRDP). There is no significant instantaneous association between GRDP and PROMAN ($F_{X\cdot Y}$ is not significant for both directions). However, as seen from each feedback direction, there is a significant feedback (at 10% level of significance) for $F_{Y\to X}$ when GRDP was considered as X and PROMAN was considered as Y. Similarly, a significant feedback (up to 10% level of significance) can be seen for $F_{Y\to X}$ when PROMAN was considered as X and GRDP as Y.

In the multi-variate analysis, both the independent variables (Y1 and Y2) were incorporated as Y and its association with the dependent variable (X) was tested. The multi-variate results are presented in Table 9.9.

Table 9.9 shows that when SECSEC and PROMAN were incorporated, there is a significant total association between X (GRDP) and Y (SECSEC and PROMAN) at the 5% level of significance. About 33.9% of that association (0. 1518 out of 0.4474) takes place between X and Y instantaneously (significant at the 5% level). Meanwhile, 42% of the feedback (0. 1882 out of 0.4474) takes place from Y going towards X (significant at the 10% level). The feedback going from X towards Y, however, is not significant.

Thus, it can be concluded that in the case of North Maluku, both the percentage of secondary sector in GRDP and productivity of the manufacturing sector contribute to the province's level of GRDP growth, but not the other way around. The feedback direction is not mutual, as we *cannot* say with enough confidence that North Maluku's change in GRDP contributes to higher percentage of the secondary sector and productivity of the secondary sector.

3.3.6 *Policy Implications*

The Geweke causality analysis for North Maluku shows that low manufacturing activities and low productivity of the manufacturing sector are highly associated with the province's small economic mass. This highlights the importance of a dynamic economic structure within an area to trigger economic cluster development.

As seen with the case of North Maluku, consistently low manufacturing activities does not contribute to a higher level of GRDP growth, which is needed to increase the critical mass of the province's economy. As an implication, more value-added economic activities in North Maluku need to be encouraged through focusing more on developing the manufacturing sector. Opportunities are already abound to create more value–added products from agriculture (spices) and fishery.

The North Maluku Geweke tests also show that productivity is important to enable economic growth. Currently, the manufacturing sector in the province is dominated by small cottage industries with low productivity. There is a limited number of companies operating with big capitals. The limited availability of cold storage facilities is a critical issue for a maritime province. There is much potential to improve productivity through value-adding, but this requires substantial investment in the infrastructure (e.g. roads, ports, and power) and facility (e.g. cold storage).

Increasing manufacturing productivity does not mean neglecting agriculture productivity. For a province with potential in agriculture and fishery, the productivity of the manufacturing sector also depends on the productivity of the agriculture and fishery sector. With low agriculture and fishery output, there is limited input for the subsequent processing activities. Maluku and North Maluku have been identified in the Master Plan for Acceleration and Expansion of Indonesia's Economic Development 2011–2025 (MP3EI) as the nation's primary fish source and reservoir. Therefore, the strategy would be to improve the secondary sector and primary sector productivity simultaneously.

Increasing productivity in North Maluku can be achieved through upgrading local small medium-sized enterprises (SMEs) and attracting many potential investors. Local SME's are already familiar with the province's potential and the economy would benefit much by keeping them as part of the strategies in pursuing higher economic growth.

3.4 East Nusa Tenggara

3.4.1 *Key Characteristics*

East Nusa Tenggara is another archipelagic province and is located in the south-eastern part of Indonesia, bordering with Timor Leste. It is part of the Lesser Sunda Islands, which lie to the east of Java, and include three provinces, namely Bali, West Nusa Tenggara, and East Nusa Tenggara. Unlike many other Indonesian areas, the Nusa Tenggara Islands are relatively dryer with semi-arid climate and receive only around four months of rain in a year. Savannah, instead of tropical rainforests, forms a substantial part of the mountainous landscape.

East Nusa Tenggara's economic structure is dominated by the primary and tertiary sectors, with very small secondary sector. The primary sector constituted around 38.36% of the GRDP in 2011 and was dominated by livestock products, such as cows and buffalos, and plantation products such as cassava, sweet potato, and maize. With a coastline of 5,700 km, there is a substantial fishery potential that is currently underdeveloped. The tertiary sector constituted 52.69% of the GRDP in 2011. Most of this is generated by the public service and trade, hotels, and restaurants sub-sector. East Nusa Tenggara also has a large tourism potential due to its scenic mountainous landscape and rich marine biodiversity with many islands and coral reefs. These, however, are also underdeveloped. The secondary sector constituted a meagre 8.95% of the GRDP in 2011. Industries in the province include food and beverages, textile, furniture, and metal crafts. These are mostly small-sized cottage industries, operating with limited resources.

East Nusa Tenggara had a population of 4.78 million people in 2011, which made it the 12th most populous province in Indonesia. However, the province has the lowest rate of urbanisation in the country, where only 19.34% of the population lived in urban areas. Indonesia's second least urbanised province in 2011 was West Sulawesi with an urbanisation rate of 22.88%.

Despite some of its potential, there are a number of issues challenging the province. First, East Nusa Tenggara has the least amount of GRDP per capita in Indonesia. In 2011, the province's GRDP per capita was 2,773,900 Rupiah in 2000 constant price. The provinces with the second and third least amount of GRDP per capita in 2011 were Maluku with 2,860,000 and Gorontalo with 2,955,600 Rupiah.

Related to East Nusa Tenggara's low GRDP per capita is its low labour productivity. The province has the lowest overall labour productivity, generating only 6.32 million Rupiah per worker per year in 2011. When broken down into sectors, East Nusa Tenggara's productivity is not very encouraging either. The province retains the lowest labour productivity for the primary sector, the third lowest for the secondary sector, and eighth lowest for tertiary sector.

East Nusa Tenggara is one of the provinces with the highest poverty rate in Indonesia. About one-fifth (20.48%) of the population lived under the poverty line in 2011. This is actually an improvement from the recorded ~30% in 2006. The HDI is similarly low, and the province is ranked 31st out of the 33 provinces. Despite the high poverty rate, East Nusa Tenggara had a low unemployment rate of 2.69 % in 2011, which means that most of the labour force were working, although perhaps were not fully employed.

Labour relations present another problem for East Nusa Tenggara as the ACI's annual competitiveness analysis found that the province is in the last place among the 33 provinces in terms of labour relations.

Figure 9.17 underscores the province's relatively weak performance compared to the median province. In all 12 sub-environments, East Nusa Tenggara is generally performing below the median province. However, the performance level varies from one sub-environment to another. In Openness to Trade and Services; Government Policies and Fiscal Sustainability; and Labour Market Flexibility, East Nusa Tenggara is not doing too far behind the median province. However, for Competition, Regulatory Standards and Rule of Law; Technological Infrastructure; and Standard of Living, Education and Social Stability, the province still needs to work hard to catch up.

Figure 9.17. 2014 Median Competitiveness Web for East Nusa Tenggara

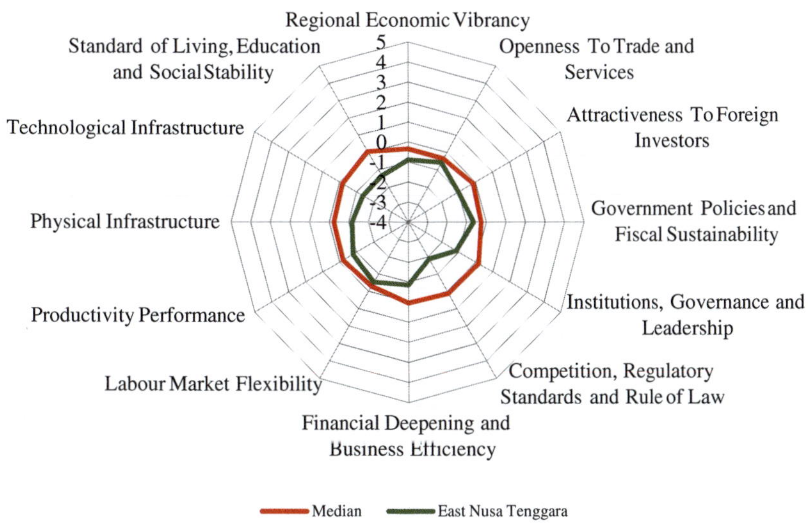

Source: Asia Competitiveness Institute

3.4.2 *Economic Development Patterns*

As shown in Figure 9.18, East Nusa Tenggara's economic development has been characterised by small size economy compared to that of other provinces. In 2011, East Nusa Tenggara's GRDP was 12,531 billion Rupiah while that of the average Indonesian province was 67,321 billion Rupiah in 2000 constant price. This means that East Nusa Tenggara's GRDP was only about 18% of the average.

For East Nusa Tenggara to compete meaningfully with other Indonesian provinces, it needs more economic mass. Within a 10-year period, we see that East Nusa Tenggara's economy has grown by 59.6%, from 7,850 billion in 2000 to 12,531 billion Rupiah in 2010. The average province, for comparison, has grown by 62.7%, from 41,378 billion to 67,321 billion Rupiah.

With a closer observation, Figure 9.19 shows that agriculture still forms the largest component of East Nusa Tenggara's GRDP. The province's main products are cattle and plantation products. Other service sector, which includes public services, is the second largest component of the GRDP in East Nusa Tenggara and is also the fastest growing sector. Trade, hotel and restaurant sector forms the third largest component, which is also growing relatively fast. Meanwhile, the manufacturing sector has remained small with very slow growth.

East Nusa Tenggara's unemployment rate was low at 2.69 % in 2011. However, if both unemployment and underemployment were taken into consideration, there was quite a proportion of East Nusa Tenggara's labour

Figure 9.18. East Nusa Tenggara's GRDP at 2000 Constant Price

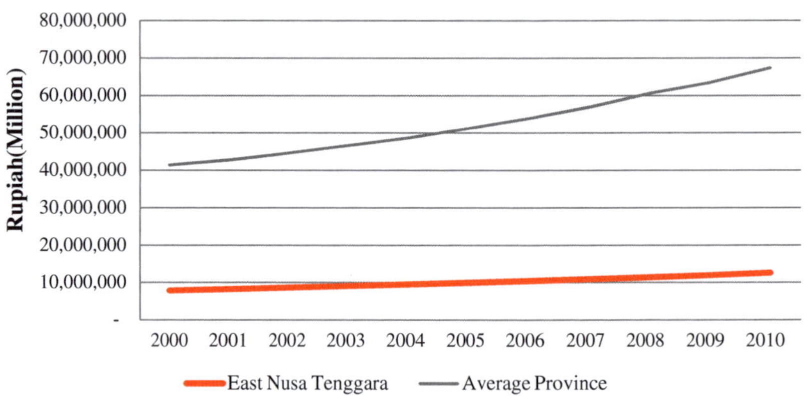

Source: Asia Competitiveness Institute using data from World Bank INDO-DAPOER

Figure 9.19. East Nusa Tenggara's GRDP by Sector (2000–2011)

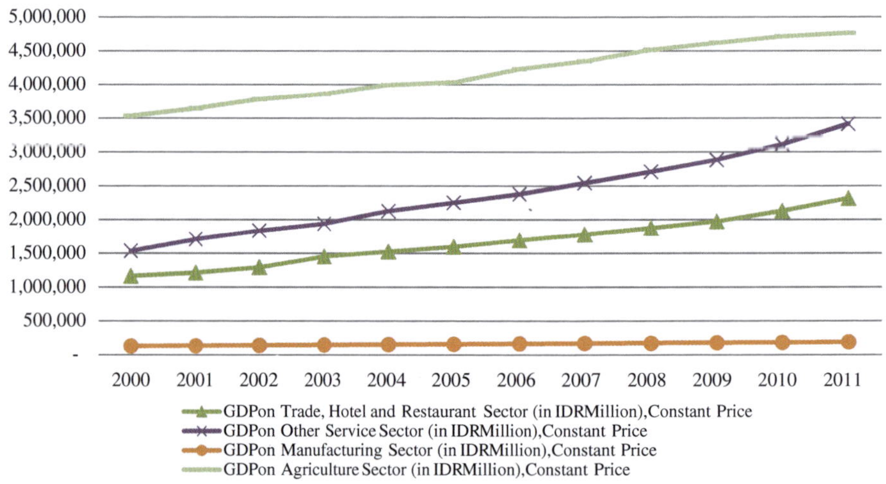

Source: Asia Competitiveness Institute using data from World Bank INDO-DAPOER

Figure 9.20. East Nusa Tenggara's Unemployment and Underemployment Rates

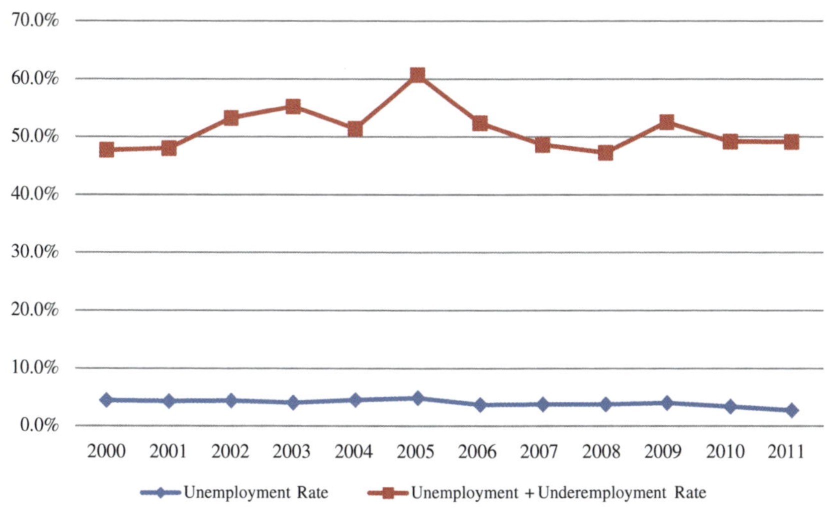

Source: Asia Competitiveness Institute using data from World Bank INDO-DAPOER

force that was underemployed. In 2011, the combined rate of unemployment and underemployment in East Nusa Tenggara was 49.2%, and throughout the past decade, as observed from Figure 9.20, the province's combined unemployment and underemployment rate constantly hovered around 50%.

The following Geweke causality analysis explores the factors that may prevent East Nusa Tenggara from achieving a larger economic mass.

3.4.3 *Hypothesis Testing*

Upon review of East Nusa Tenggara's economic development trends, it is notable that the province's GRDP remains small, with growth that is slightly slower than an average province. Among the avenues through which an agricultural economy can grow faster, one of them is by transitioning itself to become more manufacturing-oriented. East Nusa Tenggara has been a largely agricultural (including fisheries) province for a long time and it is now fitting to engage in more manufacturing activities to improve the economic growth. The manufacturing sector can absorb labour from the agricultural sector, creating higher value-added products that are labour-intensive, and thus, is more likely to create employment opportunities.

Currently, East Nusa Tenggara's agriculture sector is largely subsistence in nature, and the contribution of the agriculture sector to the GRDP is declining relatively (offset by the faster rise of services sector, more particularly the public service). This means that most food is grown for own consumption, rather than for commercial purpose. Therefore, most agriculture products are not linked with value-added activities unless the subsistence agriculture changes. A large number of the labour force could still find work in the subsistent agriculture, but it is insufficient. Although they seek other jobs, the surplus labour from low-productivity agriculture cannot be absorbed by the less than vibrant local economy. Furthermore, partly due to low skills and education level, they could not be absorbed into the highly sought after public service sector jobs either. This represents a missed opportunity for the province where a large proportion of its labour force is underemployed. We therefore proposed to test the following hypothesis that **East Nusa Tenggara could have generated higher GRDP growth, but it is hampered by low value-adding activities (as represented by small presence of manufacturing sector) and large number of underemployed and unemployed labour force who are underutilised by the local economy.**

3.4.4 *Data Description*

The selected dependent variable in the Geweke causality analysis is the change in GRDP (overall) of East Nusa Tenggara. It is chosen to represent the growth of East Nusa Tenggara's economy. Here, the change (Δ) is derived from first order difference.

The independent variables are change in contribution of secondary sector to GRDP (measured in percentage), which represents the structure of East Nusa Tenggara's economy, and number of unemployed and underemployed labour force (measured in persons), which represents the missed opportunity of underutilised workers. The data for all three variables were sourced from World Bank INDO-DAPOER.

Considering the following issues: (i) limited availability of data at the province level from the previous 30 years, and (ii) the presence of several structural breaks in Indonesia's political economic history, we have opted to use quarterly (instead of yearly) data for a period of 12 years (from 2000 to 2011).

To conduct the Geweke causality analysis, we need time series data with at least 30 data points for each indicator. The yearly data therefore had to be converted into quarterly data such that 48 data points would be obtained. The conversion was conducted using Eviews software. The method of conversion from yearly to quarterly data was "Quadratic Match Sum" for the change in GRDP and "Quadratic Match Average" for change in contribution of secondary sector to GRDP and number of unemployed and underemployed labour force. All variables used in empirical estimations were subjected to statistical checks and stationarity tests.

As seen from Figure 9.21, East Nusa Tenggara's economic structure, between 2000 and 2011, has changed, to some extent, with the relative increase in the tertiary sector and relative decline in the primary sector. The secondary sector (SECSEC), however, remained stagnant in terms of percentage contribution to GRDP. In the

Table 9.10. Variables used in East Nusa Tenggara Geweke Causality Analysis

Variable	Notation	Definition
X	GRDP	Δ GRDP
Y1	SECSEC	Δ Percentage of Secondary Sector in GRDP
Y2	UNDEMP	Number of Unemployed and Underemployed Labour Force

Source: Asia Competitiveness Institute

Figure 9.21. East Nusa Tenggara's Economic Structure

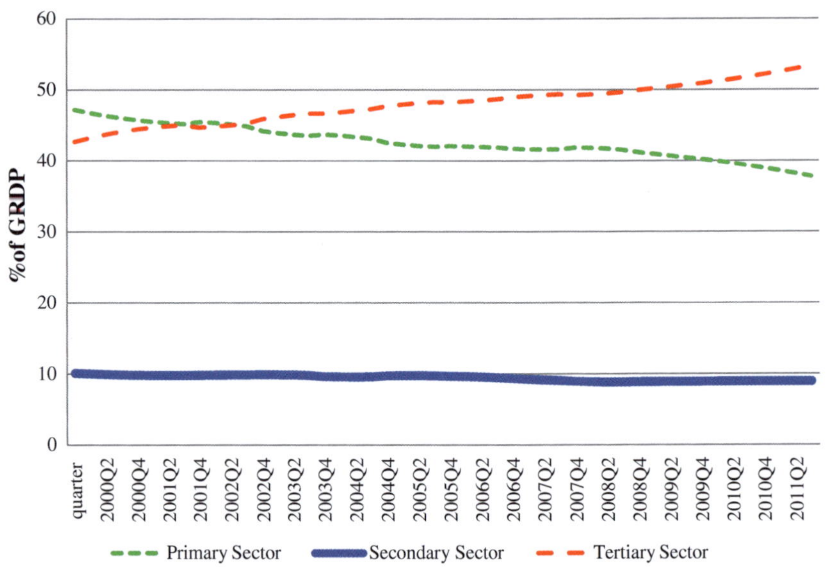

Source: Asia Competitiveness Institute using data from World Bank INDO-DAPOER

Figure 9.22. East Nusa Tenggara's Unemployed and Underemployed Labour Force

Source: Asia Competitiveness Institute using data from World Bank INDO-DAPOER

first quarter of 2000, manufacturing contributed to about 10.11% of East Nusa Tenggara's GRDP. In the fourth quarter of 2011, however, its contribution has declined slightly to 8.9%.

Figure 9.22 shows the number of labour force that was either unemployed or underemployed (UNDEMP) over a period of 12 years. There have been some fluctuations; for example, in 2005 and 2009, there were more underemployed people than in other years, reaching a peak of around 1.2 million people. However, there is an overall growing trend in the number of people who were underutilised in East Nusa Tenggara's local economy.

3.4.5 *Empirical Results*

The Geweke causality analysis was conducted in both bi-variate and multi-variate models. In the bi-variate analysis, both directions of association between the dependent variable (X) and independent variables (Y1 and Y2) were tested separately. This means that Geweke tests were conducted between X and Y1, as well as between X and Y2. In terms of direction, the tests were also conducted separately from X towards Y1 and vice versa and from X towards Y2 and vice versa.

Table 9.11 shows that there is a significant total association between GRDP and SECSEC in either direction ($F_{X,Y}$ is significant at 1% level for both directions). Most of the association takes place instantaneously between GRDP and SECSEC ($F_{X \cdot Y}$ is significant at 1% level for both directions). As seen from each direction, there is a significant feedback (at 1% level of significance) for $F_{Y \to X}$ when GRDP was considered as X and SECSEC was considered as Y. However, there is no significant association (either for $F_{X \to Y}$ or $F_{Y \to X}$) when SECSEC was considered as X and GRDP as Y.

There is also a significant total association between GRDP and UNDEMP in either direction ($F_{X,Y}$ is significant at 1% level for both directions). Most of the association takes place instantaneously between GRDP and UNDEMP ($F_{X \cdot Y}$ is significant at 1% level for both directions). As seen from each direction, there is a significant feedback (at 5% level of significance) for $F_{Y \to X}$ when GRDP was considered as X and UNDEMP was considered as Y. Similarly, a significant feedback (up to 5% level of significance) is present for $F_{X \to Y}$ when UNDEMP was considered as X and GRDP as Y.

Table 9.11. Estimated measures of bi-directional feedback between Change of Economic Output (GRDP), Percentage of Secondary Sector in GRDP (SECSEC), and Number of Unemployed and Underemployed Labour Force (UNDEMP) for East Nusa Tenggara, Indonesia, 2000–2011[ab]

Economic aggregates		$H_0(F_{X,Y} = F_{X\to Y} + F_{Y\to X} + F_{X\cdot Y})$			
X	**Y**	$F_{X,Y}$	$F_{X\to Y}$	$F_{Y\to X}$	$F_{X\cdot Y}$
GRDP	SECSEC	1.5640*** (0.0000)	0.0122 (0.4592)	0.2073*** (0.0023)	1.3445*** (0.0000)
SECSEC	GRDP	1.3606*** (0.0000)	0.0094 (0.5158)	0.0068 (0.5813)	1.3445*** (0.0000)
GRDP	UNDEMP	1.4365*** (0.0000)	0.1038 (0.1073)	0.2048** (0.0122)	1.1278*** (0.0000)
UNDEMP	GRDP	1.3257*** (0.0000)	0.1893** (0.0171)	0.0085 (0.8325)	1.1278*** (0.0000)

[a] *, ** and *** denote 10%, 5% and 1% level of significance, respectively.
[b] Confidence interval will be provided upon request.
Source: Asia Competitiveness Institute

Table 9.12. Estimated measures of multi-directional feedback between Change of Economic Output (GRDP), Percentage of Secondary Sector in GRDP (SECSEC), and Number of Unemployed and Underemployed Labour Force (UNDEMP) for East Nusa Tenggara, Indonesia, 2000–2011[ab]

Economic aggregates		$H_0(F_{X,Y} = F_{X\to Y} + F_{Y\to X} + F_{X\cdot Y})$			
X	**Y**	$F_{X,Y}$	$F_{X\to Y}$	$F_{Y\to X}$	$F_{X\cdot Y}$
GRDP	SECSEC UNDEMP	2.3500*** (0.0000)	0.1242 (0. 2543)	0.2446** (0.0326)	1.9812*** (0.0000)

[a] *, ** and *** denote 10%, 5% and 1% level of significance, respectively.
[b] Confidence interval will be provided upon request.
Source: Asia Competitiveness Institute

In the multi-variate analysis, both the independent variables (Y1 and Y2) were incorporated as Y and its association with the dependent variable (X) was tested. The multi-variate results are presented in Table 9.12.

As seen from Table 9.12, when SECSEC and UNDEMP were incorporated, there is a significant total association between X (GRDP) and Y (SECSEC and UNDEMP) at the 1% level of significance. Most or 84% of that association (1.9812 out of 2.3500) takes place between X and Y instantaneously while 10.4% of the feedback (0. 2446 out of 2.3500) takes place from Y going towards X. These directions of feedback are significant at 1% for the former and at 5% for the latter. The feedback going from X towards Y, however, is not significant.

Thus, it can be concluded that in the case of East Nusa Tenggara, both the percentage of secondary sector in GRDP and number of unemployed and underemployed workforce contribute to the province's level of GRDP growth, but not the other way around. The feedback direction is not mutual, as we *cannot* say with enough confidence that East Nusa Tenggara's change in GRDP contributes to higher percentage of the secondary sector and number of unemployed and underemployed workforce.

3.4.6 *Policy Implications*

The Geweke causality analysis for East Nusa Tenggara shows that low manufacturing activities and under-utilised workers are highly associated with the province's small economic mass. This highlights the importance of manufacturing as a labour-intensive sector that can drive higher productivity in an agricultural-based economy.

As seen from the case of East Nusa Tenggara, increasing value-adding activities through manufacturing is important to boost East Nusa Tenggara's economy. Low percentage of the secondary sector contributes to the province's low GRDP. East Nusa Tenggara needs to upgrade itself from relying on subsistence farming. Opportunities are abound to develop the cattle industry and processing of cattle and plantation products. Infrastructure in the form of roads and ports, as well as a good business environment and local economic governance would help the rise of this sector.

East Nusa Tenggara's Geweke tests also show that underutilisation of labour force is hampering the province's economic growth. By looking beyond unemployment and underemployment rate, we found that underemployment led to lost opportunity for the province as well as the people. It contributes to East Nusa Tenggara's low productivity, which reduces the attractiveness of the province in generating investment. The creation of full-time, long-term jobs is critical for the province. Manufacturing provides opportunity to absorb large number of labour force. However, the labour force needs to be prepared. Vocational education and on-the-job trainings can help to improve East Nusa Tenggara's quality of labour.

4. CONCLUSION

The Geweke causality analysis exercises were conducted on four Indonesian provinces. Two of the provinces were chosen from the more competitive provinces, while the remaining two were chosen from the less competitive ones. The exercise was conducted to understand better the underlying explanations as to why certain provinces have become very competitive (or otherwise) over time.

For the more competitive provinces, East Java and East Kalimantan's Geweke causality analysis demonstrate the importance of tertiary sector growth as the engine of development, and that tertiary sector growth is highly associated with infrastructure development and favourable labour market.

For the analysis of both East Java and East Kalimantan, the chosen dependent variable was the growth of trade, hotel, and restaurant sub-sector. Both provinces used an infrastructure-related variable, which was access to electricity for East Java and length of paved roads for East Kalimantan. Both provinces also used a labour market-related variable, which was employment rate for East Java and employment in financial sector for East Kalimantan.

The Geweke causality analysis for both highly competitive provinces show that good infrastructure development and labour market contribute significantly to the growth of the province's trade, hotel, and restaurant sub-sector.

For the less competitive provinces, North Maluku and East Nusa Tenggara's Geweke causality analysis demonstrate the importance of overall GRDP growth as the key to increasing the provinces' economic mass, and that the deficiency of sufficiently high growth is highly associated with a stagnant manufacturing sector and low productivity.

For the analysis of both North Maluku and East Nusa Tenggara, the chosen dependent variable was the GRDP growth. Both provinces used the same economic structure variable, which was the percentage of manufacturing sector contribution to the GRDP over a period of 48 quarters. Both provinces also used a productivity-related variable, which was productivity of the manufacturing sector for North Maluku and number of unemployed and underemployed workers (which could also be seen from a productivity perspective) for East Nusa Tenggara.

The Geweke causality analysis for the less competitive provinces show that the manufacturing sector and productivity contribute significantly to the level of GRDP growth. Therefore, to increase GRDP growth, less competitive provinces should consider value-adding to their products and do so in more productive manners.

REFERENCES

Geweke, John. "Measurement of linear dependence and feedback between multiple time series." *Journal of the American Statistical Association* Vol. 77, No. 378 (1982): 304–313.

Granger, C.W.J. "Investigating Causal Relations by Econometric Models and Cross-Spectral Methods." *Econometrica* Vol. 37 (1969): 424–438.

Sims, Christopher A. "Money, Income, and Causality." *The American Economic Review* Vol. 62, No. 4 (September 1972): 540–552.

Tan, Khee Giap and Mulya Amri. "Subnational Competitiveness and National Performance: Analysis and Simulation for Indonesia." *Journal of Centrum Cathedra (JCC): The Business and Economics Research Journal* Vol. 6, No. 2 (2013): 173–192.

Tan, Khee Giap, Mulya Amri, Linda Low, and Tan Kong Yam. *Competitiveness Analysis and Development Strategies for 33 Indonesian Provinces*. Singapore: World Scientific, 2013a.

Tan, Khee Giap, Mulya Amri, Linda Low, and Tan Kong Yam. *Analisis Daya Saing dan Strategi Pembangunan untuk 33 Provinsi Indonesia*. Singapore: World Scientific, 2013b.

Discussant Notes: Geweke Causality Analysis on Indonesia's Most and Least Competitive Provinces

Mr Umar Juoro
Member of the National Economic Council (KEN)
Indonesia

1. INTRODUCTION

In the Asia Competitiveness Institute's (ACI) study on Indonesia's provincial competitiveness, 33 provinces are ranked based on four criteria, namely macroeconomic, governance, microeconomic, and infrastructure development. Since the first study, the capital city of Jakarta has always ranked first and followed by East Java. Java's provinces are usually in the Top 10 and certain provinces outside Java, usually those with rich natural resources, are also in the Top 10. Meanwhile, several provinces in eastern part of Indonesia remain at the lowest rank.

The ACI study explores causal relationship between economic development with Gross Regional Domestic Product (GRDP) as a dependent variable and employment and infrastructure as independent variables. It is insightful in understanding the relationship and for deriving appropriate policy recommendations. This study widens the perspectives, as aside from looking at the provincial rank, it also seeks to explain the factors determining the high (or low) growth in each province.

2. INDONESIA'S PROVINCIAL COMPETITIVENESS

Based on the ACI's study, provinces in Java dominate the top ranks. There have been some changes in the Top 10 ranking. In 2013, Riau Islands was in the Top 10, but has dropped out of the ranks in 2014. This is also the case for Banten. This shows the dynamic of the ranking where provinces that are able to maintain their competitiveness will keep their position in the top rank, while those with declining performance will lose their position in the top rank.

The time series data on the competitiveness of Indonesia's provinces can be utilised to shed light on factors that determine economic development in certain provinces. The analysis can also lead to the formation of more appropriate policies.

3. CAUSALITY METHODOLOGY

Researchers typically use Granger causality method to determine causality between two time series data or variables, which is useful when the data are frequent. However, if the availability of data is infrequent (for example, annual data), this method cannot capture the causality accurately. In this situation, Geweke proposed a measure of instantaneous correlation, calculated from the residuals of standard Granger type of causality test that capture "instantaneous feedback". By using Geweke causality method, we can analyse not only the causality between two set data of time series, but also their instantaneous interactions. The contributions of each variable can also be seen. For this reason, the ACI's study has proceeded further than to just rank Indonesia's 33 provinces. Adopting Geweke causality analysis is very useful to better understand the underlying factors that determine the competitiveness of the provinces.

However, Geweke causality test has its limitations. As with all of econometric methods, it is very much dependent on how the model is specified and how the dependent and independent variables are determined.

In addition, the quality of the data is important in order to get useful results. To get reasonable conclusions and policy recommendations, there should be a descriptive explanation of the competitiveness of certain province. With this, conclusions and policy recommendations will be more accurate.

4. SELECTION CRITERIA

The ACI's study has selected four provinces to be analysed using Geweke methodology to determine the relationship between economic development and factors of production, including infrastructure. The selection was based on geographic diversity, population, economic structure, and economic corridor. These criteria are related to the effort in determining why certain provinces are at the top rank, while other provinces are less competitive.

To get more variety on the type of provincial economic development, it would be good to include a province that is categorised as a centre of growth and is located outside Java. In view of this, Riau Islands is a good option. By including this province in the analysis, we can get a better understanding on how to develop a province as a centre of growth and the challenges it encounter, as many provinces would like to develop a growth centre of their own.

5. EAST JAVA AS A COMPETITIVE PROVINCE

Just as Jakarta always be at the top, East Java is always the second in Indonesia's provincial competitiveness study. The province is second in GRDP (for primary, secondary and tertiary sector) and has the second largest population in the country, with the highest labour market flexibility but mediocre Human Development Index (HDI). East Java can be a good example for other provinces to learn from to improve their competiveness because this province positions itself in the top rank for all categories. Different from Jakarta, which was historically developed as the centre of administration and politics during the colonial era, East Java with Surabaya as its capital city has been developing itself as a business region with a strong agriculture hinterland.

The study found that there is a relationship between the difference in GRDP and employment rate, as seen from the Geweke causality analysis. The causality test was conducted on both directions, from GRDP to employment and the other way around. The coefficient and statistical significance is higher in the direction of employment to the economy (GRDP). The coefficient for interaction of the variables is also high and significant.

This study also shows that factors of production, which include employment and access to electricity, contribute to economic development. In other words, labour and infrastructure support higher economic growth. This means that maintaining labour market flexibility and improving the quality of human resource and infrastructure development would increase the development in East Java. Improvement in human resource is also important socially, as East Java is relatively low in HDI.

Other provinces can also learn from East Java in improving their competitiveness, through labour participation in a flexible labour market and improving infrastructure. This is different from Riau Islands province whose rank has dropped from the Top 10 and is characterised by rigid and even radical labour activities. Indonesia, in general, is still an attractive location of labour-intensive manufacturing because of the presence of a large number of youth and relatively low wages. However, rigid labour regulation that increases minimum wage steeply and the trend of labour radicalism discourage investment in manufacturing.

The study should look at manufacturing sector closely, because East Java is one of the main areas for manufacturing development. East Java would be able to further develop manufacturing sector by improving labour productivity, infrastructure and better governance. Similar characteristics can be observed in Central Java. Although Central Java is not as developed as East Java, the province also has flexible labour market, good governance and the potential to be the centre of manufacturing growth. Central Java also has a strong agricultural hinterland. Although Banten and West Java are strong in the manufacturing sector and agricultural hinterland, their competitiveness are hampered by poor governance and inflexibility of the labour market.

6. EAST KALIMANTAN AS A COMPETITIVE PROVINCE

East Kalimantan has the largest primary sector (mainly oil, gas and mining), although the population is relatively small. East Kalimantan is very rich in natural resources. As the outer island province in the eastern part of Indonesia, East Kalimantan's achievement in the top three of competitiveness ranking is indeed outstanding. The province has positioned itself as the second place in infrastructure-related environment. As for the remaining environments (macroeconomic, governance and microeconomic), East Kalimantan ranks fourth. In terms of governance environment, East Kalimantan successfully jumped rank from 17th to fourth. However, only provinces with similar wealth in natural resources, such as Riau, Aceh, and Papua, can learn from East Kalimantan's performance. Other provinces in Kalimantan, namely Central Kalimantan, West Kalimantan, and the newly created province of North Kalimantan, can also learn from the experience of East Kalimantan, but it is perhaps less relevant for provinces with smaller natural resources.

The study found that there is a relationship between the tertiary sector (trade, hotel and restaurant) with employment in financial sector and infrastructure. The result shows that the coefficient and statistical significance is higher for causal relationship that runs in the direction of employment and infrastructure to the economy (tertiary sector).

Unfortunately, this study did not explore the primary sector and secondary sector, especially manufacturing. Clearly, the primary sector, especially oil, gas and mining (mainly coal), is the main contributor for the economy of East Kalimantan, but it did not contribute much to employment. East Kalimantan is rich with energy and raw material and the government should put in effort to increase the value-adding activity through processing of raw materials. It is important to recognise the potential that East Kalimantan has to develop industrial processing and thus, promote the manufacturing sector.

The experience from East Kalimantan is particularly relevant to other provinces with rich natural resources such as Riau, Aceh, and Papua. Despite so, there are still some differences among the provinces, especially in terms of demography. To derive appropriate policy recommendations for each of these rich natural provinces, it is very important to understand the special characteristics of each province.

7. EAST NUSA TENGGARA AS A LESS COMPETITIVE PROVINCE

East Nusa Tenggara is a poor province, with the least GRDP per capita, lowest in labour productivity, lowest percentage of urban population, smallest amount of Foreign Direct Investment (FDI), and is the second lowest in electricity access. East Nusa Tenggara is a classic example of a poor province in Indonesia. Its position is very remote from the main economic activities, and the province is poor in natural resources with high incidence of poverty. East Nusa Tenggara ranks close to the bottom for all environments.

The study found that there is a relationship between the difference in GRDP with the percentage of secondary sector in the economy and employment. The result shows the importance of secondary sector and employment in supporting economic development in East Nusa Tenggara.

It is difficult, however, to develop secondary sector in poor provinces such as East Nusa Tenggara. It is not only due to inadequate resources, but also poor infrastructure. This province is still very much reliant on the support from the central government. The policy recommendation from this study to develop cattle farm is difficult to achieve due to inadequate infrastructure that will subsequently lead to high cost. The cost to transport cattle from East Nusa Tenggara to main markets in Java will be higher compared to that of importing cattle from Australia.

For a poor province like East Nusa Tenggara that is also poor in resources, the focus should be more on the development of basic infrastructure that are related to basic needs, such as health care, water, and opening access to isolated rural areas, which are important for poverty alleviation. Maluku, West Sulawesi, Gorontalo, and Bengkulu can also fall into this category of provinces.

8. NORTH MALUKU AS A LESS COMPETITIVE PROVINCE

North Maluku has the second lowest GRDP and the lowest GRDP per capita. The province is also the third lowest in the number of population, the second lowest in labour relation, and the second lowest in quality of infrastructure. The poor condition of North Maluku is different from East Nusa Tenggara's, although its position in the ranking is similar to East Nusa Tenggara. Even though North Maluku is very remote from the main economic activities, the province has significant natural resources.

The study explored the relationship between the difference in GRDP and percentage of secondary sector in the economy and manufacturing productivity. The result shows the importance of secondary sector and manufacturing productivity for economic development.

North Maluku as a poor province is different compared to East Nusa Tenggara. North Maluku is richer in natural resources. For cash crops, nutmeg is a popular commodity. Fruit plantation such as banana also has potential. Fishery used to be quite developed in the province, but the social disruption in early 2000 destroyed the fishing industry. Mining such as bauxite and its processing facility can potentially be developed in this province. West Nusa Tenggara, Jambi, and Southeast Sulawesi are similar to North Maluku in that these provinces have significant natural resources but also with high incidence of poverty, and these provinces are at the Bottom 10 of the ranking.

9. EXPLANATION ON THE COMPETITIVENESS OF CERTAIN PROVINCE

The ACI's study focused on the ranking of Indonesia's 33 provinces based on macroeconomic, governance, microeconomic, and infrastructure development-related environments. The study went further to explain the underlying factors that determine why certain provinces are at the top of the ranking while others are at the bottom. This study has certainly provided better understanding and more accurate policy recommendations. In order to get further insights on how a province is able to excel in certain criteria based on the indicators of competitiveness, the study should continue to look closely at this direction.

As Indonesia's provinces are diverse in terms of economy, population, and geography, a province should be directed to develop itself based on their strengths. For example, Yogyakarta is currently leading in the quality of life environment. As a province with special administrative status, it would be very difficult for Yogyakarta to get to the top of overall ranking in competitiveness. Focusing on quality of life renders Yogyakarta as a special province in the country. Bali is another province that has a strong position in the quality of life environment. Similarly, a province at the top of the governance-related ranking should be a good example for certain provinces to learn from. In this way, other provinces can learn from each other to improve certain indicators. Furthermore, Indonesian provinces can develop in a more diversified manner, yet able to improve the overall competitiveness of the country.

For future study, human development factor and physical infrastructure under the environment of quality of life should be separated. This is necessary in order to get a better understanding on the role of human development in a province that has a different contribution of physical infrastructure. For example, Yogyakarta is strong in human development, while East Java, East Kalimantan, and Riau Islands are strong in physical infrastructure, but relatively weak in human development.

The importance of governance to support economic development should be explored further. In the causality study, it should be examined whether governance significantly influences economic development and if so, how does the causality takes place. If the causality analysis that runs in the direction of governance to economic growth is significant, then this supports the view that the improvement in governance is a prerequisite for economic development. Thus, governance should come first to support economic development and not as a result of economic development.

Similarly, further exploration on the relationship between economic growth and human development is very important in order to understand the contribution of human development to economic development in the provincial level. If the causality that runs in the direction of human development index to economic growth is significant, then this strengthens the view that human development is a necessary factor for economic development. There may be a possibility that the causality runs in the other direction, which implies that higher economic development also supports higher human development.

Chapter 10
Concluding Remarks and Future Research Agenda

The book has offered distinct insights into Indonesia's competitiveness landscape at both provincial and regional levels. Given Indonesia's vast and diverse archipelago, culling overgeneralised analysis at national level is even more relevant. This is in line with a widespread global trend to put more emphasis on policy-making by the local governments to further advance the competitiveness of each locality.[1] Building upon the first flagship publication,[2] Chapter 1 updates the competitiveness trend of each province. It is a pioneering effort by the Asia Competitiveness Institute (ACI) to track the competitiveness of provinces using the comprehensive methodological framework. The results confirmed that provinces in Java Island continue to dominate in the Top 10 list. As a whole, disparities between top- and bottom-performing provinces continue to surface at all aspects, from governance, macroeconomic and microeconomic standpoints to infrastructure gap.

In the spirit of a more balanced regional development, Indonesia launched the Master Plan for Acceleration and Expansion of Indonesia's Economic Development 2011–2015 (MP3EI). The MP3EI mapped the economic potential for the six economic corridors. In Chapters 2 to 8, ACI adopted this classification to make its inaugural regional competitiveness studies. We found that, within Indonesia, its western versus eastern dichotomy is less profound. Aligned with more newcomers from Kalimantan and Sulawesi Regions joining the Top 10 list in provincial competitiveness ranking, these two regions leapt to second and third position, respectively, ahead of the Sumatra Region. The results highlighted the importance of taking into account a holistic view of competitiveness that covers four important environments. Each region has its own strengths (e.g. Sulawesi Region for its governance and regulatory landscape) and weaknesses (e.g. Java Region's standard of living is less favourable than its achievements on the economic front). Hence, learning opportunities are abundant from inter-regional friendly rivalry to lift Indonesia's competitiveness as a whole.

The ACI's regional grouping still follows island-based concept, which is a reflection of the legacy in prioritising land connectivity. With the new leader, President Joko Widodo, advancing Maritime Vision to restore *Jalesveva Jayamahe* spirit (at sea we are victorious), inter-island provincial grouping is not impossible with seamless sea-based connectivity. This game-changing policy will eventually leverage Indonesia's presence in enhancing regional connectivity, including in the Asia Economic Connectivity Vision 2030.[3]

Through our findings in Chapter 9 on Geweke Causality Analysis, we found varying competitiveness drivers in the top performing provinces. Overall, infrastructure and productivity are the underlying key factors that determine competitiveness (or lack thereof). Changing economic structure from primary towards higher value-added in manufacturing and service sector ensures consistent growth in productivity level.[4] Nevertheless, productivity improvement within sectors is as important. Productivity enhancement in agricultural sector further creates demands in the downstream processing of finished goods that pave the way for the birth of manufacturing sector as well as services.[5] Technology and innovation adoption to ramp up the quality of inputs while ensuring streamlined post-harvest logistic chain can eventually lift up the productivity level.

[1] Organisation for Economic Cooperation and Development (OECD), *Regional Development Policy Trends in OECD Member Countries* (OECD Publishing, 2010).

[2] Tan Khee Giap *et al.*, *Competitiveness Analysis and Development Strategies for 33 Indonesian Provinces* (Singapore: World Scientific Publishing, 2013).

[3] Tan Khee Giap *et al.*, *2014 Annual Competitiveness Ranking and Simulation Study for ASEAN-10 and Development Strategies to Enhance Asia Economic Connectivity Vision 2030* (Singapore: World Scientific, 2015).

[4] Margaret S. McMillan and Dani Rodrik, "Globalisation, Structural Change and Productivity Growth," *NBER Working Paper Series* No. 17143 (June 2011): 1–32.

[5] Joe Studwell, *How Asia Works: Success and Failure in the World's Most Dynamic Region* (New York: Profile Books, 2013).

FUTURE RESEARCH AGENDA

In line with the ACI's strong interest in providing robust and rigorous analysis of Indonesia's competitiveness, our research in going forward would include more specialised topics on decentralisation and governing institution, agricultural productivity and potential middle-income trap at provincial level.

1. Decentralisation, Governing Institutions and Economic Development

Theories of decentralisation argue that bringing decision-making down to more local levels will push public officials to be more accountable to citizens. This, in turn, should improve public services and propel local economic development. Ten years after Indonesia embarked on decentralisation, it is still very difficult to trace causal relationships between these variables and thus, the debate continues. The study will investigate empirically the micro-foundation linking decentralisation and economic development in Indonesia. We will utilise the ACI's business perception survey conducted in 2013–2014 to more than 700 business executives in 33 Indonesian provinces to explore the tendency of firms to innovate and invest locally given their perception of the quality of various governing institutions. Analysing these correlations, in light of the 10-year data on fiscal decentralisation, will provide valuable insight into how governing institutions play a critical intervening role between decentralisation and economic development.

2. Agricultural Productivity for Indonesian Provinces

Indonesia has a significant potential in agricultural production, not only for it to be self-sufficient in terms of food, but also to be the "food basket" for the ASEAN and the world. Over time, though the agriculture share to GDP has been declining, the sector still absorbs two-fifths of the labour force. Poverty remained intact at rural level and is often associated with subsistence farming. Raising agricultural productivity holds promising role for achieving food sovereignty, which is also the current government's top priority. With Malmquist Index-Data Envelopment Analysis (DEA), we can identify the Total Factor Productivity (TFP) change of each province and to what extent it is contributed by Technological Change (TC) or Technical Efficiency Change (TEC). From such findings, the ACI can further generate policy recommendations from implications that span from better resource allocation to ensuring effective adoption and adaptation of new technology at local level.

3. Potential Middle-Income Trap for Selected Indonesian Provinces

Through the MP3EI, Indonesia has firmly stated its ambitious goal to progress into the high-income group of countries by 2025, hence, succeeding in avoiding middle-income trap. While studies at the national level are abundant, more needs to be done at the provincial level. Delving into provincial level analysis in the context of diversifying performance of local economies provides value-added contribution to the literature in the first instance. By first identifying the relevant provinces to explore economic opportunities, such improvements will further help to lift more people out of poverty and avert risks of the middle-income trap. The pathway towards these goals requires provinces to adopt a sustainable growth strategy to unleash the productivity potential and continuity in terms of implementing top priority structural reforms for achieving the prosperity of all citizens. [6]

REFERENCES

McMillan, M. S., and Dani Rodrik. "Globalisation, Structural Change and Productivity Growth." *NBER Working Paper Series* No. 17143 (June 2011): 1–32.

Organisation for Economic Cooperation and Development (OECD). *Regional Development Policy Trends in OECD Member Countries*. OECD Publishing, 2010.

[6] World Bank, "Indonesia: Avoiding the Trap," *Indonesia Development Policy Review 2014* (May 2014): 2–19.

Studwell, J. *How Asia Works: Success and Failure in the World's Most Dynamic Region.* New York: Profile Books, 2013.

Tan, Khee Giap, Mulya Amri, Linda Low, and Tan Kong Yam. *Competitiveness Analysis and Development Strategies for 33 Indonesian Provinces.* Singapore: World Scientific, 2013.

Tan Khee Giap, Linda Low, Tan Kong Yam, and Sangiita Yoong Wei Cher. 2014 Annual Competitiveness Ranking and Simulation Study for ASEAN-10 and Development Strategies to Enhance Asia Economic Connectivity Vision 2030. Singapore: World Scientific, 2015.

World Bank. "Indonesia: Avoiding the Trap." *Indonesia Development Policy Review 2014* (May 2014).

Appendix 1
List of Indicators

2014 Competitiveness Ranking and Simulation Study for 33 Provinces and Six Regions in Indonesia

No	Indicator	Unit	Reversed Indicator
1	MACROECONOMIC STABILITY		
1.1	*Regional Economic Vibrancy*		
1.1.01	Gross Regional Domestic Product (GRDP)	Rupiah (Million), 2000 Constant Prices	
1.1.02	Gross Regional Domestic Product (GRDP), Non-oil & gas	Rupiah (Million), 2000 Constant Prices	
1.1.03	GRDP Growth	Percentage Change Per Annum, 2000 Constant Prices	
1.1.04	GRDP Per Capita	Rupiah (Million), 2000 Constant Prices	
1.1.05	GRDP Per Capita, Non-oil & gas	Rupiah (Million), 2000 Constant Prices	
1.1.06	GRDP of Primary Industry	Rupiah (Million), 2000 Constant Prices	
1.1.07	GRDP of Secondary Industry	Rupiah (Million), 2000 Constant Prices	
1.1.08	GRDP of Tertiary Industry	Rupiah (Million), 2000 Constant Prices	
1.1.09	Gross Domestic Fixed Capital Formation	Rupiah (Million), 2000 Constant Prices	
1.1.10	Inflation	Percentage Change Per Annum	R
1.2	*Openness To Trade and Services*		
1.2.01	Exports	Rupiah (Million), 2000 Constant Prices	
1.2.02	Exports, Non-oil & gas	Rupiah (Million), 2000 Constant Prices	
1.2.03	Imports	Rupiah (Million), 2000 Constant Prices	
1.2.04	Imports, Non-oil & gas	Rupiah (Million), 2000 Constant Prices	
1.2.05	Openness To Trade	Ratio	
1.3	*Attractiveness To Foreign Investors*		
1.3.01	Foreign Direct Investment, Last 3 Year Average	US Dollars (Million), Current Market Prices	
1.3.02	Domestic Direct Investment, Last 3 Year Average	Rupiah (Billion)	
1.3.03	Investment Promotion and Management	Index (Survey Data)	
2	GOVERNMENT AND INSTITUTIONAL SETTING		
2.1	*Government Policies and Fiscal Sustainability*		
2.1.01	Government Revenue	Rupiah (Thousand), 2000 Constant Prices	
2.1.02	Tax Revenue	Rupiah (Thousand), 2000 Constant Prices	
2.1.03	Tax Revenue/Government Revenue	Ratio	
2.1.04	Government Expenditure	Rupiah (Thousand), 2000 Constant Prices	
2.1.05	Fiscal Balance	Rupiah (Thousand), 2000 Constant Prices	
2.2	*Institutions, Governance and Leadership*		
2.2.01	Corruption Perception Index	Index	
2.2.02	Lack of Corruption	Index (Survey Data)	
2.2.03	Crime Rate	Rate Per 100.000 population	R
2.2.04	Security	Index (Survey Data)	
2.2.05	Government Inclusiveness and Accountability	Index (Survey Data)	
2.2.06	Government Progress & Expectation	Index (Survey Data)	

(*Continued*)

(*Continued*)

No	Indicator	Unit	Reversed Indicator
2.2.07	Government Efficiency	Index (Survey Data)	
2.2.08	Coordination of Local Governments	Index (Survey Data)	
2.2.09	Provincial Governing Capacity	Index (Survey Data)	
2.3	*Competition, Regulatory Standards and Rule of Laws*		
2.3.01	Regulatory Governance	Index (Survey Data)	
2.3.02	Rule of Law	Index (Survey Data)	
2.3.03	Vibrancy of Competition and Collaboration	Index (Survey Data)	
3	FINANCIAL, BUSINESSES AND MANPOWER CONDITIONS		
3.1	*Financial Deepening and Business Efficiency*		
3.1.01	Bank Deposits	Rupiah (Million), 2000 Constant Prices	
3.1.02	Bank Loans	Rupiah (Million), 2000 Constant Prices	
3.1.03	Non-Performing Loans	Rupiah (Million), 2000 Constant Prices	R
3.1.04	Non-Performing Loans per Total Bank Loans	Ratio	R
3.1.05	Number of Bank Branches or Offices	Number	
3.1.06	Population per Number of Bank Branches or Offices	Ratio	R
3.1.07	Ease of Dealing With Banks	Index (Survey Data)	
3.1.08	Firms' Performance	Index (Survey Data)	
3.1.09	Firms' Strategy	Index (Survey Data)	
3.1.10	Firms' Human Resource Capacity	Index (Survey Data)	
3.1.11	Firms' Equipment Capacity	Index (Survey Data)	
3.1.12	Firms' Application of IT	Index (Survey Data)	
3.1.13	Firms' Innovation	Index (Survey Data)	
3.2	*Labour Market Flexibility*		
3.2.01	Labour Force	Number	
3.2.02	Labour Force Participation Rate	Ratio	
3.2.03	Employment	Number	
3.2.04	Employment in Primary Industry	Number	
3.2.05	Employment in Secondary industry	Number	
3.2.06	Employment in Tertiary Industry	Number	
3.2.07	Unemployment Rate	Percentage	R
3.2.08	Minimum Wage Per Month	Rupiah, Current Market Prices	R
3.2.09	Labour Relations	Index (Survey Data)	
3.3	*Productivity Performance*		
3.3.01	Overall Labour Productivity	Rupiah (Million) per person-year, 2000 Constant Prices	
3.3.02	Overall Labour Productivity, Non-oil & gas	Rupiah (Million) per person-year, 2000 Constant Prices	
3.3.03	Primary Industry Productivity	Rupiah (Million) per person-year, 2000 Constant Prices	
3.3.04	Secondary Industry Productivity	Rupiah (Million) per person-year, 2000 Constant Prices	
3.3.05	Tertiary Industry Productivity	Rupiah (Million) per person-year, 2000 Constant Prices	

(*Continued*)

(*Continued*)

No	Indicator	Unit	Reversed Indicator
4	QUALITY OF LIFE AND INFRASTRUCTURE DEVELOPMENT		
4.1	*Physical Infrastructure*		
4.1.01	Population	Persons, Year-end	
4.1.02	Population Growth	Percentage Change Per Annum	
4.1.03	Urban Population	Percentage of Total Population	
4.1.04	Length of Paved Roads	Kilometres	
4.1.05	Registered Motor Vehicles	Number	
4.1.06	Registered Motor Vehicles per KM of paved road	Ratio	R
4.1.07	Cargo at Inter-island Seaport	Tons	
4.1.08	Cargo at International Seaport	Tons	
4.1.09	Passengers of Domestic Air Traffic	Number	
4.1.10	Passengers of International Air Traffic	Number	
4.1.11	Households with pipe water services	Percentage of households	
4.1.12	Households with state electricity services	Percentage of households	
4.1.13	Ease of Acquiring Property	Index (Survey Data)	
4.1.14	Quality of Physical Infrastructure	Index (Survey Data)	
4.2	*Technological Infrastructure*		
4.2.01	Telephone Ownership	Percentage of households	
4.2.02	Handphone Ownership	Percentage of households	
4.2.03	Desktop Computer Ownership	Percentage of households	
4.2.04	Laptop Computer Ownership	Percentage of households	
4.2.05	Internet Access at Home	Percentage of households	
4.2.06	Internet Access at Office	Percentage of households	
4.2.07	Internet Access at School	Percentage of households	
4.2.08	Internet Access in Handphone	Percentage of households	
4.2.09	Quality of Technological Infrastructure	Index (Survey Data)	
4.3	*Standard of Living, Education and Social Stability*		
4.3.01	Adult Illiteracy Rate	Percentage of Adults	R
4.3.02	Mean Years of Schooling	Years	
4.3.03	School Enrolment Rate (Primary)	Percentage	
4.3.04	School Enrolment Rate (Junior High)	Percentage	
4.3.05	School Enrolment Rate (Senior High)	Percentage	
4.3.06	Student-Teacher Ratio (Primary)	Ratio	R
4.3.07	Student-Teacher Ratio (Junior High)	Ratio	R
4.3.08	Student-Teacher Ratio (Senior High)	Ratio	R
4.3.09	Human Development Index	Index	
4.3.10	Life Expectancy at Birth	Years	
4.3.11	Gini Ratio	Ratio	R
4.3.12	Urban Population Growth	Percentage Per Annum	
4.3.13	Population Per Health Facility	Ratio	R
4.3.14	Population Per Medical Worker	Ratio	R
4.3.15	Environmental Quality Index	Index	

(*Continued*)

(*Continued*)

No	Indicator	Unit	Reversed Indicator
4.3.16	Fatalities due to Natural Disaster	Number	R
4.3.17	Quality of Education	Index (Survey Data)	
4.3.18	Quality of Healthcare	Index (Survey Data)	
4.3.19	Affordability and Accessibility of Goods	Index (Survey Data)	

Source: Asia Competitiveness Institute.

Appendix 2
Computation of Rankings: The Algorithm

A step-by-step description of the ranking process is described below for *N* regions (or provinces respectively), *M* indicators and *C* environments, with each environment comprising *S* sub-environments.

Algorithm: Ranking Methodology

(1) Compute the mean value of indicator j ($j = 1, \ldots, M$),

$$\bar{X}_j = \frac{1}{N}\sum_{i=1}^{N} X_{ij}$$

where X_{ij} represents the value that region i ($i = 1, \ldots, N$) takes for indicator j.

(2) For each indicator j ($j = 1, \ldots, M$), calculate its standard deviation (SD),

$$SD_j = \sqrt{\frac{1}{N}\sum_{i=1}^{N}(X_{ij} - \bar{X}_j)^2}$$

(3) Compute the standardised value of indicator (SVI) that each region i ($i = 1, \ldots, N$) takes under each of the indicators j ($j = 1, \ldots, M$),

$$SVI_{ij} = \frac{X_{ij} - \bar{X}_j}{SD_j}$$

(4) Compute the 'ranked' standardised value of indicator (RSVI) that each region i ($i = 1, \ldots, N$) takes under each of the indicators j ($j = 1, \ldots, M$):

$$RSVI_{ij} = \begin{cases} SVI_{ij}, & \text{if a higher value is better} \\ -SVI_{ij}, & \text{if a lower value is better} \end{cases}$$

(5) For each indicator, j ($j = 1, \ldots, M$), a ranking can be obtained for regions: regions with a higher value of RSVI for indicator j are ranked ahead of those with a lower value.

(6) For each region i ($i = 1, \ldots, N$), calculate the RSVI for each sub-environment k ($k = 1, \ldots, S$) belonging to environment l ($l = 1, \ldots, C$),

$$Raw\_RSVI_{i,lk} = \frac{1}{y_{lk}}\sum_{p=1}^{y_{lk}} RSVI_{i,jlk,p}$$

$$Mean\_RSVI_{lk} = \frac{1}{N}\sum_{i=1}^{N} Raw\_RSVI_{i,lk}$$

$$SD\_RSVI_{lk} = \sqrt{\frac{1}{N}\sum_{i=1}^{N}(Raw\_RSVI_{i,lk} - Mean\_RSVI_{lk})^2}$$

$$RSVI_{i,lk} = \frac{Raw\_RSVI_{i,lk} - Mean\_RSVI_{lk}}{SD\_RSVI_{lk}}$$

where y_{lk} is the total number of indicators under sub-environment *k* of environment *l* and ($RSVI_{i,jlk,1}$, . . . , $RSVI_{i,jlk,ylk}$) are the RSVIs for region *i* that make up sub-environment *k* of environment *l*.

(7) For each region *i* (*i* = 1, . . . , *N*), calculate the RSVI for each environment *l* (*l* = 1, . . . ,*C*),

$$\text{Raw\_RSVI}_{i,l} = \frac{1}{S_l}\sum_{k=1}^{S_l} \text{RSVI}_{i,lk}$$

$$\text{Mean\_RSVI}_l = \frac{1}{N}\sum_{i=1}^{N} \text{Raw\_RSVI}_{i,l}$$

$$\text{SD\_RSVI}_l = \sqrt{\frac{1}{N}\sum_{i=1}^{N}(\text{Raw\_RSVI}_{i,l} - \text{Mean\_RSVI}_l)^2}$$

$$\text{RSVI}_{i,l} = \frac{\text{Raw\_RSVI}_{i,l} - \text{Mean\_RSVI}_l}{\text{SD\_RSVI}_l}$$

where ($RSVI_{i,l1}$, . . . , $RSVI_{i,lS}$) are the RSVIs for the *S* sub-environments under each environment *l*.

(8) Overall rank score of region *i* (*i* = 1, . . . , *N*),

$$\text{Raw\_R}_i = \frac{1}{C}\sum_{l=1}^{c} \text{RSVI}_{i,l}$$

$$\text{Mean\_R} = \frac{1}{N}\sum_{i=1}^{N} \text{Raw\_R}_i$$

$$\text{SD\_R} = \sqrt{\frac{1}{N}\sum_{i=1}^{N}(\text{Raw\_R}_i - \text{Mean\_R})^2}$$

$$R_i = \frac{\text{Raw\_R}_i - \text{Mean\_R}}{\text{SD\_R}}$$

Regions with a higher Ri are ranked ahead of those with lower value of *Ri*, and the region with the highest *Ri* is the most competitive region.

Step (5) provides the ranking of each region for each individual indicator. To achieve this ranking, Step (4) adjusts the value of the SVIs so that a higher value will lead to a better ranking in terms of 'competitiveness'. Depending on the nature of the indicator in question, a higher or lower value may reflect a more 'competitive' region. Take for instance the sub-indicators 'Gross Regional Domestic Product (GRDP)' and 'Unemployment Rate'. A higher GRDP but a lower 'unemployment rate' suggest better economic performance, which makes a region more 'competitive'. In most cases where a higher value is better (e.g. GRDP), the SVIs of regions are considered, and those with a higher SVI value will have a better ranking. However, for indicators where the inverse is true (e.g., Unemployment Rate), the 'negative SVI' values are compared between regions and a lower SVI value will lead to a better ranking. Step (4) thus seeks to make all standardised values of all indicators consistent for ranking purposes.

Step (6) determines the sub-environment rankings of each region. The average RSVI of all the indicators in the sub-environment are calculated, re-standardised across all the regions and compared to other regions. Regions with a higher average RSVI rank better in the sub-environment. Although the number of indicators varies for each sub-environment, for the Indonesian study, there are three sub-environments for each of the four environments. The aggregate score for each sub-environment is given an equivalent weighting: 33.33% of their respective environment's score.

To arrive at the ranking for each environment, the RSVIs of the sub-environments are averaged and re-standardised across all the regions as detailed by Step (7). Finally, Step (8) requires the RSVI values of each environment to be averaged and re-standardised across all the regions to determine the overall ranking of the region. Regions with a higher RSVI are ranked ahead of those with a lower RSVI.

Identical weights are assigned to each environment as they represent equivalent significance to the computation of Indonesias Regional Overall Competitiveness Index. This method is repeated and applied consistently across all the regions to ensure precision of the rankings. Mathematically, this can be illustrated as follows:

Indonesia Regional Overall Competitiveness Index:

= 25% × (Macroeconomic Stability)
+25% × (Government and Institutional Setting)
+25% × (Financial, Businesses and Manpower Conditions)
+25% × (Quality of Life and Infrastructure Development)

Appendix 3

Notes on Data Aggregation from Provincial Level to Regional Level

No	Indicator	Unit	Reversed Indicator	Calculated as in
1	MACROECONOMIC STABILITY			
1.1	*Regional Economic Vibrancy*			
1.1.01	Gross Regional Domestic Product (GRDP)	Rupiah (Million), 2000 Constant Prices		Approach 1
1.1.02	Gross Regional Domestic Product (GRDP), Non-oil & gas	Rupiah (Million), 2000 Constant Prices		Approach 1
1.1.03	GRDP Growth	Percentage Change Per Annum, 2000 Constant Prices		Approach 2
1.1.04	GRDP Per Capita	Rupiah (Million), 2000 Constant Prices		Approach 2
1.1.05	GRDP Per Capita, Non-oil & gas	Rupiah (Million), 2000 Constant Prices		Approach 2
1.1.06	GRDP of Primary Industry	Rupiah (Million), 2000 Constant Prices		Approach 1
1.1.07	GRDP of Secondary Industry	Rupiah (Million), 2000 Constant Prices		Approach 1
1.1.08	GRDP of Tertiary Industry	Rupiah (Million), 2000 Constant Prices		Approach 1
1.1.09	Gross Domestic Fixed Capital Formation	Rupiah (Million), 2000 Constant Prices		Approach 1
1.1.10	Inflation	Percentage Change Per Annum	R	Approach 3
1.2	*Openness To Trade and Services*			
1.2.01	Exports	Rupiah (Million), 2000 Constant Prices		Approach 1
1.2.02	Exports, Non-oil & gas	Rupiah (Million), 2000 Constant Prices		Approach 1
1.2.03	Imports	Rupiah (Million), 2000 Constant Prices		Approach 1
1.2.04	Imports, Non-oil & gas	Rupiah (Million), 2000 Constant Prices		Approach 1
1.2.05	Openness To Trade	Ratio		Approach 2
1.3	*Attractiveness To Foreign Investors*			
1.3.01	Foreign Direct Investment, Last 3 Year Average	US Dollars (Million), Current Market Prices		Approach 1
1.3.02	Domestic Direct Investment, Last 3 Year Average	Rupiah (Billion)		Approach 1
1.3.03	Investment Promotion and Management	Index (Survey Data)		Approach 3
2	GOVERNMENT AND INSTITUTIONAL SETTING			
2.1	*Government Policies and Fiscal Sustainability*			
2.1.01	Government Revenue	Rupiah (Thousand), 2000 Constant Prices		Approach 1
2.1.02	Tax Revenue	Rupiah (Thousand), 2000 Constant Prices		Approach 1
2.1.03	Tax Revenue/Government Revenue	Ratio		Approach 2
2.1.04	Government Expenditure	Rupiah (Thousand), 2000 Constant Prices		Approach 1
2.1.05	Fiscal Balance	Rupiah (Thousand), 2000 Constant Prices		Approach 1
2.2	*Institutions, Governance and Leadership*			
2.2.01	Corruption Perception Index	Index		Approach 3
2.2.02	Lack of Corruption	Index (Survey Data)		Approach 3

(*Continued*)

(*Continued*)

No	Indicator	Unit	Reversed Indicator	Calculated as in
2.2.03	Crime Rate	Rate Per 100.000 population	R	Approach 3
2.2.04	Security	Index (Survey Data)		Approach 3
2.2.05	Government Inclusiveness and Accountability	Index (Survey Data)		Approach 3
2.2.06	Government Progress & Expectation	Index (Survey Data)		Approach 3
2.2.07	Government Efficiency	Index (Survey Data)		Approach 3
2.2.08	Coordination of Local Governments	Index (Survey Data)		Approach 3
2.2.09	Provincial Governing Capacity	Index (Survey Data)		Approach 3
2.3	*Competition, Regulatory Standards and Rule of Laws*			
2.3.01	Regulatory Governance	Index (Survey Data)		Approach 3
2.3.02	Rule of Law	Index (Survey Data)		Approach 3
2.3.03	Vibrancy of Competition and Collaboration	Index (Survey Data)		Approach 3
3	FINANCIAL, BUSINESSES AND MANPOWER CONDITIONS			
3.1	*Financial Deepening and Business Efficiency*			
3.1.01	Bank Deposits	Rupiah (Million), 2000 Constant Prices		Approach 1
3.1.02	Bank Loans	Rupiah (Million), 2000 Constant Prices		Approach 1
3.1.03	Non-Performing Loans	Rupiah (Million), 2000 Constant Prices	R	Approach 1
3.1.04	Non-Performing Loans per Total Bank Loans	Ratio	R	Approach 2
3.1.05	Number of Bank Branches or Offices	Number		Approach 1
3.1.06	Population per Number of Bank Branches or Offices	Ratio	R	Approach 2
3.1.07	Ease of Dealing With Banks	Index (Survey Data)		Approach 3
3.1.08	Firms' Performance	Index (Survey Data)		Approach 3
3.1.09	Firms' Strategy	Index (Survey Data)		Approach 3
3.1.10	Firms' Human Resource Capacity	Index (Survey Data)		Approach 3
3.1.11	Firms' Equipment Capacity	Index (Survey Data)		Approach 3
3.1.12	Firms' Application of IT	Index (Survey Data)		Approach 3
3.1.13	Firms' Innovation	Index (Survey Data)		Approach 3
3.2	*Labour Market Flexibility*			
3.2.01	Labour Force	Number		Approach 1
3.2.02	Labour Force Participation Rate	Ratio		Approach 2
3.2.03	Employment	Number		Approach 1
3.2.04	Employment in Primary Industry	Number		Approach 1
3.2.05	Employment in Secondary industry	Number		Approach 1
3.2.06	Employment in Tertiary Industry	Number		Approach 1
3.2.07	Unemployment Rate	Percentage	R	Approach 2
3.2.08	Minimum Wage Per Month	Rupiah, Current Market Prices	R	Approach 3
3.2.09	Labour Relations	Index (Survey Data)		Approach 3
3.3	*Productivity Performance*			
3.3.01	Overall Labour Productivity	Rupiah (Million) per person-year, 2000 Constant Prices		Approach 2
3.3.02	Overall Labour Productivity, Non-oil & gas	Rupiah (Million) per person-year, 2000 Constant Prices		Approach 2
3.3.03	Primary Industry Productivity	Rupiah (Million) per person-year, 2000 Constant Prices		Approach 2

(*Continued*)

(*Continued*)

No	Indicator	Unit	Reversed Indicator	Calculated as in
3.3.04	Secondary Industry Productivity	Rupiah (Million) per person-year, 2000 Constant Prices		Approach 2
3.3.05	Tertiary Industry Productivity	Rupiah (Million) per person-year, 2000 Constant Prices		Approach 2
4	QUALITY OF LIFE AND INFRASTRUCTURE DEVELOPMENT			
4.1	*Physical Infrastructure*			
4.1.01	Population	Persons, Year-end		Approach 1
4.1.02	Population Growth	Percentage Change Per Annum		Approach 3
4.1.03	Urban Population	Percentage of Total Population		Approach 3
4.1.04	Length of Paved Roads	Kilometres		Approach 1
4.1.05	Registered Motor Vehicles	Number		Approach 1
4.1.06	Registered Motor Vehicles per KM of paved road	Ratio	R	Approach 2
4.1.07	Cargo at Inter-island Seaport	Tons		Approach 1
4.1.08	Cargo at International Seaport	Tons		Approach 1
4.1.09	Passengers of Domestic Air Traffic	Number		Approach 1
4.1.10	Passengers of International Air Traffic	Number		Approach 1
4.1.11	Households with pipe water services	Percentage of households		Approach 3
4.1.12	Households with state electricity services	Percentage of households		Approach 3
4.1.13	Ease of Acquiring Property	Index (Survey Data)		Approach 3
4.1.14	Quality of Physical Infrastructure	Index (Survey Data)		Approach 3
4.2	*Technological Infrastructure*			
4.2.01	Telephone Ownership	Percentage of households		Approach 3
4.2.02	Handphone Ownership	Percentage of households		Approach 3
4.2.03	Desktop Computer Ownership	Percentage of households		Approach 3
4.2.04	Laptop Computer Ownership	Percentage of households		Approach 3
4.2.05	Internet Access at Home	Percentage of households		Approach 3
4.2.06	Internet Access at Office	Percentage of households		Approach 3
4.2.07	Internet Access at School	Percentage of households		Approach 3
4.2.08	Internet Access in Handphone	Percentage of households		Approach 3
4.2.09	Quality of Technological Infrastructure	Index (Survey Data)		Approach 3
4.3	*Standard of Living, Education and Social Stability*			
4.3.01	Adult Illiteracy Rate	Percentage of Adults	R	Approach 3
4.3.02	Mean Years of Schooling	Years		Approach 3
4.3.03	School Enrolment Rate (Primary)	Percentage		Approach 3
4.3.04	School Enrolment Rate (Junior High)	Percentage		Approach 3
4.3.05	School Enrolment Rate (Senior High)	Percentage		Approach 3
4.3.06	Student-Teacher Ratio (Primary)	Ratio	R	Approach 3
4.3.07	Student-Teacher Ratio (Junior High)	Ratio	R	Approach 3
4.3.08	Student-Teacher Ratio (Senior High)	Ratio	R	Approach 3
4.3.09	Human Development Index	Index		Approach 3
4.3.10	Life Expectancy at Birth	Years		Approach 3
4.3.11	Gini Ratio	Ratio	R	Approach 3

(*Continued*)

(*Continued*)

No	Indicator	Unit	Reversed Indicator	Calculated as in
4.3.12	Urban Population Growth	Percentage Per Annum		Approach 3
4.3.13	Population Per Health Facility	Ratio	R	Approach 3
4.3.14	Population Per Medical Worker	Ratio	R	Approach 3
4.3.15	Environmental Quality Index	Index		Approach 3
4.3.16	Fatalities due to Natural Disaster	Number	R	Approach 3
4.3.17	Quality of Education	Index (Survey Data)		Approach 3
4.3.18	Quality of Healthcare	Index (Survey Data)		Approach 3
4.3.19	Affordability and Accessibility of Goods	Index (Survey Data)		Approach 3

Source: Asia Competitiveness Institute.